The European Heritage in Economics and the Social Sciences

Volume 19

The European heritage in economics and the social sciences is largely locked in languages other than English. Witness such classics as Storch's Cours d'Economie Politique, Wicksell's Finanztheoretische Untersuchungen and Geld, Zins und Güterpreise or Pareto's Trattato di Sociologia Generale. Since about 1937, partly caused by the forced exodus of many scholars from the German language countries and the international reactions to this event, English has become the undisputed primary language of economics and the social sciences. For about one generation, this language shift did not result in a loss of access to the European non-English sources. However, after foreign language requirements were dropped as entry pre-requisites for receiving the PhD at major research universities, the European heritage in economics and the social sciences has become largely inaccessible to the vast majority of practicing scholars.

In this series, we hope to publish works that address this problem in a threefold manner. An aspect of the European heritage in a language other than English should be critically documented and discussed, reconstructed and assessed from a modern scientific point of view, and tested with respect to its relevance for contemporary economic, social, or political discourse.

We welcome submissions that fit this bill in order to make the European heritage in economics and the social sciences available to the international research community of scholars in economics and the social sciences.

More information about this series at http://www.springer.com/series/5902

Jürgen Backhaus · Günther Chaloupek
Hans A. Frambach
Editors

On the Economic Significance of the Catholic Social Doctrine

125 Years of Rerum Novarum

Springer

Editors
Jürgen Backhaus
Krupp Chair in Public Finance and Fiscal Sociology
University of Erfurt
Erfurt, Thüringen
Germany

Günther Chaloupek
Chamber of Labour
AK Wien
Vienna
Austria

Hans A. Frambach
Microeconomics and the History of Economic Thought
Schumpeter School of Business and Economics, Faculty of Management and Economics
University of Wuppertal
Wuppertal
Germany

ISSN 1572-1744 ISSN 2197-5892 (electronic)
The European Heritage in Economics and the Social Sciences
ISBN 978-3-319-52544-0 ISBN 978-3-319-52545-7 (eBook)
DOI 10.1007/978-3-319-52545-7

Library of Congress Control Number: 2017930160

Printed on acid-free paper

This Springer imprint is published by Springer Nature
The registered company is Springer International Publishing AG
The registered company address is: Gewerbestrasse 11, 6330 Cham, Switzerland

Contents

Introduction

Ursula Backhaus, Günther Chaloupek and Hans A. Frambach

In 1891 Pope Leo XIII published the first social encyclical, *Rerum novarum*. In the preceding decades of the 19th century, several papal encyclicals had dealt with social and political problems of the time under different aspects, but *Rerum novarum* was the first encyclical in which the Catholic Church spoke out about the economic and social situation of the workers and thereby directly addressed the Social Question. With *Rerum novarum* a tradition of Catholic social theory came into being that still holds good today: in the 125 years after *Rerum novarum* almost a dozen papal social encyclicals have been issued which mirror the social, economic and political developments.

At the time when *Rerum novarum* appeared, working conditions were still grueling. Factors like dirt, noise, stench, and heat, together with poor light and lack of air, seriously impaired health. Hygienic facilities were inadequate, danger protection was minimal, and working hours were oppressive. Workers' associations and labor movements emerged and gained great popularity. In the 70s and 80s of the 19th century at the latest, the labor movement organized in trade unions and socialist parties gained such importance that no social institution could bypass the issue. An official positioning had been expected from the Vatican, which waited, however, for a long time. Late, then, but with corresponding ardor and empathy, a workers' movement emerged in the church, exemplified in the workers' pilgrimages

U. Backhaus (✉)
Institute for the State and the Social Sciences, Bonn, Germany
e-mail: ursula_backhaus@yahoo.de

G. Chaloupek
Austrian Chamber of Labor, Vienna, Austria
e-mail: guenther@chaloupek.eu

H.A. Frambach
Schumpeter School of Business and Economics, Faculty of Management and Economics, University of Wuppertal, Wuppertal, Germany
e-mail: frambach@wiwi.uni-wuppertal.de

J. Backhaus et al. (eds.), *On the Economic Significance of the Catholic Social Doctrine*, The European Heritage in Economics and the Social Sciences 19, DOI 10.1007/978-3-319-52545-7_1

to Rome of 1887 and 1889. Pope Leo XIII addressed the pilgrims and expressed his sympathy with them, emphasizing the need for state intervention to improve their conditions. In 1887 several Catholic study circles dealing with the social questions of the time petitioned Pope Leo for a social encyclical. Their wish was fulfilled and suggestions and opinions sought on this subject throughout the world. In the end it was public pressure that led to the publication of *Rerum novarum*.

From the perspective of economic theory the first social encyclical appeared against the background of an ongoing debate about the advantages and disadvantages of capitalist and socialist economic systems that would recur in further encyclicals. If, on the one hand, capitalism was more efficient as an economic system, there were adverse social consequences which called for remedy. Whereas socialism aimed for a fundamental change of the economic system, the church took a middle course between capitalism and socialism.

The First World War left Europe in a serious crisis. The miseries caused by war and its consequences confronted the nations of Europe and the world with new challenges. When the war had ended, the demand of workers and their political parties for participation in the political process could no longer be ignored by the prevailing governments. A wave of social legislation swept through Western and Central European countries which brought with them a significant advancement towards a welfare state. The search for compromise generated various middle courses between economic capitalism and socialism. In the East, the course of events took a different turn. After the October Revolution of 1917 a socialist economic system was established in Russia which claimed to be wholly tailored to the interests of the workers.

After a brief period of economic stabilization, the Great Depression of the 1930s again threw the capitalist system into a deep crisis, to which parliamentary democracy fell victim in Germany and Austria. In the democratic countries, political and economic debates resumed about how to overcome the deficiencies of capitalism.

This was the situation in which the second social encyclical, *Quadragesimo anno*, was published by Pope Pius XI in 1931 (i.e. 40 years after *Rerum novarum*). It extended the perspective from the labor question to the more general analysis of the economic system, placing special emphasis on the role of private property. Private property, it argued, provided an incentive for performance, because the acquisition of property encouraged individuals to foresight and careful planning and served as a life insurance, e.g. for retirement provision. At the same time, private owners of capital and land should be obligated to responsible treatment of their workers and dependents. Also, the distribution issue depended on private property, because as long as the distribution of income and assets was excessively unequal it would arouse discontent, disturbance and strife. The distribution issue had systemic relevance because it was crucial for the sustainability of the capitalist system. The authors of *Quadragesimo anno*, nevertheless, suspected the danger of granting real entitlements to the individual against the state. This might, they thought, put the principle of individual responsibility at risk, and at the same time overwhelm the state with obligations toward its citizens. It was a warning against developments that might lead to a welfare state in the wake of social individualization processes, an obvious contradiction to the principle of subsidiarity introduced in this encyclical. As a proposal for a solution a third way was suggested. This entailed the reduction of the existing unequal distribution and polarization between social classes on the one hand, and a social revaluation of industrial workers and professions. As an alternative to existing capitalism, *Quadragesimo anno* envisaged a "corporatist" system, based on the concept of "professional order", as opposed to the class society of existing capitalism. Free competition was not believed capable of steering the market successfully, so regulatory intervention in the economy, governed strictly by the idea of social equity, would inevitably be required. Fascist political systems in Italy and in Austria claimed support for themselves from the concept of corporatism as proposed by *Quadragesimo anno*.

The Second World War brought immense suffering and misery. With its end, the political, social and economic structures of the world changed yet again. Europe lost political importance, the USA and the Soviet Union advanced to the position of global superpowers. However, the world also began to grow together, with the emergence of institutions such as the UNO, the International Monetary Fund (IMF), the World Bank and the OEEC (later OECD) for Western industrialized countries. Social equity was widely accorded the status of a basic right. Schemes of social security were extended and upgraded. The modern welfare state was built up on the basis of sustained economic growth in the "golden age" of post-war prosperity (1950–1975).

In Germany the social market economy experienced its prime. However, although the mechanisms of allocation and control of the market were meaningful, the social market economy, as a concept of order, had both an economic and a sociopolitical impact. It envisioned a market-based economy extended by a guiding "social idea", which brought together the different values perceived as existing in society. Here, Catholic social doctrine was used by the idea of the "social irenic", and this principle of reconciling interests—which involved the consideration and assessment of alternative social and economic conditions—flowed into the concept of the social market economy. The foundation of this concept in the higher perspective of the values of Christian faith was, however, decisive; for the economy was seen as only one aspect of human existence and not of exclusive significance.

Pope John XXIII published two social encyclicals in quick succession: *Mater et Magistra* in 1961 and *Pacem in terris* in 1963. He named social realities more directly than ever, discussing the organization of work processes, improvement of the quality of work, the relationship between employers and employees, employee involvement etc. The relationship of the industrial nations to the developing countries was mentioned in detail for the first time: wealth and material prosperity on one side, hunger and misery on the other. Closer cooperation for the support of the poor was demanded, and the great powers were called upon to stop the arms race and cut back their military budgets. The idea of the common good was defined anew: in Catholic social theory it no longer described only the welfare of a nation or its people; from now on it covered the whole world and the welfare of all mankind.

With the third major social encyclical, *Populorum progressio* of 1967, it became definitively clear that the social question had changed. Once used as a paraphrase for the situation of the working classes in the advancing industrial nations, it now expressed a global phenomenon. The world, it was stated, belonged to all its people, and no nation had the right to live at the expense of others. The world would be richer and more just if the wealthy would take account of the poor.

A phase of economic stagnation appeared again in the 1970s and 1980s, and with it the problems of underdeveloped countries and of income distribution between the richest and poorest countries intensified. Together with stagnating growth, high rates of inflation and growing unemployment doubts arose as to whether the state could provide enough growth impulses and high levels of employment with the instrument of expansive fiscal policy. Pope John Paul II published three social encyclicals. In *Laborem exercens* (1981) the working person again became the focus of consideration—an aspect to which the disturbances in the Eastern-bloc countries and the foundation of the Polish trade union movement *Solidarność* contributed. The central theme was now extended from purely economic aspects, such as a just wage, to the "dignity of work". Capitalism required urgent correction and comprehensive reform, and in *Sollicitudo rei socialis* (1987) John Paul II made the development concept virtually synonymous with peace, emphasizing social inequality as a danger for the absolute value of world peace. The industrial nations took great responsibility for the poverty in the world; real improvement could only occur if people developed and showed a deeper understanding of existing world problems; it must be clearly recognized that material consumption did not suffice for happiness, and that profit and lust for power were to be found not only on an individual, but has also on a national level.

At the beginning of the 1990s the Soviet Union dissolved; socialism seemed at an end, and this radical change was largely achieved nonviolently. In his third social encyclical, *Centesimus annus* (1991), John Paul II warned the putative "winners" (i.e. the western industrial countries) of arrogance. In developing structures of "national safety" and expanding state power, they might well damage liberal values, and a situation might arise embodying what socialism was always reproached for. The encyclical exposed an exclusive focus on the economic superiority of the market over a planned economy as potentially reducing the human being to an economic instrument and human life to the satisfaction of material needs: totalitarianism and authoritarianism also exist in capitalist and market-based systems, and democracy itself could run into danger.

In 2009, amidst the global financial crisis and the ensuing economic crisis, Pope Benedict XVI published the social encyclical *Caritas in veritate*. With astonishment it was recognized that after decades of economic liberalization the states most acutely involved corrected the undesirable development of the economy at enormous financial expense during the financial crisis, the economy itself claiming astronomical state aid, but the burdens being financed by the general public. Benedict allotted responsibility for the failure neither to the market nor to the economic system as such—hence, not to abstract mechanisms—but to the persons acting within them. The dependence culture of many people in rich states was considered totally exaggerated, and the encyclical insisted not only on compliance with liberties and rights, but also on social obligations—i.e. on responsibility to society and the community.

After intensely criticizing the prevailing economic system and the situation in the poor countries of the world in his apostolic letter *Evangelii Gaudium* (2013), Pope Francis continued his critique in the encyclical *Laudato si'*, the current social encyclical, published in summer 2015 and sometimes described as the "environmental encyclical". Here, in drastic words, Francis describes the hopeless situation of many millions of people in the countries of the so-called Third World. He deplores the irresponsible use of nature with regard to wastage of resources, the negative consequences of climate change, the disposable culture of rich countries, the deterioration in the living conditions of people in poor countries, the (despite ongoing financial crises) unabated flourishing of financial capitalism, the blind belief in technology ruling the industrial nations, and the everlasting quest for economic growth without showing any consideration for the environment. As a solution, changes are required in production methods and consumer behavior, based on radical change in attitudes and lifestyles.

The market mechanism is not believed to have sufficient potential to protect the environment and a planned economy. Francis demands nothing less than a reconsideration of the basic principles of the economy defining its meaning and aims, backed by an ecological turnaround accompanied by a style of economy and life oriented towards sustainability. For this an understanding is presupposed that freedom is much more than freedom to consume; it is inseparably connected with responsibility. Francis seeks holistic progress and the aim that people may be able to live in peace and dignity, free from the struggle for survival—always keeping in mind the preservation of basic living conditions in the form of a healthy environment and the situation of the poor.

On the basis of a system of values deeply rooted in the Christian faith, the Vatican has, then, in its social encyclicals, adopted a clear position on the fundamental problems of the economy and society. In this book specific issues referring to the social encyclicals, and in particular to *Rerum novarum*, are discussed. The first chapter starts with the time before *Rerum novarum*, when many measures to improve the situation of workers and the poor were also taken by the church. In his article "An Economist's View of the Work of Wilhelm Emmanuel von Ketteler and its Influence on the Encyclical *Rerum novarum*" Daniel Eissrich takes Bishop Ketteler as an outstanding example of the fight against injustice and for the improvement of the disadvantaged. Eissrich introduces the life and thought of Bishop Ketteler, and shows, by comparing Ketteler's writings with passages in *Rerum novarum*, how Ketteler influenced the emergence of the encyclical. Doing so, he also illustrates how Catholic social teaching was by no means a centralized Vatican issue, but was widely influenced by the regional churches.

Besides the principles of personality, subsidiarity and the interest in the common good, one of the central concepts of Catholic social theory is solidarity. The principle of solidarity was developed by the Jesuit Heinrich Pesch, together with Carl von Vogelsang known as the founder of Catholic social theory, in his concept of solidarism. Pesch saw his mission in life as an active commitment to greater justice, in particular in improving the situation of the workers. Closely related to this were further focal points of his work, the comparison of individualistic capitalism and collectivist socialism, the conflict of the social classes, and the family as the basis of the state. Pesch grasped the family, the state, and private property as the pillars of the social order, indispensable for cultural development. Hans A. Frambach shows that this was the basis for a different perception of national economics. Pesch's economic system, his *solidarism*, stood in the intellectual tradition of *Rerum novarum* and was decisive for the development of the second social encyclical, *Quadragesimo anno*, and following encyclicals. *Solidarism* was a social philosophy that saw the working human being as central to economic life, employing the principle of subsidiarity to determine the role of the state in economic activity, and subordinating economic activity to the social virtues of justice and charity. The central socio-political thrust of Pesch's solidarism is the construction of a strong welfare state based on principles of order, authority and morality. He regarded this as a legal obligation. In this way, Pesch's *solidarism* can be understood as a middle way, mediating between individualism and socialism.

The pope's efforts to find a middle (or third) way between the contradictory approaches of liberalism and socialism was, of course, not a unique venture. From the viewpoint of the history of economic thought it can be seen as one of several attempts to develop the concept of public economy ("Gemeinwirtschaft") as a principle of social development policy. Precisely this is what Karl-Heinz Schmidt analyzes in his contribution to this volume, commenting on the different meanings of the central terms "Gemeinwirtschaft" and "Gemeinsinn" and classifying important German writers on social development at the time of *Rerum novarum*—especially those who leaned toward the churches, namely Franz Hitze, Carl von Vogelsang, Johann Heinrich Wichern, and Victor Aimé Huber.

The ambivalent character of Catholic social doctrine is exemplified in the life of the famous historian and Catholic activist Lord Acton in the article by Frits L. van Holthoon. On the one hand an adherent of old Catholic principles, Acton fought, on the other hand, against the papal claim to secular power. Acton wished the Catholic Church to infuse religious liberty into the daily lives of the common people. He did not understand the modern concept of liberty, meaning freedom from restraint, disregarding moral consequences. Although the Catholic Church cared in *Rerum novarum* for the personal hardships and practical problems of ordinary people, Acton despaired of its doctrinal rigor and absolutist claims.

Further criticism of the social question as answered in *Rerum novarum* came from the Austrian sociologist August Knoll. Assuming a distinction in principle between the religious and moral sphere and the social sphere, Knoll argued that the church was only able to solve the social question on the religious and moral level, not on that of sociology, social technique or economic organization. Günther Chaloupek presents Knoll's arguments about the changing positions of the Catholic Church in history, its ability to adapt to economic and political circumstances, but also his stance among the different approaches to the social question and the debate about Catholic social doctrine. At the end of his life Knoll took a critical view of the clerical hierarchy. To break through its false pretensions with respect to social doctrine, Knoll calls for a "dualism of the two orders". While clerics have the decisive voice in spiritual matters, the competence rests with laymen in worldly issues.

Describing aspects of the historical background of *Rerum novarum*, including the relation between natural law and Christian anthropology, Peter Schallenberg begins his contribution "125 years *Rerum novarum*—the Theological Perspective" from the viewpoint of Catholic theology. In *Rerum novarum*, as in later social encyclicals, the position of the church vis à vis society, politics and the economy was based on the perceived good for the life for every human being—a holistic concept bonding together the dimensions of the material (or quantitative) and the spiritual (or qualitative). At the center of this perception is the conviction that Christian love can influence the structure of societies. All societal systems and institutions in the world should support the human vocation to receive and to give love. Men and women are believed to be created by God in his own image with an immortal soul binding them to him and his eternal love. Because it is not realistic to transfer this vision to economic life, the church has developed a system of social ethics based on the just development of the person. This development can already be found in *Rerum novarum*, where a third way between pure capitalism and socialism is proposed, containing many ideas of what later became known as social market economy. Schallenberg argues that Catholic social teaching since *Rerum novarum* aims to enable man to live a successful life. Social justice, inclusion, participatory equity and subsidiarity are emphasized as ethically required concepts to fulfill the ideas of Christian anthropology in the market economy.

The influence of *Rerum novarum* in the Netherlands is exemplified by Robert W. J. Jansen in the figure of Johannes Antonius Veraart, an early 20th century Catholic economist committed to parliamentary democracy. Veraart emphasized the distinction between the *realist* and the *ethical* approach, concepts which he had adopted from the German economist Adolph Wagner and the Austrian economist Eugen Philippovich. While the realist approach allowed the investigation of the effectiveness of measures to achieve given objectives, it did not discuss the social desirability or ethics of these objectives. In the "realist" discussion of wages, for example, the wage level was determined on a purely theoretical basis derived from the interaction of supply and demand. Hence the result depended solely on the power of the subjects and the market policies of the parties involved. Ethical considerations, on the other hand, would lead to processes of state intervention like the setting of a minimum wage, immigration policies etc. Although Veraart and his ideas have been largely neglected in Dutch economics, the literature describes him as the "auctor intellectualis" of the Dutch variant of corporatism—i.e. of industrial organization and regulation of relations between labor, capital and the state. In his writings and lectures on corporatism Veraart referred extensively to the encyclicals *Rerum Novarum* and *Quadragesimo Anno*. *Rerum Novarum* was in his view a historical document, a child of its time. Its ideas about humanity and human values were eternal but their application to capitalism was essentially temporary.

Amid the struggles between liberalism and socialism at the turn of the 20th century, *Rerum novarum* sought a middle way for the Catholic Church. At the same time, however, the seeds of a more politically oriented Catholicism also existed, envisaging a society and a state system in which labor and capital would cooperate peacefully in self-governing vocational associations: the corporative state. Although by now almost forgotten, the corporative state was an early 20th century ideal. Again focusing on the Catholic Dutch economist Johannes Antonius Veraart, Andries Nentjes takes up the story of corporatism in the Netherlands from another point of view. With reference to the discussion of the class struggle in *Rerum novarum*, and the demand for its end, Veraart outlined a corporatist economic system, called the "statutory organization of business", which he proposed as an alternative to the market system. In this system, guild-like organizations and businesses uniting employers and workers in a specific industry would make the major economic decisions. The main ideas of this proposal can be found in *Rerum novarum* and *Quadragesimo anno*. Nentjes tells the story of the varying and eventful history of the statutory organisation of business from the time immediately after the First World War until its end in the 1950s, when the corporatist movement was overtaken by the beginnings of the welfare state and the reconstruction of the market economy.

In the USA the critical discussion of the works of Henry George caused a stir. The worker priest Edward McGlynn got into trouble with his church because of the stand he took on behalf of the workers—a position he derived from George. This was reason enough for the church to investigate George's writings and conclusions. A long-lasting and fundamental debate about the role of property, especially landed property, and the issue of justice opened. George saw private property as the prime cause of poverty and called for the absorption for the common good of all profits from property (well known in economic theory under the name of "single-tax"). This was for the church the same as expropriation and a clear case of socialism. Nicolaus Tideman discusses and evaluates these issues in his article on "The Justice and the Economics of *Rerum Novarum* on Land", arguing that, as George suggested at the time of its publication, *Rerum novarum* is weak as a theory both of justice and of economics.

The principle of just taxation of immovable property (real estate) as discussed in *Rerum novarum* was thematically closely connected to Henry George's suggestions. It is the subject of the article by Francesco Forte, Flavio Felice and Elton Beqiraj. After a comprehensive presentation of the concept of property rights as natural rights in *Rerum novarum*, and of George's reaction (he thought that the relevant passages in *Rerum novarum* were written to refute his suggestions), the authors seek to evaluate the different positions by the application of econometric analysis. They estimate the effect of Henry George's taxation of immovable property on GDP along data of OECD countries from 1965 to 2013 and compare it with the position of the social encyclical *Rerum novarum*, which considers immovable property an inviolable right. The authors show that taxation of immovable property is generally in negative relation to GDP growth and hence support the position of *Rerum novarum*.

It is an interesting but at the same time astonishing thesis that Catholic social thought has decisively framed living and working conditions in Europe during large parts of the 20th century, and has done so in a what might be called a secret manner—i.e. that neither the contents nor the protagonists of Catholic social thought are much remembered in contemporary Europe. This thesis is proposed is proposed by André Habisch. He focuses on the emergence of this body of thought in the context of industrialization, and stresses the pioneering role of Christian entrepreneurs like the French textile magnate Léon Harmel and the German Franz Brandts. With their employee-friendly work and activities, based on Christian principles, and their endeavors to "acculturate" the Christian faith into modern society, they showed a wise practical commitment and exemplary leadership that paved the way for a new paradigm of Christian social ethics and even influenced contemporary discussion in both church and society. Many important figures in politics and society—Franz Hitze, Heinrich Brauns, or Heinrich Pesch—were influenced by Catholic social ethics, and this line of thought can without exaggeration be described as an important moral and intellectual tradition, a vessel of social-economic thought and wisdom.

On behalf of the entire Heilbronn group, we would like to thank the city council and the Lord Mayor of the city of Heilbronn for their continued generous support.

An Economist's View of the Work of Wilhelm Emmanuel von Ketteler and Its Influence on the Encyclical *Rerum novarum*

Daniel Eissrich

1 Introduction

Sometimes the Catholic Church is accused of having been silent for too long about the social problems of the 19th century, only breaking its silence with Pope Leo XIII's encyclical *Rerum novarum* in 1891. An example often cited against this statement is Wilhelm Emmanuel von Ketteler, Bishop of Mainz. Bishop Ketteler was a contemporary of Karl Marx, Friedrich Engels and Ferdinand Lassalle. His first essays on questions of property rights appeared in the same year as the Communist Manifesto.

> …this direction that one should look for the true origins of the social movement which would gain momentum in the heart of the Catholic Church during the second half of the century, culminating in the solemn publication, in 1891, of the encyclical *Rerum novarum*. It is a German prelate, Wilhelm Emmanuel von Ketteler, bishop of Mainz, who had the honor of being the first to present the social question very clearly as a problem of justice and not of charity, and even to face head on the necessity of basic reform (Aubert 2005, 23).

The influence of his writings on the encyclical *Rerum novarum* is certainly also significant. It is known that Leo XIII, before his election as Pope, studied the writings of Ketteler in French translation during his time as Archbishop of Perugia, and Pope Leo XIII called Bishop Ketteler his great predecessor in the field of social reform (Mueller 1971, 119, 125, 149).

The paper gives a brief overview of the work of Bishop Wilhelm Emmanuel von Ketteler and tries to show some examples of commonalities to justify the conclusion that important elements of the work of von Ketteler have been included in the encyclical Rerum novarum.

D. Eissrich (✉)
Deutsche Bundesbank, Frankfurt am Main, Germany
e-mail: daniel.eissrich@yahoo.de

J. Backhaus et al. (eds.), *On the Economic Significance of the Catholic Social Doctrine*, The European Heritage in Economics and the Social Sciences 19, DOI 10.1007/978-3-319-52545-7_2

2 The Early Years

Wilhelm Emmanuel Baron von Ketteler was born on December 25, 1811 in Münster as the sixth of nine children of Baron Friedrich von Ketteler and his wife Clementine (for a biography see Pfülf 1899). He came from an old Westphalian noble family. After completing his education at a Swiss Jesuit boarding school, he studied law and political science, starting in 1828 in Göttingen, then in Berlin, Heidelberg and Munich. In 1833, he completed his exam and, after his military service, began his career in 1835 as a Prussian civil servant. During the conflict between the church and the Prussian state, the Cologne archbishop Clemens August Droste von Vischering was arrested and, shortly thereafter in May 1838, Ketteler resigned state service. In the spring of 1839, Ketteler moved to Munich, where he quickly came into contact with the circle surrounding Joseph Görres. Here his decision to become a priest matured and, in 1841, Ketteler started studying theology in Eichstätt and Munich, finally being ordained as a priest in Münster in 1844. As early as the first station of his ecclesiastical career, Ketteler's concern for people in need became evident. As chaplain in Beckum in 1845 and 1846, he provided for the construction of a hospital. After assuming his position as pastor of the small and very poor community Hopsten in November, he campaigned massively for the poor members of his municipality during the last major famine in Germany in the winter of 1846/47. He also procured considerable funds from his noble relatives. Owing to the reputation he acquired for himself within a short time, he was urged to run for the Paul's Church assembly, for which he was elected by a clear majority in his constituency of Tecklenburg/Warendorf. Ketteler's public appearances were very limited, and he maintained his independence during the assembly. In the debates, he only once took to the floor with a contribution on the matter of schools. However, what he wrote one day before on September 17, 1848 in an open letter to his municipality is noteworthy:

> My view is based on the simple principle that every individual should be allowed to exercise those rights which he is in power to exercise. For me the state is not a machine but a living organism with living limbs, in which each limb has its own rights and its own functions and shapes its own, free existence. In my opinion, the individual, the family, the community, etc. are such members. Each lower limb moves freely within its sphere and enjoys the right of self-determination and self-government. Only when the lower limb is no longer able to achieve his aims himself or independently to avert the danger threatening his development does the higher limb enter into force on its behalf (Ketteler 1848a, 403, see also Höffner 1962, 10–13).

Here, still at the beginning of his church career, Ketteler outlines the principle of subsidiarity that would later become well known by means of the encyclical *Qudragesimo anno* and still has a high level of relevance, e.g. in the context of European law. It seems that Ketteler was the first to use the term "subsidiarity" in his 1871 publication "The Catholics in the German Empire. Draft of a Political Program". Here, also connected with questions of public education, he notes: "By contrast, it is hard absolutism … if the state abuses what I would call subsidiary rights" (Ketteler 1873, 210). The idea accompanied Ketteler throughout his life: Joseph Höffner speaks of "an almost passionate commitment to subsidiarity", but also refers to the history of this idea in the Catholic tradition. Thomas Aquinas already pointed out the fact that excessive forcing into line and standardization would only threaten a community, "as symphony and harmony of the voices dwindle if everybody sings the same tone" (Höffner 1962, 10–11).

During the September riots of 1848, the representatives General Hans von Auerswald and Prince Felix von Lichnowsky were murdered, and the funeral speech at the burial was held by Wilhelm Emmanuel von Ketteler. The impressive speech, in which he called demagogues and revolutionaries the real culprits behind the murders, was immediately printed and distributed throughout the country, and the Westphalian peasant Pastor became a national celebrity overnight (Marx 2011, 29). Only two weeks later, Ketteler urged the Church and its followers to dedicate themselves to the social question in an impromptu speech at the first German Catholics Day in Mainz (Ketteler 1848b).

3 The Advent Sermons (1848)

Subsequently, the Mainz cathedral priest invited him to deliver the Advent sermons of 1848 in the Mainz Cathedral. The following eight Advent sermons dealt in detail with the social question and were published shortly thereafter under the title "The Major Social Questions of the Present". As early as his first sermon in November 1848, Ketteler calls the social question the most important problem of the time (Ketteler 1849, 5; Ederer 1981, 10). The first two sermons deal with property right, which is decisive for the social question because "today the haves and the have-nots confront each other with animosity, and the poverty of the masses grows daily … On the one side we witness a stubborn, narrow interpretation of property rights, and on the other a determination to abolish those rights completely. We look desperately for moderation between these extremes" (Ketteler 1849, 5; Ederer 1981, 10). For Ketteler, the Catholic doctrine of property is the appropriate basis for such a position, and this is based on the writings of St. Thomas Aquinas. From the principle of faith that God created the earth, he derives the notion that God is the owner of all earthly goods. St. Thomas concludes that man can only have a right to use these earthly goods, that this right is limited to the divinely intended use of the goods, and that the goods may not be withdrawn from the purpose for which they are intended. This purpose is derived from the book of Genesis, in which God gives earthly goods to men and says, "you shall have them for food" (Gen. 1, 29, Ketteler 1849, 6–7).

Ketteler states that St. Thomas makes a distinction within property rights between the right to care, manage and maintain goods and usufruct. With regard to the administration of goods, the property rights of individuals should be recognized:

> First, only by private ownership will goods be properly cared for. Everyone takes better care of things that belong to him than of those things that men hold in common. Over and above this, every man avoids work where possible, and where things are held in common a man would just as soon leave tasks to his fellow man … Secondly St. Thomas wrote, only by the private ownership of property will that order be preserved which is necessary for the efficient exploitation of the goods of this earth. If everyone is in charge of everything, there will be general confusion … Finally, St. Thomas argued that only by acknowledging the right of private property can peace be preserved among men. Experience teaches how easily common ownership leads to quarrels and disputes… St. Thomas, by virtue of these irrefutable arguments, defends the right of private ownership in the sense of administering and caring for property; and thus his position is in complete agreement with the law of God: 'Thou shalt not steal,' and with the teaching of the Catholic Church, all of which stand completely and inalterably opposed to the communism proposed in our time (Ketteler 1849, 9–10).

Likewise, the "false doctrine of stare rights of property" is also rejected, specifically when it comes to the right to consume the fruits of the administration of the property, because "God has … determined some goods of the earth for the use of people, and it is his will that these earth goods are mainly used to allow all people to satisfy their necessary needs" (Ketteler 1849, 18). Hence, "everybody should regard his property as a common good and everybody should be willing to contribute to fulfill God's will that each person receives from nature what is necessary" (Ketteler 1849, 18). Ketteler sees no legal obligation in this context "… which could be enforced by police regulations or state laws …", but he emphasizes the aspect of human freedom and the role of the Christian virtues (Ketteler 1849, 14). Here, at the beginning of his disputes regarding the social problems of his time, Ketteler recognizes only a return to Christian values as a solution (Große Kracht 2011, 66–67), and it is the turning away from faith which has led to these social problems:

> Only since men who call themselves the friend of humanity while at the same time working to destroy humanity … have shattered man's faith in God has it been possible for such an unholy concept of private property to gain currency. We refer to a concept of ownership whereby man in effect arrogates to himself the right which only God possesses over property. Once divorced from God, man pictured himself as the exclusive lord and master of all that he possessed, considering it merely as a way of quenching his evergrowing hedonism … Thus a gap between rich and poor appeared as the Christian world had never seen before … While the wealthy indulge themselves in a lavish and wasteful satisfaction of every sensory whim, they are indifferent to the plight of their less fortunate confrères who must often do without even the bare necessities of life. Thus the rich man is in fact depriving his brother of the things which the Creator meant for him to have (Ketteler 1849, 7–8).

Yet Ketteler is already ahead of the view then predominant in Catholic mentality that only a return to medieval forms of government and estate-based society could succeed in solving social problems: "It even appears to be the task of the epoch of world history in which we live to prove to the world that all forms of government are not capable of establishing the welfare of humanity, and that this requires another, higher power" (Ketteler 1849, 17).

43 years later, Pope Leo XIII writes the following in his encyclical *Rerum novarum* concerning property rights:

> Private ownership, as we have seen, is the natural right of man, and to exercise that right, especially as members of society, is not only lawful, but absolutely necessary. "It is lawful," says St. Thomas Aquinas, "for a man to hold private property; and it is also necessary for human existence." But if the question be asked: How must one's possessions be used? - the Church replies without hesitation in the words of the same holy Doctor: "Man should not consider his material possessions as his own, but as common to all, so as to share them without hesitation when others are in need. Whence the Apostle with, 'Command the rich of this world… to offer with no stint, to apportion largely.'" True, no one is commanded to distribute to others that which is required for his own needs and those of his household; nor even to give away what is reasonably required to keep up becomingly his condition in life, "for no one ought to live other than becomingly." But, when what necessity demands has been supplied, and one's standing fairly taken thought for, it becomes a duty to give to the indigent out of what remains over (Leo XIII 1891, 22).

The similarity to Bishop Ketteler's statements is very clear. The alignment of Catholic social teaching towards Thomas Aquinas's doctrines of natural right and property, as Ketteler already expressed it in his first sermon at the Mainz Cathedral, is pioneering (Höffner 1962, 9).

4 The Labor Question and Christianity (1864)

After the discussions in the St. Paul's Church assembly about topics important to Ketteler such as fundamental rights, the Church and educational issues, he resigned his delegated mandate in January 1849. However, he returns only for a short time to his parish in Hopsten because, as early as August 1849, he assumes the politically important position of provost of Berlin and prince-episcopal delegate for the Brandenburg March and Pomerania. After also drawing attention to himself here because of his political engagement, he took over, also at the explicit wish of Pope Pius IX, the episcopate in Mainz and was consecrated Bishop of Mainz on July 25, 1850 (Marx, 31–32). He devoted himself to the internal structure of his diocese with great zeal: the education of theologians at the Mainz seminary, the foundation of the Congregation of the Sisters of Divine Providence and promotion of the establishment of other sister organizations, the appointment of the Capuchins and Jesuits to Mainz. In Mainz, the new bishop increasingly developed into the "combative leader of German Ultramontanism", and his work during the 1850s was dominated by the cultural war between the church and the state. In 1854, Ketteler published his essay "The Right and the Legal Protection of the Catholic Church" in which he complains about state despotism against the Catholic Church, and eight years later, in 1862, he published his book "Freedom, Authority and the Church" (Große Kracht 2011, 80; Marx 2011, 34–36).

The stormy public discussion about social policy during the years 1863/64, which saw the emergence above all of liberal Hermann Schulze-Delitzsch and Ferdinand Lassalle, and the fact that the social question was once again on the agenda of the Catholics Day in Frankfurt in 1863, shifted the Bishop of Mainz's focus once again to the social problems of the time. Ketteler's main contribution to the social question then appears in the year 1864: "The Worker Question and Christianity".

Immediately, Ketteler makes it clear that the situation of workers is the central point of the social problems of the time: "All in all, the condition of labor represents one aspect of the great social problem which is an inevitable consequence of the false religious, political, and economic principles stemming from the anti-Christian liberalism at large in our time" (Ketteler 1864, 371; Ederer 1981, 312). Bishop Ketteler also states: "The so-called labor problem is essentially a question of the worker's livelihood. Therefore, it is first of all a question of providing for the basic needs: food, clothing, and shelter. Secondly it is of critical importance because it pertains to the largest percentage of mankind" (Ketteler 1864, 372, Ederer 1981, 313).

Ketteler expressly affirms the correctness of Ferdinand Lassalle, who presents the iron wage law, known since Ricardo, saying that "… only an overt intention to deceive would lead one to deny it" (Ketteler 1864, 377–378). It must there be concluded that: "… the wage rate in our time is determined by subsistence in the strictest sense of that word, i.e., the minimum food, clothing, and shelter that a person needs to sustain a bare physical existence" (Ketteler 1864, 377).

Ketteler laments "…that, for us, work has completely become a commodity" and thus, like other wares, is subject to the laws of the market (Ketteler 1864, 378). As a result, "The very subsistence of almost the entire working class … the very question of daily bread necessary to sustain the worker and his family is now at the complete mercy of caprice of the market place like the price of any other commodity" (Ketteler 1864, 380; Ederer 1981, 323). Especially when unable to work, the worker "…will immediately find himself lacking even the bare necessities for himself and for those who depend on him. Such unfortunate persons are simply no longer able to help themselves and must now depend upon support from their fellow human beings" (Ketteler 1864, 374; Ederer 1981, 317).

According to Ketteler, "modern economic principles" and humane, enlightened, anti-Christian liberalism are to blame (Ketteler 1864, 377, 380). The transition from mandatory guild membership to freedom of trade is also at fault, as free trade leads to a high degree of competition, and competition forces the price of commodities to the lowest level. Production costs and freedom of trade have transferred this to work, turning work into a commodity and driving down its price to its outer limit (Ketteler 1864, 380–381).

Ketteler describes guild coercion and freedom of trade as mirror images of authority and liberty. Both have the "divine thought as a foundation" but are also "unspeakably abused". The attempt to reconcile these two opposites reflects the divine purpose. The obligation to join a guild, which Ketteler expressly seeks not to defend, represents, as a limitation on freedom, authority and prevents the abuse of liberty. In his opinion, "guild rules were designed to offer protection to the workers—as a kind of contract between the working classes and the rest of society. According to this pact, the working class performed certain necessary services, and society, by placing a restriction on competition, assured the workers a higher wage than would otherwise have been possible—so as to provide them with a decent standard of living and to protect them from day to day uncertainty and insecurity." Although the guild system was subject to numerous abuses, it is justified in principle (Ketteler 1864, 382–384; Ederer 1981, 328–329). Yet freedom of trade also has its positive sides. It has led to a reduction in the prices of goods, an increase in supply and an improvement in product quality, thus providing poorer social strata the opportunity to satisfy needs, from which they were previously excluded (Ketteler 1864, 385).

Another reason for the workers' plight in Ketteler's opinion is the excessive power of capital. This leads to a situation in which more and more self-employed must close their businesses because they cannot compete with companies with a strong capital base, thus increasing the number of workers and day laborers. Furthermore, because of production with capital-intensive machinery, workers must not only compete with other workers, but ultimately also with machine production (Ketteler 1864, 385–386).

After identifying liberalism as an essential reason for the social problems of the time, Ketteler now confronted the solutions proposed by the "liberal party", that is, the "German Progress Party" founded in 1861 (Münstermann 2013, 39). Ketteler perceives their call for workers to take the matter into their own hands, a "means for the multiplication of bread" according to the liberal approach, above all as an attack on charitable assistance, especially that of the churches. Ketteler maintains that they are trying to persuade the workers that charity would violate their dignity but have no solution to the problems of incapacity for work, disability and illness (Ketteler 1864, 390). Ketteler also does not accept the arguments that social welfare encourages abuse and "idleness". "This contempt which people are now trying to attach to charity is frequently a hidden greed, which seeks to conceal its lack of brotherly love beneath such expressions". The workers' education associations proposed by the liberal party are also "true humbug", offering cultural and sporting events, but "on the whole do not alter the material situation of the working class in the slightest" (Ketteler 1864, 396). According to Ketteler, cooperatives such as those suggested by Schulze-Delitzsch are a good idea, but ultimately nothing new. They are also opposed to actual liberal principles. Ultimately, a cooperative is no longer "true aid for the proud, independent self"; they too introduce, inasmuch as they are meant to constitute a protection for its members, "…a kind of trade barrier or constraint…" and also "…modify…general competition" (Ketteler 1864, 399–400).

Ketteler views the program of the "radical party", or the General German Workers' Association founded by Ferdinand Lassalle in 1863, in a much more positive light (Münstermann 2013, 39). Lassalle's statements concerning the inadequate effect of the suggestions proposed by the liberal party are "unrefuted and irrefutable" (Ketteler 1864, 402). His party also deserves credit for having exposed the worker's plight "with relentless acuity and truth" and of showing "with the same correctness" that assistance for workers is only possible if "…a richer source of income is opened up besides the meager wage" (Ketteler 1864, 405):

> In every business, the total revenue is divisible into three parts. First, there is the daily wage of the worker, which equals subsistence. Then there is the interest on capital which is used up in the productive process. Finally, there is profit from the sale of the product after the wages, interest on capital, and whatever other costs of doing business have been deducted. This profit goes to capital without the worker getting even the slightest share of it. Such a distribution of profit does not seem to conform to natural justice or to any other reasonable criterion. The worker contributes his flesh and blood and uses up the most valuable of the earthly endowments he possesses - his health. Each day he uses up a part of his remaining lifetime. The capitalist, on the other hand, is contributing only a dead sum of money. It seems unfair, therefore, that surplus revenue should accrue entirely to dead capital and not to those who expend their flesh and blood in the productive process (Ederer 1981, 356–357; Ketteler 1864, 405–406).

While the intelligence and diligence of the entrepreneur also contribute to the success of a company, and these hardly quantifiable factors make it scarcely possible to divide profit from the standpoint of natural justice, this does not change the obvious injustice of the status quo: "...Therefore, if one could discover a more equitable kind of distribution whereby the worker might get a decent share of business profits, ... it would appreciably improve the worker's condition" (Ederer 1981, 356–357; Ketteler 1864, 405–406).

The question that now arises is how workers can get access to capital so as to acquire a share of the company. Ketteler refers to productive associations in France and England, which represent a possible solution, but only have a marginal effect if workers have to raise the required capital themselves (Ketteler 1864, 407–408). Yet Ketteler rejects Lassalle's proposal of advancing the development of productive associations with government aid. The state may and should only intervene if someone is in extreme distress, in which case it can call on proprietors to raise essential resources for such persons. Beyond such essential supplies, there is no obligation, from neither a legal nor a theological standpoint, for further aid, only the moral obligation of Christian brotherly love (Ketteler 1864, 415). "Lassalle would like to actuate this plan through capital subsidies provided by the state. We have explained that we regard this notion, if one is considering it for universal application by means of a direct legal enactment that would tax the wealthy to provide the necessary capital for the working class, as an incursion on the legitimate bounds of the state's right to tax. We also indicated that we would have grave doubts about the practical feasibility of the approach in a manner that would permit peaceful and orderly development of the body politic" (Ederer 1981, 411–412; Ketteler 1864, 449–450, see also Nothelle-Wildfeuer 2002, 638–640).

Ketteler puts much more trust in the return to Christian values: "... since the spirits and strength of Christendom no longer holds egotism with its accompanying passions in check, we now have to experience the development of such ominous conditions in the social order. The cure for this can and will come only from within. To the degree that eternal truths once again will enlighten men's spirits, we will once more discover the correct principles and their proper application in the economic scheme of things ..." (Ederer 1981, 386; Ketteler 1864, 431). With this in mind, Ketteler trusts that the development of workers' associations can be furthered by means of voluntary, private financial support. Ketteler also recommends the formation of support facilities for people incapable of work (432), the strengthening of marriage and family (Ketteler 1864, 435), educational efforts in the Christian sense, and the consolidation of workers (Ketteler 1864, 444).

Like Ketteler, Leo XIII bemoans the fact that work has become a commodity (also see Johannes XXIII 1961, 18) and, like Ketteler, he sees the social changes and resulting isolation and defenselessness of workers as the starting point (Leo XIII 1891, 3, 38). Pope Leo XIII criticizes, like Ketteler, the increasing concentration of capital (Leo XIII 1891, 1) and demands a wage that goes beyond the level of the mere essential, whereby Leo's demands go further than Ketteler's (Leo XIII 1891, 13). Both agree that it should be made possible in some way for workers to provide for their own futures and those of their families (Leo XIII 1891, 5). Pope Leo XIII also shares Ketteler's skeptical view of tax-funded social programs (Leo XIII 1891, 47).

5 Sermon at the Liebfrauenheide (1869)

A practical episode may be partially to blame for Bishop Ketteler's subsequent loss of optimism regarding the private financing of workers' associations: in January 1864, Ketteler turns to Ferdinand Lassalle in an anonymous letter in which he presents his intention to raise 50,000 guldens for the establishment of 5 productive worker associations in the areas of cigar production, manual labor and factory production, by means of which workers will receive a share of the capital gain in addition to their wages. He also requests Lassalle's practical support, which the latter's written reply does not promise, however. Instead, Lassalle first demands the writer lift his anonymity, which Ketteler cannot bring himself to do despite Lassalle's promise of confidentiality (Müller 1947, 26–28).

Held in high esteem by Ketteler, Ferdinand Lassalle, who generally assumed neutral position vis-à-vis the Catholic Church, died as the result of a pistol duel in 1864. Their apparent mutual esteem was certainly viewed critically by the public. "When Ferdinand Lassalle, during a triumphant speaking tour in 1864, cited the support of Bishop Wilhelm Emmanuel von Ketteler of Mainz, both Roman Catholics and socialists were startled, and many were shocked" (Walker 1967, 47). In any case, Ferdinand Lassalle's successors had no interest in becoming close to the Catholic Church or to Bishop Ketteler, with revolutionary socialism of the Marxist school becoming increasingly important.

In 1865, Ketteler argues, in an address to the Catholic Gessellenverein in Mainz, in favor of government assistant for workers for the first time (Große Kracht 2011 147–148; Ketteler Ketteler 1865, 685–688). This stronger shift towards the state is also present in his paper "Germany after the War of 1866", which appeared in 1867. Ketteler associated the outcome of the war with the hope that there might be more leeway for the Church in a Prussian-dominated Germany (Brauer 1927, 99). While the social question tends to stand on the sidelines in his 1867 paper, he vehemently attacks the "liberal economics" of John Stuart Mill and Thomas Robert Malthus.

Ketteler is appalled by their doctrine: "Economics without religion and without Christ has taken us so far that it is already possible to utter horrifying principles. In the event of overpopulation, 'a portion of humanity must perish'" (Ketteler 1867, 122).

Bishop Ketteler's sermon at the Liebfrauenheide pilgrimage site near Offenbach on July 25, 1869 before thousands of workers has become famous and is still regarded today as the "Magna Carta of the Christian labor movement" (Grosse Kracht 156).

From the start of his sermon, it is apparent that Ketteler is increasingly relying on organized consolidations of workers to reach a solution to the social question: "The basic objective of the labor movement, that which provides its motive force, in fact, its very essence, is the effort to unite, to organize workers so that by solid united effort their interest may be promoted" (Ketteler 1869a, 4–5; Ederer 1981, 441). This could result in a development that counteracted the actual causes of the social problems. "Absolute freedom in all areas of economy" was accompanied on the one hand by the dissolution of old social structures, which led to the isolation of the individual worker. On the other hand, it also led to major tendencies of concentration in terms of capital, so that workers have wound up in a "desperate position" with respect to "monetary power". The problem is complicated to the same extent as the proprietor of capital power, which "…is without conscience, without religion, and uses it merely as a means to satisfy his egoism" (Ketteler 1869a, 5). Ketteler sees the development of essentially apolitical, religiously neutral trade unions in England as prototypical: "It is from the same England where the corruption began that the greatest pressure to organize labor originated. By such collective effort workers may protect their rights and interests and this is entirely legitimate and beneficial, if the working class is not completely vanquished by the power of centralized capital" (Ketteler 1869a, 5–6; Ederer 1981, 442).

Yet Ketteler warns unequivocally that the workers' efforts require a Christian orientation because labor organizations need leaders, and only an alignment towards Christian values offers workers a "…guarantee that these leaders and representatives will not turn out to be their deceivers and betrayers …"—there is indeed even a risk that workers will be exploited just as badly by their leaders as they had been previously by the capitalists, if the labor leaders are such who "… not only have no respect for Christianity, but who in fact despise it …" (Ketteler 1869a, 6; Ederer 1981, 442–443). In general terms, "… we all fall prey to egotism; it makes no difference whether we are rich or poor, capitalists or workers. We will take advantage of our fellow man as soon as we have the power to do so" (Ketteler 1869a, 6; Ederer 1981, 443).

Bishop Ketteler supports the demand for higher wages corresponding to "the true value of labor" because, ultimately, work should not simply be treated like a commodity, the price of which is determined merely by supply and demand. Yet it is exactly this situation, in which work is seen as a commodity, and the entire human being as a machine in the process of production, which Ketteler views as given. As a result, human workforces are treated like a machine, which is bought as cheaply as possible and exploited uninterruptedly until its destruction. On the other hand, he saw some initial improvements being made in England, changes which he attributed to the trade unions and whose most important instrument, the strike, he explicitly endorses. Ketteler designates objections to strikes, such as that workers are harming themselves by causing losses to the company and loss of income, as "untrue on the whole" and refers to empirical evidence from the then recently published book "On Labour" by William Thomas Thornton. Above all, Ketteler stresses the effect described by Thornton that workers generally appear defeated after strikes, but that such activities subsequently frequently lead to extensive wage increases that go well beyond the actual enterprise affected by the strike. Consequently, Ketteler now also welcomes the formation of cooperatives in Germany according to the model of English trade unions (Ketteler 1869a, 7–8). However, he also warns workers against having excessive expectations, because wage increases must also have their limits if the employer's business is to remain profitable. Excessive wage demands can have catastrophic results. If profitability is not maintained, the capital will migrate, and the "horrible debt management of our modern states" has led to a situation, in which "in the end every speculator on the exchange and in government stocks retains an immense territory for his operations" (Ketteler 1869a, 10). In contrast, workers will not find a new source of income so easily, and so it is they themselves, along with small tradespersons, who ultimately suffer from excessive wage demands. Ketteler also cautions that the working class itself must "avoid the pitfalls of a disorderly selfishness, which it is fighting against among the capitalists", and this requires a "good, Christian" working class because, without Christian virtues, both "monetary power" and "working class power" will lead to ruin (Ketteler 1869a, 10–11). And even the highest wage that can be reached by negotiations and labor disputes only guarantees workers and their families adequate income if this is based on "great temperance and frugality" (Ketteler 1869a, 8–9). Ketteler emphasizes the possibility of companies, in which the workers are co-owners. He again stresses his idea of implementing this in cigar manufacture, where it is possible to produce significant amounts with a relatively small amount of capital (he suggests 20,000 Thalers, Ketteler 1864, 21).

Even when Ketteler criticizes existing conditions in terms that could not be clearer—"The godlessness of capital, which exploits the worker as manpower and machine to the point of destruction, must be broken. It is a crime against the working class…"—his pursuit of balance is also distinctly recognizable: "The objective must not be the struggle between the employer and the worker, but a lawful peace between them" (Ketteler 1869a, 10). "We would see everywhere that the demands of the working class, insofar as they are justified, have their true basis in religion and morality" (Ketteler 1869a, 21). Concerning the person who stands against Christian beliefs, one can "assume without further ado that he understands nothing about the labor questions or is a fraud" (Ketteler 1869a, 22).

Shortly after his sermon at the Liebfrauenheide, Bishop Ketteler held three lectures at the 1869 Bishops Conference in Fulda. The lecture concerning the "Care of the Church for Factory Workers" was later published under the title "The Charitable Concern of the Church for the Working Class". In it, Ketteler enumerates the reasons why the Catholic Church should intervene to help

> … The social problem touches on the deposit of faith. Even if it is not immediately apparent, the leading principle of modern economics which has been aptly characterized as, 'The war of all against all' 'stands in direct opposition to our Faith … Furthermore, it is within the competence of the Magisterium to rise in opposition to the materialistic conception of things, according to which man is treated no longer as a person, but as representing a certain amount of labour - a machine - and whereby he is regarded as a commodity which one exploits for egoistical purposes. … The Church must get involved in this social problem in an especially urgent manner if it is to work for the salvation of mens' souls. At stake here are the souls of vast numbers of the working masses who find themselves placed in a proximate occasion of sin … Out of consideration for simple Christian charity, the Church is obliged to come to workers' rescue … Finally the Church must get involved in the workers' problems, because otherwise they will fall prey to other elements which either are indifferent to Christendom or are downright hostile to it (such as Schulze-Delitzsch or the Social Democrats) … (Ederer 1981, 475–478; Ketteler 1869b, 435–438).

Ketteler warns that the Church could evade its responsibility by asserting that the issue was still too confused and that it should take a stand later with more peace and security. On the contrary, the topic is "a ripe one". It is also unrealistic to expect that the entire system might be overturned, so "… one must do what one can to soften its ill effects and to come up with appropriate remedies and see to it that the workers also share in whatever benefits the system is capable of generating" (Ederer 1981, 478; Ketteler 1869b, 438).

Ketteler thus presented a catalog of measures, most of which he had already touched upon in his sermon at the Liebfrauenheide. He attaches special importance to the demand for "state legislation for the protection of workers". This was to include the prohibition of child labor, the regulation of working time, Sunday rest, the closure of operations that are hazardous to health, and compensations for occupational incapacity that can be attributed to the work itself.

The measures described would also later be demanded by Pope Leo XIII in similar form (Leo XIII 1891, 41–42, 48). The formation of workers' associations, the self-help of workers and the founding of charitable institutions are also central concerns of the *Rerum novarum* encyclical (Leo XIII 1891, 29, 43–45, 48). However, the Pope insists on the argument that strikes are not well-suited instruments, above all damaging the workers themselves (Leo XIII 1891, 38).

6 Later Years

The Bishop of Mainz subsequently dedicated himself again to political questions concerning the relationship between church and state. Although he was a representative of Ultramontanism in Germany, Ketteler opposed the dogmatization of the Pope's infallibility at the First Vatican Council in 1870. However, he accepted the decision of the majority at the council and announced the corresponding pronouncements in his diocese. In 1871, Ketteler was elected representative of the constituency of Tauberbischofsheim in Baden in the first German Reichstag and founded the Center Party together with Ludwig Windthorst. From 1870 at the latest, it appears that Ketteler's skeptical sympathy for a brand of socialism such as was heralded by Ferdinand Lassalle had finally given way to a rejection of a potentially violent revolutionary communism of a Karl Marx. It also becomes clear how a third alternative for Catholic social doctrine emerged with the rejection of liberalism and socialism. In his 1871 paper "Liberalism, Socialism and Christianity", Ketteler strictly opposes liberalism and socialism, between which he sees a close connection:

> … we find another kind of liberalism in the recalcitrant offspring of mature liberalism; and in this latter form it causes much grief to its parents to the extent that the latter would gladly disown it and blame the whole thing on us Catholics. Their efforts come to naught, however, because the offspring clings to its parents, demands its rightful inheritance, and can prove that it is its legitimate progeny. I refer, of course, to socialism. (Ederer 1981, 501; Ketteler 1871, 23) … If the principles of liberalism are valid, then socialism, which is in fact one of the most perverse aberrations of the human spirit, is fully justified (Ketteler 1871, 27–28; Ederer 1981, 506).

In a pastoral letter from February 1876, published later with the title "Religion and the National Welfare", Bishop Ketteler describes how Christian living enhances the national economic welfare. While other measures, e.g. wise legislation, are important, these "… other means are by themselves insufficient and religion and morality are the first and most important prerequisites for the general welfare of a nation" (Ederer 1981, 543; Ketteler 1876).

His final rejection of both liberalism and socialism is an ultimate commonality with the encyclical *Rerum novarum* (for the position of *Rerum novarum* see Messner 1981, 12–14, Pius XI 1931, 10).

7 Closing Remarks

Bishop Ketteler died, following a trip to Rome, on July 13, 1877 in the Capuchin monastery Burghausen am Inn and is laid to rest in Mainz Cathedral. Bishop Ketteler is no longer able to experience the practical effect of his sociopolitical ideas. This is left to successors such as Frank Hitze. His nephew, Ferdinand Heribert von Galen, introduces the "Galen motion" at the Reichstag in 1877, in which demands such as Sunday rest and occupational safety represent the birth of the social policy of the Center Party. Yet it is above all in subsequent social encyclicals, particularly *Rerum novarum*, that Bishop Ketteler's ideas are again to be encountered. Especially succinct is the common insight that it is not a complete elimination of current economic systems, but rather gradual reform that can solve contemporary social problems. His orientation towards ideas of natural law and Thomas Aquinas is pioneering for Catholic social doctrine. One element of the Catholic doctrine of natural law is that decisions, be they individual or social, depend on the free will of man. This is hardly compatible with either liberalism or socialism: "In both systems, there was a lack of free choice. For the classical economist, it was folly of human laws that encumbered what ought to be a natural ordering of relations among persons. There was no choice as to the end, the end was an ordered system. … For the communist, the end was given, an historical inevitability" (Meador 2007, 59). Already at the inception of Catholic social doctrine, with Bishop Ketteler, we see the development of a third path between capitalism and socialism (see also Frambach and Eissrich 2016). Another noteworthy point about Bishop Ketteler is that, despite being a member of the church, he advances not only arguments based on faith; on the contrary, many of his arguments are based on economic necessities. This type of argumentation is later followed by the encyclical *Rerum novarum* and other social encyclicals.

Pope Benedict provided another reminder of his enduring importance by naming Wilhelm Emmanuel von Ketteler a pioneer of Catholic social teaching in his encyclical *Deus caritas est* in 2005 (Benedict XVI 2005, 27).

References

Aubert R (2005) Catholic social teaching. An historical perspective. Marquette University Press, Milwaukee

Benedict XVI (2005) Encyclical Deus caritas est. http://w2.vatican.va/content/benedict-xvi/en/encyclicals/documents/hf_ben-xvi_enc_20051225_deus-caritas-est.html. Accessed 1 July 2016

Brauer T (1927) Ketteler - Der deutsche Bischof und Sozialreformer. Hanseatische Verlagsanstalt, Hamburg

Ederer RJ (ed) (1981) The social teachings of Wilhelm Emmanuel von Ketteler, Bishop of Mainz (1811–1877). University Press of America, Washington D.C.

Frambach H, Eissrich D (2016) Der dritte Weg der Päpste. Die Wirtschaftsideen des Vatikans. UVK, Konstanz

Große Kracht H-J (2011) Wilhelm Emmanuel von Ketteler. Ein Bischof in den sozialen Debatten seiner Zeit. topos, Kevelaer

Heidenreich B (ed) (2002) Politische Theorien des 19. Jahrhunderts, Akademie Verlag, Wiesbaden

Höffner J (1962) Wilhelm Emmanuel v. Ketteler und die Katholische Sozialbewegung im 19. Jahrhundert. Franz Steiner Verlag, Wiesbaden

Iserloh E (ed) (1977a) Wilhelm Emmanuel Freiherr von Ketteler, Sämtliche Werke und Briefe, Abt. I, Bd. 1, Schriften, Aufsätze und Reden 1848–1866. v. Hase und Koehler, Mainz

Iserloh E (ed) (1977b) Wilhelm Emmanuel Freiherr von Ketteler, Sämtliche Werke und Briefe, Abt. I, Bd. 1, Schriften, Aufsätze und Reden 1867–1870. v. Hase und Koehler, Mainz

Iserloh E (ed) (1977c) Wilhelm Emmanuel Freiherr von Ketteler, Sämtliche Werke und Briefe, Abt. I, Bd. 4, Schriften, Aufsätze und Reden 1871–1877. v. Hase und Koehler, Mainz

Ketteler WE (1848a) Offenes Schreiben Kettelers als Deputierten der deutschen Nationalversammlung an seine Wähler, 17. September 1848, reprinted in Mumbauer J (ed) (1924), pp 396–407

Ketteler WE (1848b) Rede vor der ersten Versammlung des Katholischen Vereines Deutschlands in Mainz am 4. Oktober 1848, reprinted in Iserloh E (ed) (1977a), pp 17–20

Ketteler WE (1849) Die großen socialen Fragen der Gegenwart - Sechs Predigten gehalten im hohen Dom zu Mainz. Verlag von Kirchheim und Schott, Mainz, English Edition: Ederer (ed) (1981)

Ketteler WE (1864) Die Arbeiterfrage und das Christentum, reprinted in Iserloh E (1977a), pp 367–515

Ketteler WE (1865) Ansprache anlässlich der Festfeier des Mainzer Gesellenvereins vom 19. November 1865 über die Soziale Frage, reprinted in Iserloh E (ed) (1977a), pp 684–688
Ketteler WE (1867) Deutschland nach dem Kriege von 1866, reprinted in Iserloh E (ed) (1977b), pp 1–127
Ketteler WE (1869a) Die Arbeiterbewegung und ihr Streben im Verhältniß zu Religion und Sittlichkeit – Eine Ansprache, gehalten auf der Liebfrauen-Haide am 25. Juli 1869, Verlag Franz Kirchheim, Mainz
Ketteler WE (1869b) Fürsorge der Kirche für die Fabrikarbeiter, reprinted in Iserloh E (ed) (1977b), pp 429–451
Ketteler WE (1871) Liberalismus, Socialismus und Christenthum, reprinted in Iserloh E (ed) (1977c), pp 21–34
Ketteler WE (1873), Die Katholiken im Deutschen Reiche. Entwurf zu einem Politischen Programm, reprinted in Iserloh E (ed) (1977c), pp 186–262
Ketteler WE (1876) Fastenbrief - über den Zusammenhang zwischen Religion, Sittlichkeit und Volkswohlfahrt, reprinted in Reich M (ed) (1904), pp 885–902
Leo XIII (1891) Encyclical Rerum novarum. http://w2.vatican.va/content/leo-xiii/en/encyclicals/documents/hf_l-xiii_enc_15051891_rerum-novarum.html. Accessed 1 July 2016
Marx R (2011) Christ sein heißt politisch sein. Wilhelm Emmanuel von Ketteler für heute gelesen. Herder, Freiburg, Basel, Vienna
Meador DM (2007) Examining the economic foundations of catholic social thought. Umi, Kansas City
Messner J (1981) Die Magna Charta der Sozialordnung. 90 Jahre Rerum novarum, Kirche und Gesellschaft (76)
Mueller FH (1971) Kirche und Industrialisierung. Fromm, Osnabrück
Müller OH (1947) Ketteler: Auswahl aus seinen sozialen Schriften. Kompass-Verlag, Oberursel
Münstermann H (2013) Geschichte und Kapitalwirtschaft: Beiträge zur Allgemeinen Betriebswirtschaftslehre. Springer, Berlin, Heidelberg
Mumbauer J (ed) (1924) Wilhelm Emmanuel von Kettelers Schriften, vol I: Religiöse, kirchliche und kirchenpolitische Schriften. Josef Kösel & Friedrich Pustet, Munich
Nothelle-Wildfeuer U (2002) Wilhelm Emmanuel von Ketteler (1811–1877). In: Heidenreich B (ed), pp 629–647
Pius XI (1931) Encyclical Quadragesimo anno. http://w2.vatican.va/content/pius-xi/en/encyclicals/documents/hf_p-xi_enc_19310515_quadragesimo-anno.html. Accessed 3 July 2016
Pfülf O (1899) Bischof von Ketteler (1811–1877). Eine geschichtliche Darstellung, vol 1–3. Verlag von Franz Kirchheim, Mainz
Reich M (ed) (1904) von Kettelers Hirtenbriefe. Lehrlingshaus, Mainz
Walker FA (1967) Bishop Ketteler and Ferdinand Lassalle, CCHA Study Sessions (34), pp 47–56

Solidarism as the Center of Economy—The Economics of Heinrich Pesch

Hans A. Frambach

1 Introduction

In 1891, the year of Pope Leo XIII's pioneering social encyclical *Rerum novarum*, the Jesuit priest Heinrich Pesch (1854–1926) was 37 years old. He had just returned from England, where he had encountered the social problems of increasing industrialization—an experience that gave him the desire to devote his life to the improvement of the situation of industrial workers. Pesch had, of course, no influence on the emergence of *Rerum novarum*, and he was already dead when the second social encyclical *Quadragesimo anno* was published in 1931 on the 40th anniversary of the first. But a significant portion of his adult life was lived during the papacy of Pope Leo XIII (1878–1903), and although he had already discussed essential social problems in the sense of the encyclical before it was published, most of his own scholarly production came after *Rerum novarum*. Pesch refers to the encyclical in many of his works, making suggestions to improve the situation of workers and commenting on the role of private property, ethical and social obligations of the state, the relation of entrepreneurs and labor, fair wages, productivity and justice (Pesch 1914, 170, 191, 201–206, 508–516; 1922, 412–413, 522–526; 1923, 562–565, 617, 625–650, 661–662). Other even wider topics that deeply concerned him were the comparison between individualistically oriented capitalism and collectivistic socialism, the conflict of the social classes, and the family as the basis of the state (Pesch 1925, 230–232, 240, 702–705).

H.A. Frambach (✉)
Schumpeter School of Business and Economics, Faculty of Management and Economics, University of Wuppertal, Wuppertal, Germany
e-mail: frambach@wiwi.uni-wuppertal.de

J. Backhaus et al. (eds.), *On the Economic Significance of the Catholic Social Doctrine*, The European Heritage in Economics and the Social Sciences 19, DOI 10.1007/978-3-319-52545-7_3

With such ideas Pesch stood in line with the spirit of *Rerum novarum*, and his work undoubtedly inspired the emergence of *Quadragesimo anno* in a lasting manner; indeed, it can in a certain sense be understood as a bridge between those two encyclicals (Ederer 1991, 596–597, 605, 609; Grosschmid 1954, 147; Mazurek 1980, 79, 81; Mulcahy 1952, 8). Moreover, Pesch's economic system, which he called solidarism, was decisive not only for the development of *Quadragesimo anno* but also for further social encyclicals such as *Mater et Magistra* (1961), *Pacem in Terris* (1963), *Laborem Exercens* (1981), and *Sollicitudo Rei Socialis* (1987). Solidarism was a social philosophy that saw the working human person as central to economic life, employing the principle of subsidiarity to determine the role of the state in economic activity, and subordinating economic activity to the social virtues of justice and charity (Pesch 1998, viii; Ederer 1981, 82; Grosschmid 1954, 149, 152–155; von Nell-Breuning 1990, e.g. 89). Many of Pesch's concepts have remained alive and influential over time and are still valid today. Pesch ranks as the founder of Catholic social theory and as the person who first systematized Christian social considerations (e.g. Große Kracht 2007a, 9; 2007b, 59, 62–63; Fenske 1991, 729; Gülich 1991, 1, 7; Mazurek 1980, 78; Mulcahy 1952, 7; Reisz 2006, 138; Wishloff 2006, 33).

2 Stages in the Life of Heinrich Pesch

Heinrich Pesch was born on September 17, 1854 in Cologne. In 1860 his family moved to Bonn where Heinrich went to school and matriculated at the Königlich-Preußisch Rheinische Universität (Royal Prussian University of the Rhineland) in theology. In March 1873, after only one semester, he gave up theology and enrolled for jurisprudence. In winter semester 1874–75 he attended his first lecture in national economics with Erwin Nasse, one of the founders and the current president of the *Verein für Socialpolitik*. A financial theorist and deeply religious protestant, Nasse, as Mueller (1980, 12–15) remarks, strongly influenced the development of Pesch's economic thinking. In a letter to Pesch shortly before his death, Nasse expressed his conviction that the development and application of norms embedded in human conscience was much more important for economic progress than public institutions. While still a student, Pesch applied for a novitiate in the Jesuit Order, to which he was admitted on January 10, 1876. In the following two years he completed the ascetic training in the religious house in Exaeten, near Roermond (Netherlands), followed by the juniorate in nearby Valkenburg (Netherlands), where he intensified his humanistic studies as a Jesuit scholastic (Mueller 1980, 20; Pesch 1924, 191–192).

Pesch completed the compulsory three years of philosophical studies from 1879 to 1882 in the Jesuit College at Blijenbeek Castle, near Goch in the Lower Rhineland. There he learnt to appreciate scholasticism, with its fundamental principles of dialectics and syllogistic reasoning, which he began to apply to the social sciences and economics. At the end of this philosophical triennium, he was sent as a grammar school teacher to the Jesuit College of Stella Matutina in Feldkirch, Austria, where he spent a further three years in practical training as an educator and pedagogue—the so-called "regency" (Interstiz) usual in the Jesuit Order. After these three years, Pesch still had to complete his four years of theological studies, which he did at the Jesuit house at Ditton, in Lancashire, England, a small town between Liverpool and Warrington. It should be remembered that the Bismarckian laws against Jesuits forbade the Order on German territory between 1872 and 1904 (the law was finally repealed in 1907). In Ditton Hall Pesch was able to experience at first hand the reality of the Industrial Revolution, with its great economic achievements overshadowed by labor issues. In a later self-portrait he wrote that it was the fate of the working class that led him to the final decision to address himself academically to the *social question* and to devote his life to the improvement of the situation of the workers (Pesch 1924, 194–195).

On December 18, 1887, at the age of 34, Pesch was ordained priest by the bishop of Liverpool, but he had still to complete his additional year of tertianship, the third probationary period in the Jesuit training program. In 1890 he was sent back to Exaeten in the Netherlands, where he had started his novitiate some thirteen years before. There he supported his 18 year older brother, Tilmann Pesch SJ (1836–1899), in editing the monthly journal *Stimmen aus Maria Laach* (Voices from Maria Laach). Between 1890 and 1918 Heinrich Pesch wrote 98 articles and book reviews for this journal; for other journals only six articles. In the early 1890s he was invited by Count Ernst Emanuel Teles da Silva-Taroucca to Türmitz Castle in Austria to discuss socialist ideas and tendencies, especially the teachings of Johann Rodbertus-Jagetzow, the grandson of Johann A. Schlettwein. Count Silva-Taroucca was a big Austrian landowner and industrialist, a later president of the Austrian "Katholikentag" (the main gathering, every few years, of lay Catholic organizations in German-speaking countries). In Türmitz Pesch wrote his pamphlet *Die sociale Befähigung der Kirche in protestantischer Beleuchtung* ("The Social Mission of the Church under Protestantism"). From Türmitz he travelled to Vienna, visiting Christian charitable institutions there, and describing and analyzing them in a 142-page document entitled *Die Wohltätigkeitsanstalten der Christlichen Barmherzigkeit in Wien* ("The Welfare Institutions of Christian Charity in Vienna", Freiburg im Breisgau 1891) published as an extended supplement to *Stimmen aus Maria Laach*. For this, he had to visit various institutions, speak with executives and collect empirical and statistical data etc.

Heinrich Pesch
Source: Verband der wissenschaftlichen katholischen Studentenvereine Unitas e.V.;

In 1891 Pesch returned to the Netherlands, but—at the request of Paul Leopold Haffner, Bishop of Mainz and successor to Bishop Wilhelm Emmanuel von Ketteler (1811–1887)—he was in 1892 appointed "spiritual director" at the theological college in Mainz, a position he held until 1900. During his time in Mainz he worked enthusiastically in social adult education. Among other things he studied the writings of Ketteler and wrote the book *Liberalismus, Socialismus und christliche Gesellschaftsordnung* ("Liberalism, Socialism and the Christian Social Order"). Published in 1901 in two volumes, this saw liberalism as the root of all evil, directly followed by its offshoot, socialism. In this book Pesch took up the contemporary discussion within social and political Catholicism and provided it for the first time with a comprehensive theoretical foundation (Mueller 1980, 28–38). He left Mainz for a stay at the writers' centre at Bellevue Castle in Luxembourg, where he immersed himself in preliminary studies for the *Lehrbuch der Nationalökonomie* ("Textbook of Economics") that was to become his lifework: an exposition of the theoretical foundations of economics in light of the benevolent pragmatism of the Catholic social movement. At Bellevue Castle he found a first-class library stocked by the Jesuits with thousands of books and leading journals, and perfect conditions for academic work (Pesch 1924, 198).

Among the different places offered to him by the Order to deepen his knowledge in economics Pesch had chosen Berlin, and in April 1901, at the age of 46, he enrolled in the philosophical faculty of the Friedrich-Wilhelm-University to study economics, attending the lectures of such famous teachers as Gustav von Schmoller, Max Sering, Adolf Wagner, Karl Helfferich, Konrad Bornhak and Ladislaus von Bortkiewicz. In 1903 he returned to Luxembourg to start work on his *Lehrbuch*. He began intensively to study the first volume of Karl Marx's *Capital*—incidentally, a book with an excellent reputation in Catholic circles (Große Kracht 2007a, 17–18; Mueller 1980, 40–41, 47–48). In 1910 Pesch again moved from Luxembourg to Berlin, where he stayed for fifteen years. In Berlin he lived in the Good Shepherd Convent in the suburb of Marienfelde, whose nuns cared for prostitutes and unmarried mothers and undertook the education and support of vulnerable children. There he wrote the four remaining volumes of his *Lehrbuch*, along with *Ethik und Volkswirtschaft* ("Ethics and Economics") and some pamphlets on the relationship between Catholic workers and current revolutionary events (Große Kracht 2007a, 22–23).

In Berlin Pesch had the opportunity to combine theory and practice, seeking in pastoral care both a balancing factor to his academic work and stimulation from the pulsating life of the city. In one respect, especially, one can draw a direct line from his practical experience to his writings. For where the original intention of the Marienfelde convent was to contribute to the social question by the exercise of charity and private-law agreements without the support of legislation, Pesch followed Leo XIII, as well as von Ketteler and Hitze, in stressing the role of the state in this area, without underestimating the part played by voluntary and charitable social welfare societies (Mueller 1980, 54, 61).

As Heinrich Pesch aged and began to lose his strength, the search for a successor began. Pesch himself wanted to have the social scientist Heinrich Lechtape as his successor, but the Order wanted a Jesuit to continue his work. Lechtape was known in particular from his 1919 book *Der christliche Sozialismus*[1] ("Christian Socialism") which expounded "the economic constitution of the future, following Heinrich Pesch" (in the second and third editions the term "socialism" was replaced by "solidarism", a concept first used by Pesch in his article of the same title in 1902). The Jesuits chose Oswald von Nell-Breuning SJ as Pesch's successor, but the two men were incompatible. As Gustav Gundlach SJ (1892–1963) mentions, Nell-Breuning at the age of 34, speaking with the 70 year-old Pesch, suggested that the master's *Lehrbuch* best be reduced from five to two volumes. In the end, Gundlach was engaged to help Pesch for the rest of his life (Mueller 1980, 61).

[1]"Der christliche Sozialismus, die Wirtschaftsverfassung der Zukunft (nach Heinrich Pesch dargestellt)".

Heinrich Pesch received many honors. For example, in 1923 the faculty of economics and social sciences of the University of Cologne awarded him an honorary doctorate, and a second one was given him in 1925 by the faculty of Catholic theology of the University of Münster. In 1925 his health was already weakening and the Jesuit Provincial decided to send him from Berlin to Valkenburg in the Netherlands because of the better healthcare provision there. For some month, Heinrich Pesch worked on the revision of the third volume of his *Lehrbuch*. He celebrated his golden anniversary as a Jesuit on January 10, 1926. On April 1, 1926 he died.

3 Theoretical Foundations and Fundamental Convictions

Human beings as individuals capable of reason govern the world, and rational nature is the common good of humankind, but the justification for this is God's will (Pesch 1914, 2). Pesch starts his *Lehrbuch* with this principle, and goes on to describe its foundations—as opposed to its concrete manifestations—as unchangeable. By his nature, man is compelled to subject the earth to his service in a purposeful and continuous manner, since it is the only way to satisfy his needs. In doing so, he is able, in contrast to the animals, to change, expand and refine his wants, as human culture and its means develop Progress appears, therefore, as an undeniable aspect of human existence from which nobody can be excluded. Everyone is entitled to participate in the material progress of culture (Pesch 1914, 3).

However, progress and the satisfaction of human needs and desires cannot and should not be driven to infinity, particularly as we have various needs, material and immaterial, cultural, existential and natural, modest and luxurious, individual and collective. Referring to Albert Schäffle's *Éléments d'Économie Politique*, Pesch calls for a moral limit to the expansion of wants. Such an expansion can only be allowed if the wants are aligned with the criteria of moral education and happiness (Pesch 1914, 8). Pure craving for enjoyment has no intrinsic limits and can easily become excessive, whereas rational striving searches for an optimal mix of competing wants, both material and immaterial, including those of morality. To attain "true welfare" man has to align himself with the spiritual and moral order, to be aware of the world as God's property, to find the right balance of values, to be able to renounce. Man can only master the world, and thus follow the divine order, if he can master himself (Pesch 1914, 8, 18; 1998, 6–7). The contradiction with the views of modern economic theory is obvious and needs no further comment.

The instrument for the fulfillment of the divine call to master the earth is human labor. Labor, a gift of God, is part of the natural endowment of the human personality. For this very reason, it would be a denial of an incontestable truth to reduce human labor to the level of material things (Pesch 1914, 9). Workers are human beings, not goods, and that is why the wage question should not be seen in purely economic terms as a bare result of the price mechanism of the supply and demand of labor (Pesch 1923, 563). The special nature and value of human labor results from this, and it includes both effort and pleasure. Of course, not everyone need take a shovel in the hand, but no one should live from the labor of others without any attempt on their part to do something useful. Such behavior is perceived as a departure from the order ordained by God (Pesch 1914, 10; 1998, 6).

A central principle of Heinrich Pesch's thought relates to the social nature of man, who is not created by God as a self-sufficient individual (Pesch 1914, 29). Oswald von Nell-Breuning (1890–1991) illustrated this idea with the metaphor of people all being in the same boat (von Nell-Breuning 1990, 17, 20–26). If the boat sinks, everyone goes down; if it reaches its destination, everyone is saved. What is undertaken to reach the goal requires the interaction of all occupants and benefits all; what is omitted—if only some occupants work and do what they want, without consideration for the purpose of the voyage—harms everyone, endangering their safety and leading in the worst case to shipwreck, which brings loss to everyone (von Nell-Breuning 1951, 361). Mutual interdependence and the strong social relations within the human community impose reciprocal obligations. To pursue the metaphor, it follows that captain, crew and passengers have rights and duties, and this as a result of moral commandments (Möhring-Hesse 2007, 236). In his book *Baugesetze der Gesellschaft* ("Constructional Laws of Society") Nell-Breuning gave shape to Pesch's central concept of solidarism, describing, among other things, solidarity as a "basic law of mutual responsibility" that supports, like a scaffold, the structure of human society—"society will be supported by solidarity as a modern skyscraper by a steel skeleton" (von Nell-Breuning 1990, 11).

A classical element of man's social nature is the division of labor. In combining their energies, people are able to achieve what could never be accomplished by an individual acting alone. One is reminded of Adam Smith's principle of the division of labor, which he derived from the motives of economic action, namely a certain "propensity to truck, barter, and exchange one thing for another" (Smith 1973, 117). There, too, the division of labor appears as the expression of mutual human interdependencies. But in contrast to Smith, who explains the propensity for barter and exchange above all in terms of the individual seeking their own selfish ends, Pesch invokes moral and ethical principles: insights into faith, reason, and moral conscience. He argues that as the division of labor proceeds, mutual interdependence is intensified, and this relationship is in accordance with the divine plan to increase the welfare of the human race. A situation follows in which individuals meet not as isolated subjects reduced to their own ego and lacking any obligation toward each other, but as connected through the duties of mutual consideration and support. The more egoistic motives appear, the more significant the moral moment becomes (Pesch 1914, 30–33). Thus Smith and Pesch agree on the advantages of the division of labor for economic and social welfare, but the approaches behind their concepts differ considerably.

In the light of the foregoing, Pesch's principle of solidarity follows from three general principles: (1) Man is master of the world, of which he himself is part, and which is given to him to satisfy his needs. (2) Man masters the world through work; labor is the essential means of his mastery; without labor there can be no satisfaction of needs and no progress; animate and inanimate nature serves working people in this task. (3) Man can exercise his mastery of the world only in and through society, by working together in a group with his equals, and with a division of labor (Pesch 1922, 2). The principle of solidarity means, however, not only social interdependence, the exchange of goods, productive cooperation etc. It also entails a broader ongoing beneficial cooperation, a reciprocal dependence on the well-being of others that is more than a mere de facto relationship, for it also represents a *moral* relationship between man and his fellows. Thus the principle of solidarity refers to the rational purpose of social life. Even though an individual may only strive for his own interests, he must at the same time have regard for the legitimate interests of others, who, as human beings, have an equal claim to happiness, well-being and the benefits of social living (Pesch 1914, 32–33; 1998, 8–9).

Pesch's concept of solidarity is descriptive, inasmuch as it derives from existing conditions. It can be interpreted as a principle of being in harmony with the divine order of creation. This allows it to be grasped as a social obligation based on natural law, specifically on what he calls the "three pillars of the social order": the *family*, the *state* and *private property* (Pesch 1914, 145–235). Rooted in nature, the *family* is the first social bond, combining human beings in their reciprocal rights and duties. It is seen as the germ-cell of social life and the initial (and smallest) socio-economic entity. The fundamentals of social life and human association—authority, the relation of superiority and subordination, the sense of right and wrong, the sense of duty, the common good, solidarity, love, work and property—all these are included in the family (Pesch 1914, 147, 152, 154; Mueller 1946, 37).

For Pesch the *state* is the direct product of history. Man as a social being seeks to live a life that befits his human dignity and directs him to his goals. For this he needs other social relationships besides the family: relationships with more power and breadth. These are provided in and by the state. Without the state, human aims would remain unattainable and man would lack a lot that is necessary and advantageous for his welfare (Pesch 1914, 160; 1998, 14):

> The purpose of the state as political society consists in providing, preserving, and fulfilling the sum total of those public conditions and institutions which provide, preserve, and enhance the potential of all its members through their combined energies, so that they may freely and independently achieve their true temporal welfare according to their own particular capacities and situations, and preserve what they have achieved in an honest manner. (Pesch 1914, 167, 1998, 23)

There are two sides to public welfare. On the one hand, the state has to make the necessary arrangements to protect its members, i.e. individuals, families and corporations. On the other hand, the support of the state is directed to the entire community and *not* to individual persons. The community of citizens and their groups are provided with the social benefits that are only possible through the combined powers of the state. Individual members of society can achieve their own private welfare while sharing in those benefits and institutional arrangements. In exceptional cases, however, and under given conditions, it may become necessary to assist and support individual persons directly. In accordance with the principle that the poor and the sick should not be left alone in misery, public intervention may be necessary, but private benevolence for the poor should never be replaced by public care. Even the best care provided by the community or the state cannot replace free charitable actions (Pesch 1914, 169, 174–184).

Pesch's interpretation of the role of the state is consistent with the exposition of the situation of working people in *Rerum novarum* (1891, 1, 2): e.g. that the state has to care for the common good in taking account of different social groups and treating them according to the principles of justice. Nevertheless, if the state provides protection and help to its members, it is self-evident that these for their part must forego the temptation to pursue their own interests at all costs without regard for others (Pesch 1914, 172). To fulfill its aims, the state has to provide an adequate system of laws, as well as appropriate economic and social policies. Here again, Pesch is in line with basic statements of Leo XIII's encyclical (e.g. 3–12).

The third pillar of the social order is *private property*, which is understood as one of the most important conditions of a modern economy. In accordance with *Rerum novarum*, Pesch sees private property as a natural right deriving from the absolute necessity of self-preservation. People must have the right to exclude others from the possession and use of the goods they need to survive—in other words the right to create private property. Foresight and provision for the future are mentioned as constituting an additional rational basis for private property (Pesch 1914, 201–202). None other than Henry George, however, raised an objection against this argument, saying that private property should only be held in goods produced by human labor: land is a product of the earth, so man should not be permitted to own it. However, Pesch, following *Rerum* novarum, puts forward further arguments: with private property, parents have an instrument in their hands to care for the future of their children. Property must be understood in this way as an expression of the natural love and care of parents for their children, and as a means to strengthen the welfare of the family as an institution. Moreover, only private property can guarantee that laborers retain some fruits of their work. Finally, the best individual and social use of goods results from private property (Pesch 1914, 203–204), because it produces more efficiently than common property.

However, Pesch also presented the limitations of private property. The right to private property is undoubtedly a right, but not, as such, the highest right. The rights to life and livelihood must be evaluated above property rights. Property rights are accompanied by moral prescriptions and should never be exercised without a sense of duty—in other words property (as the German Constitution still puts it) entails responsibility. Otherwise, the possession of property could end in the misuse of power. Hence, property is not an end in itself: private property is a means to enhance the welfare of the individual, the family and society, and as such it has to be organized and protected by the state (Pesch 1914, 223–224).

Pesch held these three pillars of the social order (family, state, and private property) to be the indispensable conditions of any cultural development (Pesch 1922, 3), and on this basis he suggested a different perception of national economics. Man, and not the market with its laws of supply and demand, must be the aim and subject of the economy. The economy has to serve public welfare. What is required is social equity and public welfare as regulatory principles, with the professions and their established standards on the one hand, and the subsidiary intervention of the state on the other as institutional safeguards. An important measure for realizing this is the enhancement of justice by creating a more uniform distribution of burdens—taking account of individual variations in capacity and performance (Pesch 1918a, 21–22). To achieve this, the economy has to be directed both by the competition principle and the requirement of cooperation between social partners, which again means keeping in view the aim of individual and common welfare (Pesch 1918a, 18–28). Thus, a liberal state, characterized by the capitalist market system, must be extended by components that take into account the social nature of man. This entails a normative principle that could be mediated through the social ethics of solidarism (Mulcahy 1949, 358). Adam Smith, whom Pesch concedes to be no materialist, is accused of having—in his *Theory of Moral Sentiments*—surrendered moral conduct to natural instinct, and thus of substantially contributing to the increasingly materialistic character of national economics and its consequent failure to attain true knowledge of economic laws. In contrast, Pesch emphasizes that true laws can only be derived from a full grasp of the "nature of people and society", which must take account of the intellectual and moral sphere (Pesch 1914, 407).

4 The System of Solidarism

Pesch wanted to build his ideas into an efficient and workable economic system that would, at least to some extent, also provide a sound foundation for Smith's industrial system—he called the application of solidarism to economic life the "social system of industry" to distinguish it explicitly from Smith's "individualistic industrial system" (Mueller 1946, 38; 1977, 189). For Pesch, the working people were the starting point of solidarism. His "social" or "solidarist working system" was based on the "ordered cooperation of the industries and professions", with particular approval reserved for the professional organization of the workers in large-scale industry (Pesch 1925, 214–221, 261). Although he considered competition and private property to be indispensable ("competition is fair or right if [...] neither of the contracting parties takes advantage of any unawareness or lack of information of the other"; Messner 1976, cit. 120; Briefs 1983, 237–238), Pesch sought to delimit liberalist excesses and to overcome the unbounded power position of capital ownership, which he traced back to the (in his eyes) degenerate private-sector market organization, and the unbridled greed in the amassing of wealth that had replaced moderate acquisition efforts (Pesch 1925, 227; 1914, 436–437). He firmly believed that his "solidarist aim" would gain full strength and validity only within the framework of the Christian philosophy of life (Pesch 1925, VI). In other words, to avoid the one-sidedness of both liberalist individualism and collectivist socialism Pesch introduced the group solidarity of individuals, at first descriptively in the sense of the human condition of mutual dependence, and then prescriptively and normatively in the sense of a goal to be achieved. Solidarity means that men and women must also consider the vital interests of others (Briefs 1983, 239–240).

In his system Pesch distinguished various types of solidarity: (1) "The universal solidarity of the human race" that should enable us "to see in our fellow man a natural companion and, in fact a brother, assuring him of just and charitable treatment because of the common relationship which we all share toward God and Christ" (Pesch 1914, 414–415; 1998, 68). This universal type of solidarity deserves application in all situations where man approaches man, i.e. in the family, the state, economic life, international relations between countries etc. It is argued that Christian reasoning knows no difference of race, nation or class, and that within the "general family of God" justice and love should define interpersonal relationships. Hence: (2) "Solidarity of the family". (3) "Solidarity among citizens of the same state", which creates the organic unit of individual existences necessary for the purposes of the state. And: (4) "Solidarity among colleagues at the level of occupational and vocational groups", understood as representing the common interests of the profession (Pesch 1914, 414–415; 1998, 68–69, see also Pesch 1922, 3–5; 1925, 218–224).[2]

Applied to political society and the national economy as distinct aspects of social life, the concept of solidarity "can have no other goal than that of political society itself". The same cannot be said, however, if solidarity is directed to the concealment of the egoistic actions of individuals and social classes (Pesch 1914, 397–398; 1998, 44). Since society is a union of free moral beings, the social system—or, more precisely, its underlying idea—must, for Pesch, itself be a moral postulate. Hence, solidarity, as the natural inclination of man to mutual attachment and goodwill, is to be understood ab initio not only as an empirical fact but also as an assumption about the nature and aims of human life, together with such core social and ethical components as adherence to human dignity and the obligation to mutual support (Spieß 2007, 153). Pesch described this moral claim, which stands as the supreme social law for individual, society and state, as the *idea of solidarity*, and the system built on it as the *system of solidarism* (Pesch 1902, 38).

The concept of solidarism was inspired by the French "solidarisme" and had its roots in the philosophy of positivism. Referring back to the positivism of Auguste Comte, the empiricism of John Stuart Mill, the evolutionism of Herbert Spencer, the different kinds of legal solidarism (Léon Bourgeois and Léon Duguit), sociological solidarism (Émile Durkheim), anarchistic solidarism (Peter Kropotkin), and cooperative solidarism (Charles Gide) (Große Kracht 2007b, 60; Mazurek 1980, 74; Mulcahy 1952, 9; Pesch 1902, 307–310; 1914, 392–405), it represented a "third

[2]These distinctions remind one of Émile Durkheim's division of solidarity into *mechanical* and *organic solidarity* (Durkheim 1988, 118–184). While mechanical solidarity derives from the similarities and agreements of the group, organic solidarity results from the division of labor, which is based on the diversity of individuals and follows mechanical solidarity. If societies differentiate and organize themselves cooperatively, processes of professionalization and individualization lead to high social complexity and at the same time to a stronger attachment of individuals within the whole (Durkheim 1988, 82).

way"—between liberalism and communism—to the solution of the social question (Gülich 1989, 220–221). As Pesch wrote:

> The guiding principle of individualism was the absolute freedom and autonomy of the individual economic unit seeking exclusively its own advantage. To individualistic decentralization, socialism opposed a totally unified, centralized, universal economic community which obliterates all social differentiation between occupational groups, classes, and estates. Between these two extremes of absolute centralization and absolute decentralization, there is a third system which we propose to call solidarism. (Pesch 1902, 38; 1914, 393; 1998, 39–40)

With regard to the role of the state, Pesch approved of the French concept of solidarism; however, he blamed it for being insufficiently workable if all it envisaged was temporary state intervention with the aim of gaining free cooperation. As such, French solidarism amounted merely to a weakened form of liberalism and served individual interests. Pesch intensively analyzed the theories of his highly esteemed teacher and lifelong friend Adolph Wagner (1835–1917), the advocate *par excellence* of state socialism. Wagner considered state socialism to contain many elements of socialism and held its critique to be justified in part and its claims regarding property ownership to be both possible and desirable. He contrasted state socialism with individualism, but at the same time dissociated it from socialism, because it valued the entitlement and necessity of individualism in principle as being in accordance with the common interest (Wagner 1892, 59). At the center of Wagner's political conception stands his conviction of an observable historical regularity, namely what he called the "law of the growing expansion of public state activities in advancing civilized nations" (Wagner 1893, 884). According to this law it would seem obvious to define the tasks of the state in a way that goes far beyond an occasionally intervening social authority: for example to claim the principle of state support, and with it of an offensive state taxation obliged to social and redistributional political aims etc. (Wagner 1948, 43). However, Wagner himself never went so far as to accept the abolition of private ownership of the means of production, preferring to give priority to common or state socialist solutions.

Pesch sought to perpetuate Wagner's ideas by offering a more realistic alternative to state socialism, namely his own solidarism. Thus he interpreted the increasing influence of state activity not, as Wagner did, as a law in the sense of a regularity, but as a means to an end that was itself determined by a major objective: to provide the members of society with secure conditions for their physical and mental growth. The true measure of a developing culture must be the material, intellectual and social development of its members, and of the middle classes in particular (Pesch 1914, 183–184). Everyone can, in a formal sense, profit equally from such a welfare state, and everyone is dependent on it; all are simultaneously obliged to sustain it and must contribute in accordance with their individual performative capacity, so that the purpose of the state, an increase in general welfare, can be achieved (Möhring-Hesse 2007, 239). In this respect Pesch addresses the fundamental trade-off between a "welfare state" (*Wohlfahrtsstaat*) and a "social welfare state" (*Versorgungsstaat*).[3]

Pesch's "third system" arose from a highly differentiated and detailed analysis of the strengths and weaknesses of the systems of socialism and capitalism. He rejected both systems in their pure forms but sympathized with their fundamental ideas. Thus he accepted in principle a market economy, the use of capital, and the institution of private property. Nevertheless capitalism seemed him to entail the command of the economy by an unhindered and inhibited acquisitiveness (Pesch 1918b, 18). He even surmised in the fact that so many representatives of the church followed capitalist interests and had a positive attitude toward the market system the reason for people's deep mistrust of the church. Rather than just enduring and patching up what was manifestly inadequate, he demanded an unequivocal stand against capitalism and an active contribution to a new economic constitution that would open the way to a new economic era. The time of individualistic free-market capitalism seemed to him over; what was necessary now was the socialization of people through economic, social and moral ties, rather than a socialization of the means of production (Pesch 1919a, 7–8; 1919b, 3, 15, 21–22). He deemed this break with the capitalist system necessary in order to overcome the distrust of socialist workers. At the same time, he wished to convince Christian workers of the insurmountable conflict between individualistic capitalism and Christian social and moral theory (Pesch 1919a, 7–8; 1919b, 3). Pesch was no revolutionary; despite his criticism, he wanted in principle to preserve the existing system with its prevailing structures of inequality. The state should seek gradual equality, while the responsibility of the church is for morality.

Pesch believed in the workers, the proletariat. He appreciated their striving for identity and emancipation—a core element of the organic moral concept of solidarism was to structure work in professional organizations (Pesch 1922, 268)—and he thought he saw promising signs of spiritual awareness and will among young people. He believed that an epoch would come in which the workers rather than capital would form the center of the economy, and where employers and employees would grow together in solidarity. To attain this, not the means of production but the producers—the laborers—would have to be socialized in the sense of teaching them to be effective and responsible members of society, aware of their solidarity within the social whole. Hasty socialization, communalization, expropriation,

[3]The French social Catholic movement should also be mentioned here. They were divided into non-interventionists (Angers School) and interventionists (Liège School). The first argued that personal interests should be bound to the ethical maxim of responsibility for society and that the obligation to a moral life derived from divine law. The Liège School argued for state interventionism. Both approaches refer back to the teachings of the Spanish diplomat and state philosopher Juan Donoso Cortés (1809–1853), for whom solidarity meant the responsibility of all in the mutual achievement of redemption and eternity (Cortèz 1989, 158–159; Pesch 1925, 238). The social Catholics from Liège demanded protective rights for the workers and a new economic and social order based on Christian rather than liberalist principles; they sought to influence the decisions of Catholic social politicians and had considerable impact on the emergence of the social encyclical *Rerum novarum* (Reisz 2007, 41).

irresponsible strikes and egoistic wage claims would only frustrate hopes of a better, more humanly oriented economic system (Mueller 1980, 66–67). Even state socialism must be rejected, because, among other things, it restricts private freedom and represses the positive effects of private property (Pesch 1914, 174–184).

The central socio-political thrust of Pesch's solidarism is the construction of a strong welfare state based on principles of order, authority and morality. He regarded this as a legal obligation. Voluntary charitable solidarity, together with the compassion and self-help concepts of the 19th century—all based on models of aid that were independent of the state—were valuable and indispensable additions to solidarity, but in the end it was the political intervention of the state with its laws that formed the central principle of control (Große Kracht 2007b, 68). For Pesch, free market economy was the rule, social economy the exception. Liberty of economic behavior was to be accepted if it was in harmony with the material welfare of the people and the formation of primarily smaller and medium-sized private property holdings (Pesch 1925, IX–X, 203–213, 230–231). Again in this respect, Pesch saw his solidarism as the middle way, mediating between individualism and socialism (Pesch 1902, 58).

5 The Importance of Pesch's Work

The significance of Heinrich Pesch's work may today seem somewhat ambivalent. His writings have evoked a vast literature, and his *Lehrbuch* in particular has been cited and referred to approvingly by many famous economists and social scientists, among them Sombart (1930, 36) and Schumpeter (1965, 934), the latter in his *History of Economic Analysis*. Othmar Spann (1926, 170) and Bernhard Dempsey (1958, 70) characterized the *Lehrbuch* as "a supreme intellectual achievement", and Harris (1946, 40) cited Nell-Breuning in saying that Pesch was the "only systematic Catholic writer whose work has received recognition as a scientific achievement in the general economic world." Moreover, the main principles of Pesch's work, especially his concept of solidarism, are unquestionably among the central intellectual foundations of the modern European welfare state. Located as a "third way" between individualistic liberalism and collectivist socialism, they represent the Catholic interpretation of a solidarity rooted in the German intellectual tradition and may justifiably be regarded as one of the most important steps in the development of modern Catholic social philosophy. Although many social-Romantic (Othmar Spann, August Pieper, Anton Heinen), as well as more socialist (Theodor Steinbüchel) models of society exist within what is known as German "social Catholicism", it is above all Heinrich Pesch's solidarism that typifies the Catholic approach. Pesch intended this concept—like the terms "individualism" and "socialism"—to serve as a mass slogan. In his *Lehrbuch* he sought on the one hand to present a societal model that would be politically and morally superior to both liberalism and socialism, and on the other to better explain the changing economic and social realities of the 20th century (Große Kracht 2007b, 61).

Pesch's "third way" is not, however, a simple compromise between the extremes of individualism and collectivism. It is, rather, based on his recognition of the true nature of man as an individual person and—in consequence of the essentially dialogical nature of the human mind—at the same time a thou-related social being. In other words, solidarism is rooted in the human condition: it is primarily a matter of "being" in the metaphysical sense of the term, and only secondarily, as a consequence, a matter of action or operation (Mueller 1977, 190).

In his monumental work Heinrich Pesch developed solidarism as a fully fledged economic and social theory. His economic analysis was based on the factual and moral bond that unites the members of society with one another and with the social whole, and the whole with its members. In contrast to the theories of individualism and collectivism, solidarism is, however, more than a theory: it is a directive based on the moral reality of the common good, an ethical as well as an explicatory system. Pesch's solidarism was later taken up by his younger fellow Jesuits, especially Gustav Gundlach and Oswald von Nell-Breuning (see e.g. Ebner 2007, 109). It spread widely and successfully within the church and had a great impact on social theory and political decision making, as well as on economic and social policy. Modern principles of solidarity are in fact unthinkable without the Catholic social teachings of Heinrich Pesch.

However, no serious efforts were made during the 20th century to develop Pesch's solidarism further. Today, there are problems in basing the idea of the state on solidarity and justifying it from natural law. Current social problems like the refugee issue have pushed economic arguments increasingly to the fore. Even eighty years ago Abram Harris observed that "there is little in the writings of Pesch that warrants serious attention from the standpoint of theoretical economics": he was mainly concerned with questions of social reform (Harris 1946, 59). In the current social debate we have the problem that not only the welfare state and its activities are criticized, but with it many aspects of solidarity (see the keywords "individual responsibility", "personal provision", "welfare state", "social welfare state2 etc.). The critique of the welfare state is concerned not only with its inefficiencies, incompleteness and unsustainability, but also with the desire to free citizens from the compulsory solidarity imposed on them by the social state, so that they can manage their own life and provide for their own future (Möhring-Hesse 2007, 246). Today's great challenge seems to be to enable citizens to understand themselves as equals among equals, on the one hand not to depend solely on the welfare state and on the other not to become so entangled in the daily struggle for survival that they sink in the ocean of individualism and egoism. Pesch—and it seems like being on another planet—fought with admirable foresight, in accordance with the social encyclicals since *Rerum novarum*, for a growing realization of the commandment of neighborly love.

Certainly, the solidarist ideas of Catholic social doctrine do not play a significant role in today's political life (Große Kracht 2007b, 85). At a more abstract level, the combination of a de facto solidarity rooted in mutual dependence and its transformation into a normative moral system unfortunately tends to appear rather quaint and improbable if human behavior is no longer bound to higher values. For Pesch the combination of both manifestations of solidarity was given by divine moral law (Spieß 2007, 138). Perhaps that is why Pesch's solidarist concept had no great success outside Christian (especially Catholic) circles, and why, as Hermann-Josef Große Kracht (2007b, 80–82) pointed out, even authors like Gundlach and Nell-Breuning replaced the concept of solidarism with that of solidarity (with regard to Gundlach 1962, see the article "Solidaritätsprinzip" in: *Staatslexikon*, ed. Hörres-Gesellschaft, 6. Ed., vol. VII, Freiburg, Herder, 119–122, 120; and for Nell-Breuning see "Gesellschaftliche Ordnungssysteme" in *Wörterbuch der Politik*, vol. V, Freiburg, Herder, 1951, 359).

So far as economic theory is concerned, Pesch is often thought of as an outsider, not least because his central concept of solidarism failed to enforce itself as a political and social guideline for 20th century societies (see e.g., Große Kracht 2007b, 59, 85). His concept of solidarism pursues a moral aim, but it remains a brainchild of the 1920s, concerned with the systematic establishment of a professional/occupational order as a middle course between capitalism and socialism. From the viewpoint of economic theory, this system fails to give convincing answers to the incentive problem and the exploitation issue. Nonetheless, Heinrich Pesch's solidarism must be given credit, not only insofar as it argues from the conditions, circumstances, and prevailing economic system of his time, but also in being set up so dynamically that further development by his pupils was possible. The accusation sometimes leveled that solidarism amounts to a type of Romantic socialism must be considered differentially.

Pesch binds his social perspective—the social development of society and the economy, the obligation to the social good—to God. Only with regard to God can laws be durable; otherwise they would be subject to change and the unpredictability of human affairs with all its unforeseen consequences. Pesch's thinking starts from a Christian awareness, a conscientious dedication to the whole, a willing conviction of the necessity to subordinate private interests to the claims of justice and the common good, and last but not least, self-restraint and the strengthening of Christian charity (Reisz 2007, 49). It becomes clear that high personal and social values, order and morality are the fundamental assumptions of his system of solidarity, in which social justice becomes the spiritual foundation and pillar of Christian solidarism (Grosschmid 1954, 155). Pesch embedded his concept of solidarism within a comprehensive economic theory, which itself corresponds to a normative set of Christian moral ideals. Pesch believed in a realm of ideal values, where progress benefits everybody: kings and subjects, factory owners and workers, poor and rich—all are human beings, united by moral ties of love and justice (Pesch 1925, 239). Any progress that fails to improve the situation of the poorest can never be seen as social progress.

As his assistant and successor Gustav Gundlach once remarked, one could not distinguish between Heinrich Pesch as a human being, a Jesuit, and an economist. He was a priest who saw the victims of a diseased social system and could not easily pass by (Mueller 1980, 58). Economics meant more to him than pure theory: it was a practical science with the task of conveying to economic and social politicians, political leaders and organizers, legislators and reformers insights into facts, structures and trends, in order that they might make wise, clear and successful decisions (Mueller 1980, 62–63).

References

Briefs G (1983) Pesch and his contemporaries: Nationalökonomie vs. contemporary economic theories. Rev Soc Econ 41(3):235–245

Cortèz JD (1989) Essay über den Katholizismus, den Liberalismus und den Sozialismus und andere Schriften aus den Jahren 1851–1853, vol I, ed. and transl, by Günter Maschke. VCH, Acta Humaniora, Weinheim

Dempsey BW (1958) The functional economy. Englewood Cliffs, New Jersey

Durkheim É (1988) Über soziale Arbeitteilung. Studie über die Organisation höherer Gesellschaften, Suhrkamp, Frankfurt

Ebner A (2007) Interkonfessionelle Ursprünge der Sozialstaatsdiskussion. Heinrich Pesch SJ und die Historische Schule der Nationalökonomie. In: Große Kracht H-J, Karcher T SJ, Spieß C (eds) Das System des Solidarismus. Zur Auseinandersetzung mit dem Werk von Heinrich Pesch. LIT, Berlin, pp 91–114

Ederer RJ (1981) Heinrich Pesch's solidarism and Boris Ischboldin's scientific reformism. Int J Soc Econ 8(7):73–86

Ederer RJ (1991) Heinrich Pesch, solidarity, and social encyclicals. Rev Soc Econ 49(4):596–610

Fenske H (1991) Politisches Denken im 20. Jahrhundert. In: Lieber H-J (ed) Politische Theorien von der Antike bis zur Gegenwart. Bonn, Bundeszentrale für politische Bildung, pp 657–880

Große Kracht H-J (2007a) … der Hebung des Arbeiters mein Leben zu widmen. Zur Lebensgeschichte von Heinrich Pesch SJ (1854–1926), In: Große Kracht H-J, Karcher T SJ, Spieß C (eds) Das System des Solidarismus. Zur Auseinandersetzung mit dem Werk von Heinrich Pesch. LIT, Berlin, pp 9–30

Große-Kracht H-J (2007b) Zwischen Soziologie und Metaphysik. Zur Solidarismus-Konzeption von Heinrich Pesch SJ. In: Große Kracht H-J, Karcher T SJ, Spieß C (eds) Das System des Solidarismus. Zur Auseinandersetzung mit dem Werk von Heinrich Pesch. LIT, Berlin, pp 59–89

Grosschmid GB (1954) Pesch's concept of the living Wage in Quadragesimo Anno. Rev Soc Econ 12(2):147–155

Gülich C (1989) "Organisation" der Wirtschaft. Von Durkheims Berufsgruppen zu Bouglés Solidarismus. Zeitschrift für Soziologie 18:220–229

Gülich C (1991) Die Durkheim-Schule und der französische Solidarismus. Deutscher Universitäts-Verlag, Wiesbaden

Harris AL (1946) The scholastic revival: the economics of Heinrich Pesch. J Polit Econ 54(1): 38–59

Mazurek FJ (1980) Die Konzeption des gesellschaftlichen Solidarismus nach Heinrich Pesch, Jahrbuch für christliche Sozialwissenschaften (JCSW), vol 21, pp 73–98

Messner J (1976) Fifty years after the death of Heinrich Pesch. Rev Soc Econ 34(2):117–123

Möhring-Hesse M (2007) Solidarismuns und Sozialpolitik. Peschs gesellschaftsweite Solidarität in der akturellen Sozialstaatsdiskussion. In: Große Kracht H-J, Karcher T SJ, Spieß C (eds) Das System des Solidarismus. Zur Auseinandersetzung mit dem Werk von Heinrich Pesch. LIT, Berlin, pp 231–259

Mueller FH (1946) The principle of solidarity in the teachings of Father Henry Pesch. Rev Soc Econ 4(1):31–39

Mueller FH (1977) Heinrich Pesch (1854–1926). Social philosopher and economist. The currency of the idea of solidarism. Jahrbuch für christliche Sozialwissenschaften 18:181–204
Mueller FH (1980) Heinrich Pesch. Sein Leben und seine Lehre, Bachem, Cologne
Mulcahy RE (1949) The welfare economics of Heinrich Pesch. Q J Econ 63(3):342–360
Mulcahy RE (1952) The economics of Heinrich Pesch. Holt, New York
Pesch H (1902) Solidarismus. In: Stimmen aus Maria-Laach, vol 63, pp 38–60, 307–324
Pesch H (1914) Lehrbuch der Nationalökonomie, vol I: Grundlegung, 2. rev. ed., orig. ed. 1905, Herder, Freiburg
Pesch H (1918a) Ethik und Volkswirtschaft. Herder, Freiburg
Pesch H (1918b) Nicht kommunistischer, sondern christlicher Sozialismus! Die Volkswirtschaft der Zukunft, ed. by the Deutsche Zentrumspartei, pamphlet vol 4, Germania, Berlin
Pesch H (1919a) Neubau der Gesellschaft, pamphlet "Flugschriften der 'Stimmen der Zeit'", vol 1. Herder, Freiburg
Pesch H (1919b) Sozialisierung, pamphlet "Flugschriften der 'Stimmen der Zeit'", vol 5. Herder, Freiburg
Pesch H (1922) Lehrbuch der Nationalökonomie, Vol IV., Allgemeine Volkswirtschaftlehre III: Der volkswirtschaftliche Prozess, 1. Deckung des Volksbedarfs als volkswirtschaftliche Aufgabe, 2. Produktion, 1. and 2. ed., orig ed., Herder, Freiburg im Breisgau
Pesch H (1923) Lehrbuch der Nationalökonomie, Vol V., Allgemeine Volkswirtschaftlehre III: Der volkswirtschaftliche Prozess, 3. Tauschverkehr, 4. Einkommens- und Vermögensbildung, 5. Störungen des volkswirtschaftlichen Prozesses, 1. and 2. ed., Herder Freiburg
Pesch H (1924) Heinrich Pesch SJ. In: Meiner Felix (ed) Die Volkswirtschaftslehre der Gegenwart in Selbstdarstellungen. Felix Meiner Verlag, Leipzig, pp 190–208
Pesch H (1925) Lehrbuch der Nationalökonomie, Vol. II: Allgemeine Volkswirtschaftslehre I, 4. and 5. unchanged ed., orig. ed. 1909. Herder, Freiburg im Breisgau
Pesch H (1998) Heinrich Pesch on Solidarist Economics. Excerpts from the Lehrbuch der Nationalökonomie, translated by Rupert E. Ederer. University Press of America. Lanham, New York, Oxford
Reisz G (2006) Solidarität in Deutschland und Frankreich. Eine politische Deutungsanalyse, Buderich, Opladen
Reisz G (2007) Der solidarische Staat. Solidaritätsdeutungen in Deutschland und Frankreich und ihre politische Bedeutung heute. In: Große Kracht H-J, Karcher T SJ, Spieß C (eds) Das System des Solidarismus. Zur Auseinandersetzung mit dem Werk von Heinrich Pesch. LIT, Berlin, pp 31–58
Rerum novarum (1891) Social Encylica of Pope Leo XIII
Schumpeter JA (1965) Geschichte der ökonomischen Analyse, 2. Vol. Vandenhoeck & Ruprecht, Göttingen. English edition: Schumpeter JA (1954) History of economic analysis. Oxford University Press, New York
Smith A (1973) An Inquiry into the nature and causes of the wealth of Nations, orig. ed. 1776. Penguin Books, Harmondsworth
Sombart W (1930) Die drei Nationalökonomien. Geschichte und System der Lehre von der Wirtschaft. Duncker & Humblot, Munich and Leipzig
Spann O (1926) Die Haupttheorien der Volkswirtschaftlehre auf lehrgeschichtlicher Grundlage. Quelle & Meyer, Leipzig
Spieß C (2007) Solidarismus und Sozialethik. In: Große Kracht H-J, Karcher T SJ, Spieß C (eds.) Das System des Solidarismus. Zur Auseinandersetzung mit dem Werk von Heinrich Pesch. LIT, Berlin, pp 137–158
von Nell-Breuning O (1951) Gesellschaftliche Ordnungssysteme, Beiträge zu einem Wörterbuch der Politik, vol V. Herder, Freiburg
von Nell-Breuning O (1990) Baugesetze der Gesellschaft. Solidarität und Subsidiarität, Herder, Freiburg
Wagner A (1892) Grundlegung der politischen Oekonomie, erster Theil: Grundlegungen der Volkswirtschaft. Leipzig, C.F, Winter

Wagner A (1893) Grundlegung der politischen Oekonomie, erster Theil: Grundlegungen der Volkswirtschaft. Leipzig, C.F, Winter
Wagner A (1948) Finanzwissenschaft und Staatssozialismus, orig. ed. 1887. Otto, Heppenheim
Wishloff J (2006) Solidarist economics: the legacy of Heinrich Pesch. Rev Bus 27(2):33–46

Public Economy ("Gemeinwirtschaft") as a Concept of Social Development Policy—Examples of German Authors of the Late 19th Century

Karl-Heinz Schmidt

1 Introduction

In Central Europe, especially in Germany, economic and social activities of state-authorities and non-profit organizations are based on long-term traditions in practice and in the history of economic thought. During the 16th and 17th century, various kings, princes, and other royal personages ruled the lands. These authorities widely dominated and regulated production, trade, and consumption in the national economies of European states. The 18th century, in particular the second half, brought about the process of liberalization of the individual from political powers and related institutions. From the point of view of the history of economic thought, the influence of state-authorities during the long-term period of feudalism and mercantilism declined, whereas the influence of markets and of non-governmental organizations increased. During the 19th century, declining state-authorities and growing private market-institutions left room for non-profit-organizations and other related institutions to emerge. Therefore, especially in German-speaking countries, not only public authorities and governmental institutions were distinguished from private market-institutions and enterprises, but also institutions and organizations "in-between". Thus, the "three-sector-structure" of the market economy emerged. The German economist Friedrich B.W. von Hermann in his studies *Staatswirtschaftliche Untersuchungen* (1832, 1870, 1924) introduced the term *Gemeinwirtschaft* in order to refer to those economic activities that were carried out jointly within a family, a monastery, a lifetime-community or a wealth-community. The term "Gemeinsinn" was introduced in order to refer to the joint element of these institutions, in contrast to individual utility and profit-oriented behaviour of actors in the market-economy. According to von Hermann the actors and institutions of "Gemeinwirtschaft" were designated by renouncing any struggles among members

K.-H. Schmidt (✉)
Department of Economics, University of Paderborn, Paderborn, Germany
e-mail: Karl-Heinz_Schmidt@wiwi.uni-paderborn.de

J. Backhaus et al. (eds.), *On the Economic Significance of the Catholic Social Doctrine*, The European Heritage in Economics and the Social Sciences 19, DOI 10.1007/978-3-319-52545-7_4

of an institution or organization about benefits and burdens (Wendt 1956, 118). But the author was convinced, that this attitude would be possible only by caritas/love ("Liebe") in families and by religious connections in monasteries. Here, the "door is open" for further discussions on the definition of "Gemeinwirtschaft"—in relation to religious documents and declarations by the Churches including *Encyclicas* by the Pope. But from the study of the former literature it should be kept in mind that von Hermann already pointed out important characteristics of "Gemeinschaft": a closed group of persons as actors of the concerned institution or organization, distinct economic thinking ("Gemeinsinn"), a specific way of distribution of wealth and a special form of property. In von Hermann's view, the term "Gemeinwirtschaft" should be focussed on small units of communities for life. They should be acknowledged as single microeconomic units within the macroeconomic system.

Later during the 19th and 20th century the meaning of the term "Gemeinwirtschaft" has changed (Ritschl 1965, 331). Nevertheless, the term was applied continuously in order to describe a sector of economic and social institutions and activities aiming at economic justice and stabilization of economic and social welfare in so-called "mixed economic systems" (Weisser 1963; von Nell-Breuning 1986, 853–857).

2 Definitions of *Public Economy* ("Gemeinwirtschaft")

Since the beginning of the 19th century different definitions of "Gemeinwirtschaft" have been proposed by authors of distinct schools of economics and social science. To point out the broad variety of approaches, apart from F.B.W. von Hermann (s.a.), the concepts by several scholars of economics and social development at the late 19th century will be compared (Stavenhagen 1969). Wilhelm Roscher, the outstanding historian of economic thought of the 19th century, later developed a much broader concept of "Gemeinwirtschaft" than von Hermann. According to Hans Ritschl, it was Wilhelm Roscher's idea to amplify the concept of "Gemeinwirtschaft" by including wide spheres such as the home economy, the economy of corporations or associations, the economy of communities, the state economy and even the total national economy (Roscher, W., System der Volkswirtschaft, I, Stuttgart 1854). Roscher based this widened definition on the term "Gemeinsinn", meaning social thought. This wider concept met with criticism, i.e. by the later member of the Younger Historical School, Adolph Wagner, who was opposed to Roscher's idea to cover the total national economy by the term "Gemeinwirtschaft" (Ritschl, 332).

Prior to Wagner, the scholar of economic and social thought, Albert E. Schäffle, developed and introduced the following distinction between two systems: first, a system of "Gemeinwirtschaft", understood as a "social system of human economy" (1867), and second, the "private, speculative and capitalistic system", based on the economic organization of productive resources by profit-oriented behaviour of capital owners (Chaloupek 2010, 177, 195; Schmidt 2010, 155–160). In a nutshell, while Schäffle circumscribed the system of "Gemeinwirtschaft" as an "economy of several or many people together" ("Wirtschaft für Mehrere oder Viele gemeinsam",

Ritschl, 332), he substituted the element "Gemeinsinn" by the form of organization as a basic characteristic of "Gemeinwirtschaft". This form of organization should be characterized by voluntary interest and freedom of decision-making. Finally, Schäffle distinguished on the one hand voluntary, free organizations, i.e. clubs pursuing the interest of public welfare ("gemeinnützige Vereine") such as cooperatives and foundations, and on the other hand enforced cooperations ("Zwangsverbindungen"), i.e. the state, communities and different kinds of corporations (Ritschl, 332). Later on, Adolph Wagner completed Schäffle's terminology by a generalized distinction of principles of organization and economic systems: the individualistic, private system; a public or enforced public system ("zwangsgemeinwirtschaftlich"); and a "caritative" ("karitatives") system (Ritschl, 332). The basic relevance of these terms for studies on "Gemeinwirtschaft", however, turned out only later. During the first half of the 20th century Schäffle's terminology became more influential (1867) as compared to Adolph Wagner's related publications at the end of the 19th century (Ritschl, 332).

Another basic distinction has to be considered in relation to "Gemeinwirtschaft": the distinction between individual and public, res collective preferences ("Einzel- und Gemeinbedürfnisse oder Kollektivbedürfnisse"). Again we find these terms at first in von Hermann's works and later—with some modifications—in Adolph Wagner's publications related to the diverse "systems" (Gross 1900, 165).

3 Examples of the Studies of German Authors on Social Development Around 1890

3.1 Driving Forces of Social Development

At the end of the 19th century different driving forces proposed and pushed forward the ideas and concepts of social development in Germany and Central Europe (Stegmann 1988, 1231–1234). According to the proposal by Heinz Lampert, two groups of driving forces may be distinguished: firstly individual persons, mainly during the first half of the 19th century, and secondly clubs, unions, cooperatives and political parties mainly during the second half of the 19th century (Lampert 1980, 77). Concerning the individual persons Lampert distinguished two subgroups: promoters of social reforms, who tried to push forward social reforms on the grounds of the existing social order ("Gesellschaftsordnung"), and promoters of social revolutions aiming at the change of the legislation and social order. Among the examples of individual persons having promoted the social movement, Lampert named "Ketteler, Kolping, Schulze-Delitzsch, Marx, Engels, Lassalle, Naumann et al." (Lampert 1980, 77). While Ketteler and Kolping represent the first subgroup of persons, Marx and Engels represent the second subgroup. Thus, social reformers are distinguished from social revolutionaries. The influences of the individual persons on the social movement in Germany are documented and widely known, but it is worthwhile to take note also of less well-known persons who contributed to social reforms. Moreover, persons should be considered who acted as authors of social studies or who contributed to general or social policy in political or social institutions or by academic activities. Concerning the second group of driving forces—clubs, cooperatives, unions etc.—individual persons should be considered, too: Kolping and Schultze-Delitzsch may be named in particular.

The persons having pushed forward social reforms included entrepreneurs, representatives of the churches and Christian organizations, university teachers and scientists, but also state-employees and members of Parliament (Lampert 1980, 78ff). For various reasons, the representatives of the Christian churches strived for different programs of social reforms. They wanted to pursue the idea of social justice, take care of handicapped and poor persons who suffered from the economic and social effects of industrialization, and intensify the activities of social policy to the benefit of the poor groups of the society. By their activities representatives of the Catholic Church and the Protestant Church wanted to contribute to the stabilization of the society.

3.2 Schools of Economic Thought and Their Interest in Social Development

Around 1890, the Central European schools of economic thought, especially in the countries "of German tongue", were heavily involved in debates and struggles for economic stabilization. Demands ranged from measures and methods to carry out efficient policy reforms to measures of enforcing revolutionary change in the national economy and society. In Germany, the proposals of authors of different schools of economic thought encompassed measures of social policy or measures aiming at the introduction of a new economic and social system—or—as a "third way"—recommendation of the organization of a specific economic sector: the public economy. The authors of the schools of economic thought being involved in related debates and publications at the end of the 19th century, included in particular members of the Younger Historical School, socialist authors, followers of the Classical School and pioneers of the Neoclassical School. The aforementioned authors Roscher, Schäffle and Wagner represented the Historical Schools; the publications by Emil Sax on the public economy should be mentioned additionally. The authors were involved in the aims and organization of *Public Economy* in the sense of "Gemeinwirtschaft". One has to keep in mind that the designated schools of economic thought included different concepts of economic policy, especially concerning the relations of the private sector, the special "public sector," and the national State. Therefore, the differences between the recommended measures of social policy and of "public development" ("Gemeinwirtschaft") are not surprising. Authors of classical economics argued in favour of free markets and a restricted segment of public institutions and related interventions. Authors of socialism differed substantively as to their demanded measures: to enforce strict regulations of allocation and distribution in specific sectors or to change the total economic and social system. Authors of the *Public Economy* ("Gemeinwirtschaft") recommended to combine interventions into the market and regulating measures (Rittig 1977), partly enforced by the state, for example according to Adolph Wagner's proposal of specific cooperatives, the so-called "Zwangsgemeinschaften".

A concise review of the history of economic thought on *Public Economy* ("Gemeinwirtschaft") has been provided by Thiemeyer (1973, 1974, 1981). In his article on "Gemeinwirtschaft" (1981) he points out the conditions of the institutional framework of economic activities taking place "between" private markets on the one hand and the State and public government on the other. He emphasized the author Karl Heinrich Rau as an important representative of the theory of "public economy" ("Gemeinwirtschaft"). Furthermore Thiemeyer pointed towards important contributions by other members of the German Historical Schools, like Bruno Hildebrand, Karl Knies, Emil Sax and the aforementioned authors Albert Schäffle and Adolph Wagner (Thiemeyer 1981, 527). In his review-article he identifies the period 1867–1900 as the "classical period of the *Public Economy* ("Gemeinwirtschaft"), beginning with Schäffle's second edition of his book "The social system of human economy" (Thiemeyer 1981, 527; Schäffle 1873). Carl Rodbertus, the founder of the concept of "State-Socialism", must also be considered. He believed, that the Prussian State would be able to bring about social justice and economic and social progress, a concept that was also acknowledged by Adolph Wagner (Thiemeyer 1981, 528). Concerning Wagner, and additionally regarding Schäffle and Sax—altogether the "three stars" of the development of the concept of "public economy" during the late 19th century—the concept of "subsidiarity" (in German also called "Lückenbüßertheorem" of public welfare) has to be considered. It was demanded by Emil Sax in his analysis of the price-policy of public enterprises, especially of railway companies in his related basic study (Sax 1887, 1918/22; Thiemeyer 1981, 529, 539).

From the considered publications on *Public Economy* ("Gemeinwirtschaft") in Germany at the end of the 19th century it may be concluded, that the institutional structures and framework conditions of developing specific concepts of "Gemeinwirtschaft" have been favourable for authors who were orientated towards the churches. In particular, it should be emphasized that these authors were the "driving forces" of the social movement around 1890. In this respect, the pontificate of Leo XIII (1878–1903) has to be reconsidered.

Pope Leo XIII (1878–1903) tried intensively to solve, or at least to reduce the conflict between the Catholic Church and the political, social and cultural activities of the modern State (Verlag DT 2006, 147; Maier 1987, 905–907). Though he was opposed to rationalism and liberalism, and also to freemasonry, he acknowledged the State as being independent from the Church. He also acknowledged democracy, though he preferred a conservative system of political government. During his pontificate new basic documents of the Catholic Social Doctrine were published, as the encyclical *Rerum Novarum* (1891) (Rauscher 1988, cols. 1250,1251; Frambach and Eissrich 2016, 29–54). He also sustained the development of the Christian social movement and of measures to solve the *Social Question*, mainly to reduce the poverty of labourers (Frambach and Eissrich 2016, 30). In this regard Leo XIII was the first Pope who kept these activities on his agenda. Concerning international relations between the Catholic Church and the States worldwide, he succeeded in diminishing the cultural conflict ("fight") with Germany and Switzerland and to reduce political differences with European and American States, but in Italy he failed to reestablish the "Church-State". Also, he did not succeed in developing new, functioning relations to the Orthodox Church in Eastern Europe. In reviews of his pontificate as a whole, he is seen as a very successful political pope, and in particular a "Labour Pope" ("Arbeiterpapst"), who sustained intensively the social movement and furthered the development of social and economic policy, even in the long run (Maier 1987, 907).

3.3 Specific Authors of Studies on Social Development and "Public Economy"

Considering the broad topic of *Public Economy* and the topic at hand of identifying driving factors of social movement, especially by the churches, in particular four important authors come to mind, apart from Ketteler (compare the chapter by D. Eissrich in this volume) and other highly respected persons. In this section, a short description of their biography and some of the relevant writings and teachings is presented.

3.3.1 Franz Hitze

The first example is *Franz Hitze* (1851–1921). He was the son of a wealthy family in the Sauerland region not far from Cologne. During his studies of philosophy and theology in Würzburg he became interested in publications by W.E. von Ketteler and in studies on the *Social Question* (Rauscher 1986, cols. 1292–1293; Bredendieck 1953; Brakelmann 1971; Lampert 1980, 86–87). On the basis of these studies he not only got into opposition to H. Schulze-Delitzsch and his concept of "liberal socialism", but also to the concept of "radical socialism" as represented by F. Lassalle and K. Marx. In opposition to these concepts F. Hitze developed and discussed his own concept of "Christian Socialism". He was introduced into the position and obligations of a priest in Paderborn (1878). During the following years (up to 1880) he continued his studies in Rome, where he worked intensively on K. Marx' ideas as outlined in his "Capital". After the return from Rome (1880), Hitze worked as general secretary of a new organization called "Labourer Welfare" ("Arbeiterwohl"). Later he established several clubs for catholic workers, es a national club for Catholics in Germany ("Volksverein für das katholische Deutschland"). The purpose of this institution was to teach catholic people the concept of social responsibility and prepare them to carry activities in line with this concept. Hitze also got involved into the movement of Christian trade unions and the German "Caritas" organization. Furthermore he cooperated with the management of the political party "Zentrum". He contributed to the related program of social policy. In 1882 he became member of the Prussian Parliament. Since 1884 he also got the membership of the German "Reichstag". In 1893, Hitze was offered a new academic chair dedicated to the teaching and research of "Christian social doctrine" ("Christliche Gesellschaftslehre") by the University of Münster (Rauscher 1986, col. 1292).

In his publications Hitze criticized the social development in the industrial society intensively. He had elaborated this point of view during his earlier stay in Rome, and on these grounds he proposed to solve the social problems. Herewith he was influenced by another academic and political journalist: Karl Freiherr von Vogelsang (1818–1890). Hitze indeed argued to some extent similarly to von Vogelsang, especially as far as the system of the economy and society is concerned. He favoured the idea to solve the social problems by renaissance of a medieval economic and social order. It should be based on guilds and related institutions, but established on amplified economic and democratic grounds. He obviously was convinced that socialism should be realized in the future, either in terms of an absolute social democratic socialism by means of the State or as a relative, conservative and stable ("healthy") socialism by the guilds (Rauscher 1986, col. 1292).

As a member of the German "Reichstag", Hitze concentrated his work on the preparation and discussions on legislative projects concerning the protection of Labour at industrial production and new laws on social security. On behalf of Hitze's first speech in Parliament (1885) Chancellor Bismarck called him the "agitating chaplain". Obviously, Hitze was clearly opposed to Bismarck's policies. Therefore, he could only carry out his ideas and proposals for social reforms after Bismarck's period of political activities in Parliament, the so-called "Bismarck-era", had ended (Rauscher 1986, col. 1292).

3.3.2 Karl Freiherr Von Vogelsang

The second author who can be considered a driving force of the social movement at the end of the 19th century was the political journalist and editor *Karl Freiherr von Vogelsang* (1818–1890). He was the member of a conservative agrarian family of Northern Germany. After studies of law, he became employed in the Prussian public service ("Staatsdienst"). He quitted that professional position, because he was opposed to the revolutionary movement in Germany in 1848. The related unrest was in contradiction to his ideal of reforms of the society on the grounds of guilds and related institutions. Therefore he decided to go to Austria and to convert to Catholicism in Innsbruck (1850). But he returned to Germany and settled with his family in Cologne (1854), where he edited a political journal (in cooperation with a second editor). After several years (1864), he changed his location again: he moved to Vienna—forever (Oeliger and Vogelsang 1989, cols. 765–766). Since 1875 Vogelsang lived in Vienna; he held a position as catholic political journalist opposed to adherents of liberal and centralism-oriented political concepts. He promoted effective reforms of the society; he was called "father of the catholic school;" became a leader of the catholic social movement in Austria; and edited a monthly journal for social science and national economy (since 1883), entitled "Monatsschrift für christliche Sozialreform". This journal successfully gave many important impulses on ideas, aims, programs, and measure of social policy and social development. He was designated to be the most well-known representative of the catholic social movement in the countries applying the German language. Von Vogelsang was continuously opposed to rationalistic liberalism. In his political publications he argued in favour of a renaissance of a former social order, based on guilds and established on the grounds of integrated economic, social and political functions of related institutions. They should be determined to form a "Parliament of Future". The State should be designated by the monarchy in terms of a "social kingdom" (Oeliger and Vogelsang 1989, col. 766). With his ideas and his proposed concept of an amplified social reform von Vogelsang was involved to develop further aims and measures of social movement. These were promoted earlier by authors of romanticism. In this respect, the best known author of romanticism in the countries of German language was Adam Müller. He is also considered in studies on the history of economic thought (Müller 1819; Andreae 1961, 465).

3.3.3 Johann Heinrich Wichern

The third example of an author, who was concerned with social reforms and social movement under the conditions of industrialization, was a representative of the Protestant Church: *Johann Heinrich Wichern* (1808–1881). He established institutions which were linked to the Protestant Church and focused on social services for poor or/and disadvantaged persons. His activities to set up Christian welfare-oriented organizations like the "Internal Mission" pursued two aims: to solve social problems by moral renovation of people, and to contribute to social resistance against a political revolution (Lampert 1980, 87).

The events in Germany during the revolutionary year of 1848 prompted Wichern to more activities such as enlargement of the institutions of the "Internal Mission" and organization of large congressional meetings. In order to support children, Wichern founded a caritative institution, called "Rauhes Haus". The Prussian King engaged him as an expert for the prison reform. Wichern also supported the

"Internal Mission" by publishing a basic document—"Denkschrift"—about "The Internal Mission of the German Protestant Church" (Talazko 1989, cols. 983–984). On the whole, Wichern's activities encompassed the following three fields of practical activities: organizing and running the institution of "Rauhes Haus", managing the "Internal Mission," and preparing and contributing to a prison reform in Prussia (Lampert 1980, 87).

3.3.4 Victor Aimé Huber

Further examples of persons who organized institutions and measures of social welfare and social development in practice might be considered, i.e. the promoter of the concept of cooperatives and of social policy: *Victor Aimé Huber* (1800–1869). He amplified Wichern's idea of love/caritas by the idea of justice and the demand for a basic reform of society (Faust 1980). Like Wichern, Huber intended to avoid an expansion of proletarian poverty in Germany by instituting practical measures of social policy. A visit to England convinced him that higher social development in society is best achieved by putting more practical measures of social policy in place (Lampert 1980, 87–88; Mundig 1984).

4 Conclusions

Though the examples of authors considered, who published studies on social development and the *Public Economy* ("Gemeinwirtschaft"), only covered a small segment of the literature on economic and social problems during the late 19th century, the following conclusions may be drawn from the sections above:

Out of the variety of driving forces of social development—entrepreneurs, individual academic persons, economic and social organizations, clubs etc.—authors of economic studies, social documents, political advice or of recommendations concerning the *Social Question* in European countries are important subjects of studies on the development of the *Public Economy* ("Gemeinwirtschaft").

The authors considered are acknowledged in relation to the schools of economic and social sciences of the late 19th century, the time period of this study. The relevant schools are mainly the following: the school of late classical economics, the German historical schools, scientific socialism and the beginnings of the neoclassical school. The schools are representing the framework conditions for the activities of the authors.

The examples of authors considered (F. Hitze, K.F. v. Vogelsang, J.H. Wichern a.o.) pursued different programs and activities, but the authors were deeply involved in the basic conflict between the social development and the State and can be interpreted as "driving forces" of social development. This is illustrated by the activities carried out by representatives of the churches and of church-oriented politicians (Hitze, Vogelsang a.o.).

Though the documents of the churches (like the encyclicals of the Pope, es *Rerum Novarum*) have not been commented on in this study directly, the relation between the churches, es the Catholic Church, and the State at the end of the 19th century is part of the background of the study. Moreover, it determined the scientific position of authors, who were involved in research and publications on *Public Economy* ("Gemeinwirtschaft"). The three outstanding economists, who paved the way for *Public Economy* in Germany, Roscher, Schäffle, and Sax, developed a new direction of economic thought during the second half of the 19th century and thus pointed towards a solution of the deep conflict, "liberalism versus socialism". Their concept of *Public Economy* was focused on promoting a "third way" in order to bring about higher economic and social development.

Appendix

Social Question—Social (Public) Economy—Economic Systems and Social Welfare	
Thesis 1	The *Social Question* appears as a *New Social Question* which concerns additional groups of society (children and pensioners in low-income-families)
Thesis 2	To the *Social (Public) Economy* ("Gemeinwirtschaft"), not only the viewpoint of the social mentality for carrying out economic activities collectively is important, but also the economic allocation of resources in order to be competitive
Thesis 3	The *Social (Public) Economy* needs flexible structures of production, innovative management and justice of distribution as strategic goals
Thesis 4	The *Social (Public) Economy* means more than a sector of public enterprises in the market-system. The economic system should consist of firms orientated towards the goal: maximization of social welfare, whatever the system will be like. Structural flexibility will be needed!

References

Andreae W (1961) Handwörterbuch der Sozialwissenschaften (HdSW), vol 7, Gustav Fischer, Stuttgart et al., pp 464–466

Brakelmann G (1971) Die soziale Frage des 19. Jahrhunderts, 4th edn. Witten

Bredendieck W (1953) Christliche Sozialreformer des 19. Jahrhunderts, Leipzig, p 1953

Brinkmann K (1956) Historische Schule, Handwörterbuch der Sozialwissenschaften (HdSW), vol 5, G. Fischer, Stuttgart et al., pp 121–123

Chaloupek G (2010) Schäffle on the economics of socialism and social democracy. In: Backhaus J (ed.) Albert Schäffle (1831–1903). The legacy of an underestimated economist. Haag + Herchen, Hanau, pp 177–198

Eissrich D (2017) An economist's view on the work of Wilhelm Emmanuel von Ketteler and its influence on the encyclical rerum novarum, this volume

Frambach H, Eissrich D (2016) Der dritte Weg der Päpste, Die Wirtschaftsideen des Vatikans, UVK, Konstanz, München

Faust H (1980) Victor Aimé Huber, ein Bahnbrecher der Genossenschaftsidee, Hamburg 1952; quoted after Lampert H, 87
Gross G (1900) Gemeinwirtschaft, Handwörterbuch der Staatswissenschaften (HdSt), 2nd edn. vol 4, Jena, pp 165–169
Lampert H (1980) Sozialpolitik. Springer, Berlin
Maier H (1987) Leo XIII. Staatslexikon, 7th edn. Freiburg et al., cols. 905–907
Müller A (1819) Von der Notwendigkeit einer theologischen Grundlage der gesamten Staatswissenschaften und der Staatswirtschaft insbesondere, Leipzig, Vienna 1898
Mundig K (1984) V.A. Hubers ausgewählte Schriften über Sozialreform und Genossenschaftswesen. Berlin
Oeliger J, Vogelsang J (1989) Staatslexikon. Herder, Freiburg et al., cols. 765–766
Rauscher A (1986) Hitze, Staatslexikon, Herder, Freiburg et al., cols. 1292–1293
Rauscher A (1988) Sozialenzykliken, Staatsexikon, Herder, Freiburg et al., cols. 1250–1257
Ritschl H (1965) Gemeinwirtschaft. HdSW vol 4, G. Fischer, Stuttgart et al., pp 331–346
Rittig G (1977) Gemeinwirtschaftsprinzip und Preisbildung bei öffentlichen Unternehmen unter volkswirtschaftlichen Gesichtspunkten. Schriftenreihe Gemeinwirtschaft Nr. 25, (Eds.). Bank für Gemeinwirtschaft AG; Europäische Verlagsanstalt GmbH, Frankfurt am Main - Cologne
Roscher W (1854) System der Volkswirtschaft, vol I, Stuttgart
Sax E (1887) Grundlegung der theoretischen Staatswirtschaft, Vienna
Sax E (1918/1922) Die Verkehrsmittel in Volks- und Staatswirtschaft, Berlin
Schäffle AEF (1873) Das gesellschaftliche System der menschlichen Wirtschaft, Tübingen
Schmidt KH (2010) Albert E. Fr. Schäffle's Contribution about "Steuerreform, Sozialpolitik und internationale Wirtschaftspolitik"—Basic ideas and actual relevance. In: Backhaus J (ed): Albert Schäffle (1831–1903), Haag + Herchen, Hanau, pp 153–176
Stavenhagen G (1969) Geschichte der Wirtschaftstheorie, 4th edn. Vandenhoeck & Ruprecht, Göttingen
Stegmann F (1988) Soziale Frage, Staatslexikon, 7th edn. vol 4, Herder, Freiburg et al., cols. 1231–1234
Talazko H (1989) Wichern, Staatslexikon, 7th edn. vol 5, Herder, Freiburg et al., cols. 983–984
Thiemeyer T (1973) Grundsätze einer Theorie der Gemeinwirtschaft, series Gemeinwirtschaft no. 3, eds.: Bank für Gemeinwirtschaft AG, Europäische Verlagsanstalt GmbH, Frankfurt am Main
Thiemeyer T (1974) Gemeinwirtschaft in Lehre und Forschung. Schriftenreihe Gemeinwirtschaft no. 13, eds. Bank für Gemeinwirtschaft AG; Europäische Verlagsanstalt GmbH, Frankfurt a. M.-Köln
Thiemeyer T (1981) Gemeinwirtschaft, Handwörterbuch der Wirtschaftswissenschaften (HdWW), vol 3, Gustav Fischer, Stuttgart et al., pp 525–540
Verlag DT (ed) (2006) dtv Lexikon, vol 13. Gütersloh, Munich, p 147
von Hermann FBW (1832, 1870, 1924) Staatswirtschaftliche Untersuchungen über Vermögen, Wirtschaft, Produktivität der Arbeiten, Kapital, Preis, Gewinn, Einkommen und Verbrauch, 3rd edn. Leipzig
von Nell-Breuning O (1986) Gemeinwirtschaft, Staatslexikon, 7th edn. vol 2, Herder, Freiburg et al., cols. 853–857
Weisser G (1963) Gemeinwirtschaft. Evangelisches Soziallexikon, Karrenberg F (ed), 4th edn. Kreuz-Verlag, Stuttgart
Wendt S (1956) Handwörterbuch der Sozialwissenschaften, vol 5. G. Fischer, Stuttgart et al., 118

Lord Acton and *Rerum novarum*

Frits L. van Holthoon

1 Introduction

Lord Acton (John Emerich Edward Dalberg-Acton), was an English Catholic historian, politician, and writer, who kept silent on the subject of pope Leo's XIII encyclical *Rerum novarum*, but why? Part of the answer is that the British political scene was not conducive to the message of *Rerum novarum*. However, Lord Acton was a special case who at a certain stage in his career had taken an active interest in the politics of his Church. By his upbringing and his family connections he acquired a continental rather than a British outlook on the affairs of church and state. During the Vatican Council of 1869–1870 he organized the opposition of those bishops who were against a decree announcing the infallibility of the Pope. He lost the battle and after 1870 he was silent on the matters of his Church. His silence shows that he was deeply hurt by what he regarded as the defeat of liberal Catholicism. He remained a devout catholic and was not excommunicated, but in a way he excommunicated his Church.

This chapter is in a sense a dialectical counterpoint to the ideas and measures connected to *Rerum novarum,* and the following procedure will be used to explain why Acton's silence gives us an insight into the world of *Rerum novarum* and the future of Catholicism.

After some introductory remarks on *Rerum novarum* as a social movement, where in a brief overview a corporatist tendency in theory as well as in practice is revealed, Acton will be discussed under two headings, a. as a politician and b. as a historian, whereby the latter subject is of interest, i.e. the nature of Acton's view on history is under special consideration. Lord Acton was an influential scholar. In a famous essay he introduced the 'German School of History' to the English reader and at the end of his life he established the groundwork for the first edition of the *Cambridge Modern History* which was an important factor in making English history writing playing such a prominent role in the twentieth century.

F.L. van Holthoon (✉)
University of Groningen, Groningen, Netherlands
e-mail: f.l.van.holthoon@home.nl

J. Backhaus et al. (eds.), *On the Economic Significance of the Catholic Social Doctrine*, The European Heritage in Economics and the Social Sciences 19, DOI 10.1007/978-3-319-52545-7_5

2 Rerum novarum

The encyclical of 1891 had an electrifying effect on Catholics who wanted to create an alternative to capitalist market economics. Leo XIII did not create the catholic social movement, but at least he gave it international status. Acton and his correspondent, the German theologian Johann Joseph Ignaz von Döllinger had a low opinion of the pope who, as Döllinger wrote "was in moral custody" (in moralischer Haft) (Conzemius 1971, 240). Neither Döllinger nor Acton were interested in the social message of the pope, they looked at the way liberal Catholics were marginalized or (as in the case of Döllinger) being excommunicated after the Vatican Council of 1870. In fact the catholic social movement was a combination of intolerance and social élan.

The social movement which started to take shape in the seventies of the nineteenth-century had two aspects: the corporatist and the collectivist aspect. It often is not easy to distinguish corporatism from collectivism, because elements of both are mixed in daily politics. We might regard them as the two poles on a sliding scale. Corporatism is the idea to order society in a special pattern according to hierarchical lines, whereas collectivism is the attempt to defend the rights of the working class and is by its nature democratic. In politics corporatism and collectivism can meet in the middle, when the idea of ordering society and collective action get fused.

Corporatism is the idea that factory owners and workers would reform the factory as an organisation that would transcend classes. Curiously enough liberal factory owners, such as Siemens and Lord Lever, had the greatest success with their welfare schemes. They realized that care for the daily lives of their workers and education resulted in greater productivity. However, their outlook was practical rather than philosophical. Some Catholic factory owners, such as the Belgian entrepreneur Léon Harmel, had the ambition to eliminate the class struggle and took a (paternalistic) interest in their personnel. Harmel was much applauded by Leo XIII. Between the two world wars, corporatism was hotly discussed by philosophers. It inspired Mussolini's fascism while the Nazis perverted it, but it did not manage to present a viable alternative to the capitalism of the market.

Collectivism on the other hand, as it manifested itself in trade unions, youth organizations, political parties and welfare organizations, has had an enormous impact. Its premise was the class struggle and the emancipation of the masses. Its success meant that—to an extent—they conquered the state which had been the exclusive domain of an elite of aristocrats, patricians and higher civil servants. These now had to cope with a totally new infrastructure of politics. The osmosis of the state and civil society became a fact and also the Catholics came to live within a situation geared to mass democracy.

Given the individualizing tendency of the Industrial Revolution corporatism has the handicap of its ambition wanting to order society totally and then according to hierarchical lines. The collective action of workers was intertwined with the industrializing process and so stood a better chance to survive the impact of a revolution, which was constantly challenging the *status quo* of the social order. However, today it seems that the heyday of collective action in its traditional form is over and that trade unions are becoming the victim of individualizing forces in society.

With *Rerum novarum* Leo XIII introduced a Trojan horse within the catholic community. And the higher clergy was fully aware of the hazards of the Pope's message. In the beginning the combination of dogmatic rigidity and social élan worked well. However, there were two problems with the response. First, the call of the Pope inevitably became a call for the emancipation of the working class and that led to loss of control of the catholic branch of the trade union movement in the long run. This hazard created tension between the higher and the lower clergy. Thomas Nipperdey describes this as

> The tension between the politically and socially more conservative episcopacy and the populist and/or socially committed pastoral clergy.[1]

The strict interpretation of dogmas and moral rules was a bonus in the short run, but in the long run they not only lost control over the catholic social movement, but they lost their flock.

In Dutch history "pillarization" is an important episode. It meant that *in the course of modernization* a catholic, a protestant and a humanist/liberal pillar[2] channelled this process. At the heyday of pillarization the segmentation of society was almost complete. Each pillar had its own organizations of party, radio station, youth-organization and trade union. Catholic boys married catholic girls; and children went to catholic schools including university. Dutch Catholics were the most loyal followers of the Roman church and catholic intellectuals heralded the social movement as an instrument of emancipation. What they meant was that the movement could free Catholics from the stigma of being second class citizens in a protestant country. When that process of emancipation had done its job Catholics *en masse* left the church and the teaching it stood for.[3]

3 Acton's Politics and Intellectual Biography

Social relations in England were not conducive to a corporatist settlement. It was generally accepted that the working classes should fight their way in, especially by making collective demands for higher wages and better working conditions. In a

---

[1]"Die Spannung zwischen dem politisch und sozial konservativeren Episkopat und den populistischen oder sozial engagierten Kapelanen" (Nipperdey 1998, 434).

[2]So it is often mentioned in the Dutch literature. Of course it was a misnomer, because it never took part in the segregation of the Dutch population. It was the "pillar" of the Dutch liberal elite which exercised its cultural hegemony during the period of pillarization.

[3]For those who can read Dutch see my essay "Verzuiling in Nederland" (Holthoon F L van 1985, 159–175).

way this social and political situation explains Acton's silence on the subject of *Rerum novarum*, but not quite. In his introduction to Acton's *Lectures on Modern History* Trevor Roper writes that "Lord Acton was one of the great Victorian misfits" (Acton 1961). And so was William Gladstone, the prime minister who fashioned the first modern mass party in Britain. Acton and Gladstone struck up a great friendship and Acton became Gladstone's political adviser. Acton wrote in one of his notes:

> If politics transcend religion that is, if you are a Liberal, it is because the ethical purposes are supreme (Butterfield 1968).

To explain the bizarre fact that Acton was a misfit some remarks on his intellectual biography are necessary.

Acton (1834–1902) was born in Naples as the son of the prime minister of the Kingdom of the Two Sicilies. His mother was a daughter of a catholic family in the Rhineland: the Dalbergs. The pedigree of the Actons was that of a catholic country squire in Shropshire since 1600. If his birth accentuated his cosmopolitan background this was enhanced by a university education in Munich and his marriage to the daughter of a well-known catholic family in Bavaria. As a catholic Acton could not get a degree in Cambridge and his wife Marie Arco-Valley was known within the family network before she married Acton. Needless to say Acton spoke English, German, Italian, and French and of course read Latin and Greek.

In an age which knew many well-known converts to Catholicism, the most famous one being John Henry Newman, Acton was an outsider among British Catholics. His family had stuck to the creed since 1600 enduring persecution and discrimination. The newly converted Catholics could not understand Acton's resistance to the decree of papal infallibility. For them Catholicism was a belief, for Acton it was a fact of life.

At the university of Munich Ignaz von Döllinger was his mentor. From this relationship sprung a friendship between professor and student. That friendship became prominent during the deliberations of the bishops, convened in Rome, on the issue of the infallibility of the pope. From November 1869 to May 1870 Acton was in Rome and tried to organize the considerable resistance of many bishops to a decree which would settle this issue. When he saw that his efforts were in vain Acton left Rome. The decree was adopted in July. In August the French troops that protected the pope left Rome and the forces of the brand new Italian national state marched in. This was the end of the Church State and the temporal power of the pope. Pius IX became an exile in Rome.

The outcome of the Vatican Council had a curious effect on the Döllinger-Acton relationshi Döllinger did not back down and his bishop excommunicated him. However, he still went to church and adopted a tolerant attitude to those bishops who did submit even while they kept their misgivings. Acton regarded this tolerance as treason, treason that is to historical truth. Afterwards the two remained friends, but Acton did no longer accept Döllinger as his mentor.

When talking about historical truth, Acton meant two things: something simple, and something prophetic. Regarding the first, popes could not be declared infallible, because history had shown that they were not. During the Counterreformation they installed the inquisition in Rome and at the same time they were involved in many criminal acts, such as the massacre of Huguenots during St. Bartholomew's day in Paris (1572). Moral truths for Acton were universal (at least since the coming of Christ). In an essay on 'Wolsey and Henry VIII' he wrote

> The argument which exonerates Wolsey [from burning heretics] by the times he lived in, is a serious fallacy. Christians must be judged by a moral code which is not invented in the eighteenth century, but is as old as the Apostles (Acton 1908, 63).

Acton stuck to this opinion to the end of his life. In a century where "historism" flourished he was a splendid exception.

In a number of essays on the eve of the Vatican Council he castigated the Church because it would not accept the authority of science, when it was evident that it was plainly wrong. Acton held strong views on the relation between science and religious doctrine and he even went further. He wrote in an essay on "Ultramontanism" (1863):

> The Church must always put herself in harmony with existing ideas, and speak to each age and nation in its own language. A kind of amalgam between the eternal faith and temporal opinion is thus in constant process of generation, and by it Christians explain to themselves the bearings of their religion, so far as their knowledge allows (Acton 1952).

If we read Acton's essays before and during the Vatican Council it is clear that Acton urged the Church to get out of doctrinal rigidity and adopt much more liberal ideas on morality and the teachings of the Church in general. Without much exaggeration Acton can be regarded as the herald of the second Vatican Council. It is a wonder that he was never excommunicated. Cardinal Manning (another convert!) was on the brink of doing so, but he did not dare. And with good reason of course. Acton belonged to the oldest catholic families in Britain. It would be strange if a man who never uttered any doctrinal heresy and whose family was responsible for the fact that Catholicism was still present in Britain would be banned. Another important reason was that, owing to Gladstone, Acton became a prominent member of the establishment. Will you ban a catholic peer created by Gladstone or a Lord in Waiting to the Queen, will you ban the first catholic *Regius* professor in Cambridge ever? It was the friendship with Gladstone which made Acton into an influential political figure in Victoria's Britain.

After the Vatican Council, Acton did no longer believe in his Church as a reforming agency. He turned his attention to liberal politics in Britain and he became Gladstone's closest adviser even to the extent that Gladstone repeatedly urged Acton, who during that period lived with his family most of the year in the South of France, to come home and help him. However Acton did not budge, he wrote letters and election speeches and framed Gladstone's policy for Home Rule in Ireland. During one term Acton was Member of Parliament for Bridgnorth (near his seat in Shropshire), but when he was defeated at the next election he was delighted. Yet Gladstone did not relax his grip and made Sir John Acton a peer of the realm as Lord Acton. He hoped that the new catholic peer would help him in promoting his Irish policy. However, Acton preferred to stay aloof and to counsel from the distance. He came home when he needed a job, because his estates did not bring in enough money. Gladstone persuaded Andrew Carnegie to buy Acton's library, and via John Morley that valuable collection of books landed in the Cambridge University Library. However selling 70.000 volumes (for £9000) was not enough to save Acton from bankruptcy. So there was talk of a post as cabinet minister or an ambassadorship. Eventually Acton became one the Lords in Waiting for Queen Victoria and he got on famously with the difficult monarch. Rosebery, Gladstone's successor after Gladstone's death, provided Acton with a proper job by making him the first catholic *Regius* professor in Cambridge. That was in 1895, seven years before Acton's death.

Owen Chadwick (in the best book on Acton's intellectual development) comments on Acton's friendship with Edmond Scherer, a Swiss protestant as follows:

There was a rapport between the minds. The one had come out of Protestant ultra-orthodoxy; both had lost faith in authority as an absolute concept; and both saw history as inseparable from the conscience of the human race (Chadwick 1998).

In the same way Acton and Gladstone were united in a sense of defeat and of moral purpose. Gladstone had written a book on Church and State, in which he regarded the Anglican state church as an ideal vehicle of reform. He came to the conclusion that the church lacked the authority and the will to perform that duty. In the same way Acton gave up his own church as a moral instrument. Both then concentrated on liberal politics. It should inject moral purpose in a policy of economic and social reform. And both regarded history as a theodicy. Providence and progress was the lodestar of history and it was the duty of the historian to find that historical truth time and again.

4 Providence and Progress

What kind of historian was Acton? Truth to Gladstone and Acton was first of all historical truth. That is the red thread of righteousness which runs through the labyrinth of history. For Acton, above all history was Christian history for which the motto was *providence* and *progress*. He said:

> [I]n 1808, it is no hyperbole to say that the progress of the world towards self-government would have been arrested but for the strength afforded by the religious motive in the seventeenth century. And this constancy of progress in the direction of organised and assured freedom, is the characteristic fact of Modern History, and its tribute to the theory of Providence (Acton 1906, 26).

Modern history, which started according to the lecturer in the Renaissance around 1495, is the story of organic change and Edmund Burke was the man who inspired him most.[4]

[4]Burke was no historian, but Acton was much impressed by an early work by Burke: *The Abridgment of English History*.

Acton gave his lectures in 1899 as *Regius* professor in Cambridge and he announced that he would start his history four hundred years ago, when as he said a new period made its way, the period of modern history. In that time of innovation a new idea of freedom was born, that is to say of Christian freedom. If we follow his version of modern history Acton portrays it as a seesaw of state—church authority and thinkers and movements that protested against the constraints of authority. In the end the "universal spirit of investigation and discovery" prevailed that "withstood the recurring efforts of reaction, until, by the advent of the reign of general ideas which we call the Revolution, it at length prevailed" (Acton 1906, 26).

Reading this leads to the interesting conclusion that Acton's lectures on general history are in the greater part religious history, or perhaps we should say that religion is the dynamic factor in Acton's general history. His lectures end with the story of the American Revolution. That, however, is not the revolution Acton had in mind in the sentence just quoted nor did he refer to the French Revolution. The great transformation when religious change became political change started with the Dutch and the British took over from them. It was the dissenters in both countries that created the revolution Acton was referring to.

What then about the nineteenth century? Is the British parliamentary system in 1808—as the supposed outcome of the "revolution"—the ultimate model of political freedom? That system went through some considerable changes during the nineteenth century. Politically it was not the model for continental parliamentary regimes. The truth is that Acton did not know how to proceed. He was scornful about the usual promoters of freedom during the Enlightenment such as Montesquieu, Locke, Voltaire and Rousseau. They lacked the religious experience necessary for understanding the true meaning of freedom. He was blind to the secular interpretation of freedom, which prevailed during the nineteenth-century in the common practice of Europeans. Think of Adam Smith's invisible hand. It invites partners in trade to cooperate for their mutual benefit and let the market do its work. That invitation opened the way to the best and most practical definition of liberty. When the Catholic Church refused to play the role which Acton had assigned to it—that of infusing religious liberty in the daily lives of the common people—, he could only pursue his ideal of freedom by supporting Gladstone's politics.

Cambridge University Library stores Acton's boxes containing his annotations and short notices with his thoughts. Acton had the plan to write a history of freedom, but as with his other books his plan did not materialize. Apparently he lacked the creative talent to compose large scale projects, but in the case of the history of freedom the truth is that the project stranded on the eve of the French Revolution and that Acton did not know how to proceed from there. He had lost his red thread.

Acton was scarcely a great historian; his style is so elliptical that sometimes his meaning is lost. Furthermore he had a method of annotating, or rather of not annotating, which even according to nineteenth century standards is unacceptable. However, he was an influential historian. During the seven years of his professorship he planned the *Cambridge Modern History* which started to publish after Acton's death. Mandell Creighton in his Introduction to the enterprise wrote: "An ordered series of monographs is the only practical scheme for a general *History of Modern Times*" (vol I, 1). This impressive set of 15 volumes set the model for the future and is undoubtedly one of the factors responsible for the bloom of English history writing in the twentieth-century.

5 Negative and Positive Liberty

In his inaugural Isaiah Berlin lectured on positive and negative liberty (Berlin 1963). Positive liberty (according to Kant) is the duty to obey the natural and rational order of things, and feel free and be free as a consequence. Negative liberty is the freedom from restraint disregarding any moral consequence.

It is clear that both the Church of *Rerum novarum* and Acton held fast to positive liberty as an ideal. According to Acton liberty should be enacted within an institutional framework and be enjoyed in a disciplined way. The catholic clergy could not agree more. The social movement attached to *Rerum novarum* dealt with the real and practical problems, but in the end under the influence of doctrinal rigour and a moral code which went out of date. Then it started to ignore the interests of Catholics and lost control of the catholic laity. The high minded liberalism of the aristocrat Acton was lost during "The Strange Death of Liberal England", when liberty unequivocally came to mean negative liberty (Dangerfield 1936).[5] Liberty, in England and elsewhere, means freedom of restraint according to Stuart Mill's classical definition. In an industrial society Adam Smith's invisible hand is the best option for using that liberty of restraint, but *laissez faire* is of course not the end of the story. Acton was right in insisting that we should lead responsible lives; on the other hand he took, like most nineteenth-century bourgeois and aristocrats, no interest in the Industrial Revolution and its consequences. I even suspect that he had a distaste of the vulgar pleasures of the common man, which that revolution made possible. And yet behind the vulgarity of the common man are the hardcore values of democracy, justice and liberty without which modern society cannot function properly.

Alfred Weber made the distinction between *culture* and *civilization*. Culture, according to him, means the moral and aesthetic practice of life and civilisation represents the business arrangement of our lives (Weber 1951). This distinction is, I think, typical for the anti-modernist sentiment that prevailed in the nineteenth-century in which business arrangements were widely regarded as a necessary evil and the real life was contained within culture. Yet, the so-called civilizational values that are necessary to run modern society also have to be

[5]See also my *The State and Civil Society, Theories, Illusions, Realities. A Survey of Political Theories in the 19th Century Western World*, Maastricht (2003: Shaker), ch.VI, "Liberal Thought, British and Continental".

cultivated for our own good and cultivation is, however you define it, an important element in culture.

References

Acton L (1906) Lectures on modern history. Meridan, New York
Acton L (1908) Wolsey and Henry VIII. Historical studies and essays and studies. Macmillan, London, p 63
Acton L (1952) Ultramontanism. Essays on church and state. Hollis and Carter, London, p 82
Acton L (1961) Lectures on modern history. Meridian, New York
Berlin I (1963) Four essays on liberty. Oxford University Press, Oxford
Burke E (1757) An essay towards the abridgement of the English history, greetings FLvH
Butterfield H (1968) Lord Acton. The Historical Association, London, p 10
Chadwick O (1998) Acton and history. Cambridge University Press, p 199
Conzemius V (ed) (1971) Ignaz von Döllinger—Lord Acton Briefwechsel 1850–1890. Becker, München
Dangerfield G (1936) The strange death of liberal England. Collins, London
Nipperdey T (1998) Deutsche Geschichte, 1866–1980, vol 1 "Arbeit und Bürgergeist"
van Holthoon FL (2003) Liberal thought, British and continental (ch.VI). In: The state and civil society, theories, illusions, realities. A survey of political theories in the 19th century western world. Shaker, Maastricht
van Holthoon FL (1985) Verzuiling in Nederland. De Nederlandse Samenleving sinds 1815. In: van Holthoon FL (ed) Assen 1985: van Gorcum, Assen. pp 159–175
Weber A (1951) Prinzipien der Geschichts- und Kultursoziologie. München

The False Pretensions of the Catholic Social Doctrine—The Critique of the Catholic Austrian Sociologist August M. Knoll (1900–1963)

Günther Chaloupek

1 August Maria Knoll—Life and Writings

In Austria the most prominent representatives of Catholic social thought were not bishops and clerics—as was the case in Germany—but laymen. The central figure was Carl von Vogelsang (1818–1890), a Prussian aristocrat converted to Catholicism, who came to Vienna to work as journalist and editor of a periodical which became an important voice in political debates during the last decades of the Habsburg monarchy. He played a dual role: at the theoretical level as founder of the Catholic social doctrine, at the political level as mentor of Christian social movement which took shape under Karl Lueger's leadership in the 1880s. Vogelsang's expectation that his radical programme for solution of the Social Question would be accepted as basis of the official social doctrine of the Church was not fulfilled by the encyclical *Rerum novarum*. For August M. Knoll, who considered himself as the master's follower, this was "Vogelsang's tragedy" which resulted from his misunderstanding of the true mission of the Church with respect to the social and economic order.

August Maria Knoll was born in Vienna on September 5, 1900, into a family of a school teacher. He studied at the University of Vienna, from which he received his Dr. rer. pol. (doctorate in state sciences) in 1924, for his thesis "Karl Vogelsang und der Ständegedanke". As a student he joined the Catholic fraternity "Nibelungia Wien". After finishing his studies Knoll worked as private tutor and journalist. In 1932 he became private secretary of prelate Ignaz Seipel (Catholic priest, Austrian Federal Chancellor 1922/24, 1926/29, died 1932). He wrote his habilitation thesis "Der Zins in der Scholastik" under Othmar Spann. From 1934 to 1938 he was a Privatdozent (unsalaried lecturer) at the University of Vienna.

G. Chaloupek (✉)
Economic Research Department, Austrian Chamber of Labor, Vienna, Austria
e-mail: guenther@chaloupek.eu

J. Backhaus et al. (eds.), *On the Economic Significance of the Catholic Social Doctrine*, The European Heritage in Economics and the Social Sciences 19, DOI 10.1007/978-3-319-52545-7_6

In 1932 Knoll published his fist book on Catholic social doctrine "Der soziale Gedanke im modernen Kapitalismus". The programmes of the Church and of Catholic organizations for a solution of the Social Question are discussed in the context of the emergence of the Social Question and other current approaches to its solution, e.g. Marxist socialism and German socialism of the chair ("Kathedersozialismus"). The book describes the evolution of Catholic social thought which led to the encyclical *Rerum novarum* in 1891. Its reception is documented by quotes from newspapers and periodicals. Although the encyclical *Quadragesimo anno* had been published in 1931, it is not subject of Knoll's book.

As member and functionary of the Christian-social Party Knoll was appointed to politically important positions after the establishment of a fascist-authoritarian regime in 1934. He became administrator of the Vorwärts-Verlag, which had been expropriated from the Social-democratic Party, and was editor in chief of two newspapers. After Austria's occupation by Nazi Germany in 1938 Knoll lost his positions at the publishing house. He was banned from his teaching position at the university and drafted for military service.

Knoll returned to Vienna in 1945. 1946 he was appointed to extra-ordinary professor, 1950 to ordinary professor of sociology at the University of Vienna. He is co-founder of the "Institut für Sozialpolitik und Sozialreform" (today Dr. Karl Kummer-Institut für Sozialreform, Wirtschafts- und Sozialpolitik), established in 1953.

Through various publications in periodicals, most notably through his books "Katholische Kirche und scholastisches Naturrecht" (1962) and "Kirche und Zukunft" (1963) Knoll became a public figure as prominent representative of "left wing Catholicism" in Austria, together with the historian and philosopher Friedrich Heer and the psychiatrist and publicist Wilfried Daim. He died in 1963.

2 Knoll's Book Der Soziale Gedanke im Modernen Katholizismus (1932) on the Relevance of the Encyclical Rerum Novarum

Knoll's basic position on the fundamental nature of a Catholic social doctrine rests on a principal distinction between the religious and moral sphere and the social sphere: "The Church solves the Social Question insofar as it is a religious and moral question, but not in as far as it is a question of sociology, of social technique, of organization of the economy".[1] Hence, the Church does not have a mission with respect to arrangements of economic systems, methods of production and distribution, but rather in matters where violations of charity and social justice in a

[1]"Die Kirche löst die soziale Frage, insofern diese eine religiöse und sittliche Frage ist, nicht aber, insofern sie eine Frage der Soziologie, der sozialen Technik, der Wirtschaftsorganisation ist".

concrete society call for its intervention. The task of the Church consists in "watching over outrages against charity[2] and justice" (Knoll 1932, 9).

This implies that there exists no particular social order that can be identified with Christianity or the Church (14). From a Christian or Catholic viewpoint, a variety of different forms and programs of social order appear possible under the condition that they do not violate justice and charity. Since the Church itself does not aim at establishing a missionary earthly kingdom, it does not provide social categories for an ideal order (8).

Knoll supports his position by referring to two millennia of historical experience which demonstrated the compatibility of Christian faith with different social orders. He quotes St. Paul whose letter to the Ephesians indicates that Christian religion accepts slavery as institution of "ancient capitalism" which was the social order in the Roman empire: "Servants, be obedient to them that are your masters, … Knowing that whatsoever good thing any man doeth, the same shall he receive of the Lord, … and ye masters do the same things unto them" (Ad Ephesios VI 5) (21). In the same vein, the Church has accepted the feudal order of land tenure and the urban handicraft system of the Middle Ages, such different economic systems as mercantilism and industrialism, small businesses and large enterprises, even socialism if it associates labour and capital in legal entities such as cooperatives, communal and state enterprises (8).

The flexibility of the Catholic Church to adapt to different orders of economy and society is reflected in official statements of authorities. Knoll demonstrates this by reviewing papal decrees on the issue of usury/interest. The position of the Church on this question changed in parallel with the changing function of money in society. It denied the legitimacy of interest for money loans in the early Middle Ages when monetary exchange was rare and the natural economy was still dominant, whereas its propensity to accept interest as price for financing productive capital goods increased with the growth of the exchange economy (26). In the conflict between the Dominicans (hostile to interest) and Jesuits (friendly) the Pope was careful not to take either side. Starting from *Cum onus* of 1569, the papal bulls discarded "usury", but at the same time not any kind of interest was qualified as usury, e.g. if the interest rate was modest (26ff).

With the rise of capitalism and socialism in the 19th century the debate about possible solutions of the Social Question intensified, within the Catholic Church as well as in other Christian confessions (see Sect. 3). If the encyclical *Rerum novarum* of 1891 was claimed by either side to give support to the Catholic-conservative or the Catholic-liberal orientation, in Knoll's view this is an expression of misleading concepts of Catholic social doctrine. At the same time, *Rerum novarum* rejects the claim of either side to represent the social doctrine to be the only one consistent with Catholic theology, while it establishes "basic programmatic principles for (social) programs. By necessity an infinite variety of such

[2]The term used by Knoll is "Liebe" by which he means "caritas"/charity.

Catholic social programmes can exist, taking into account the ever changing nature of social realities" (232).

As concerns substantial issues, *Rerum novarum* postulates a moral obligation of the state to intervene against exploitation and poverty, in order to rescue the working class from being doomed to a proletarian existence—in this respect the Church follows the critique of the conservative school of thought. At the same time, the betterment of the social position of workers should be achieved within the given system—*ecclesia vivit modo capitalistico*, as Knoll quotes his mentor Ignaz Seipel whose position was on the side of the liberal Catholics. In itself, the Catholic Church functions neither in a capitalistic nor in an anti-capitalistic mode, while it operates within a capitalist system (232). Socialism is rejected because the Church accepts man as an empirical being, and is therefore "sceptical towards all optimistic social ideals" (235). The encyclical advocates social peace instead of class struggle, compromise instead of social radicalism, mediation instead of strike (236).

If, in his book of 1932 Knoll is rather outspoken with respect to the limits of providing a religious foundation for a social programme, he appears rather hesitant to take sides either with Vogelsang's radical anti-capitalistic or Seipel's more liberal attitude, which appear both possible within these limits. We therefore proceed by discussing Knoll's position in the current debate about Catholic social doctrine.

3 Knoll's Position in the Debate About Catholic Social Doctrine Before 1938[3]

3.1 Conservative and Liberal Catholic Social Thought in Austria

The first part of Knoll's book of 1932 is a survey of the literature on the Social Question. He briefly summarizes the critique of capitalism and liberalism in the writings of German romanticist philosophers, French, English and German socialists and the German *Kathedersozialisten* (socialists of the chair), before he turns to Catholic social thought in the 19th century in Europe. The section also includes a survey of official documents of the Church dealing with the Social Question before the publication of *Rerum novarum*, and of measures of social legislation in Austria and in Germany.

In the Habsburg monarchy, political Catholicism and modern Catholic social thought emerged during the period of political and economic liberalism between 1867 and 1879.[4] At first Catholic politicians represented the class of the land-owning aristocracy, and were predominantly conservative, if not "reactionary" in their orientation. The conservative current gained strength when the phase of

[3]On the evolution of Catholic social doctrine see also Diamant (1965).

[4]On political Catholicism in this period see Fuchs (1949, 43ff).

rapid economic expansion ended in the crash of 1873. The ensuing severe recession was followed by a long period of declining prices which was—somewhat misleadingly—called "Great Depression" which ended only in the 1890s.

Catholic social thought fought against these developments on three fronts: against the negative social consequences of the capitalist mode of production; against the tendency of secularization which was the consequence of both capitalism and liberalism; and also against the emerging movement of socialism. Catholic writers saw an urgent need for political reaction to the increasing momentum of the socialist movement by offering a Christian alternative to the atheistic materialism of the latter.

In this period a profound change of political Catholicism took place. Already in 1879, the liberal government had been replaced by a coalition called "Iron Ring" ("Eisernen Ring") headed by Count Taaffe, which was composed of conservative Catholic groups of a variety of nationalities. Mainly as a consequence of reforms of electoral law through which franchise was granted to wider circles of the population, the votes of owners of small businesses and peasants became a major determinant of parliamentary elections. The representatives of those groups increasingly dominated the Catholic political movement which turned from a party of notables to the popular Christian-social party of Karl Lueger (mayor of Vienna from 1897 to 1910).

The central figure of Catholic social thought in Austria was Karl von Vogelsang, who came from a Protestant Prussian noble family. After converting to Catholicism in 1850, he worked as a journalist in Catholic Southern Germany, and finally settled in Austria in 1864. In 1875, he became editor of the Catholic newspaper *Das Vaterland* (fatherland), and of the monthly magazine *Österreichische Monatsschrift für Gesellschaftswissenschaft und Volkswirtschaft*. Vogelsang is the spiritual founder of the Christian-social movement in Austria, and thereby also of the variant of Austrian antisemitism associated with the person of Karl Lueger.

Vogelsang's pronouncedly anti-liberal and anti-capitalist views[5] were—admittedly—in central aspects indebted to Marxist and Lassallean socialism, from which it sharply diverged with respect to the alternative social order which should replace capitalism. Influenced by the German romanticist social philosopher Adam Müller, Vogelsang's model of an ideal Catholic society was medieval, when every man belonged to one of the big social groups (*Stand*) nobility, clerics, peasants, urban burghers. This model guaranteed the stability of a hierarchy of social groups based on god's will and natural law, and social solidarity by assigning a safe place in society to all its members.

Vogelsang was not only opposed to the capitalist economic and social order. He was suspicious of fundamental civil rights and liberties such as freedom of speech and freedom of science, which had destroyed traditional social structures. Deprived of its previous solid foundations, the political system was now "freely floating in the air", subjected to changes in majority opinion (Klopp 1894/1932, 240ff).

---

[5]Vogelsang never published a book with a comprehensive version of his theoretical works. This was done by his son-in-law Wiar Klopp (1894/1932) who assembled and edited essential parts Vogelsang's articles and pamphlets in systematic form.

With respect to the Social Question, Vogelsang proposed the organization of the economy in corporations, modelled after the medieval guilds. Hence, he discarded market competition and supported the craftsmen's movement (*Handwerkerbewegung*) which fought for revision of the liberal Small Business Act of 1859 (*Gewerbeordnung*) through which guilds had been abolished. For big industry, Vogelsang advocated the establishment of joint corporations of owners and workers to unite the two in the ownership of productive capital, and to pull the rug from the socialist agitation for class struggle. Like Marx, he wanted to abolish wage labour, but in opposition to socialism Vogelsang wanted all workers to participate in the ownership of the means of production, and thus receive a "just" compensation for their work. The state was assigned an essential role in the implementation of the corporatist structure of economy and society. Politically, Vogelsang's ideal was that of a social monarchy, a "social kingdom", similar to the teachings of Carl Rodbertus. The monarch is assigned the role to function as supreme head of all corporate units.

Vogelsang's book *Die materielle Lage des Arbeiterstandes in Österreich* (with Schneider 1884) had great influence on social legislation. After the dissolution of the monarchy, his ideas served as theoretical basis of anti-democratic political forces in the newly established Republic of Austria to replace parliamentary democracy with a "corporate state" (*Ständestaat*).

A liberal current in Catholic social though had first emerged in France (Knoll 1932, 70f) in the wake of Frederic Bastiat's *Harmoniés economiques* (1850) which maintained that the common good was served by a society in which individuals could freely pursue their own interests. They used the term "solidarism" for the capitalist market economy in which the individual feels responsible for himself and for the whole society. In Germany,[6] the first representative of the liberal current was Georg Graf Hertling who advocated social policy measures against the abuses of capitalism, while capitalism as a system was to be maintained. A more radical version of liberal orientation is represented by Heinrich Pesch SJ (1854–1926) who developed his own version of solidarism. Liberal Catholic thinkers were basically anti-interventionist in their economic policy concepts, while recommending only moderate social policy measures, if they did not weaken the functioning of the market mechanism. They did not deny that the social conditions of the working classes needed improvement, which had to be brought about by appealing to the moral responsibility of the capitalists and the wealthy.

In Austria, the liberal orientation among in Catholic social thought gained strength only after Vogelsangs death (Diamant, 58ff). The main representative was Franz Schindler, professor of moral theology at the University of Vienna. Schindler was opposed to Vogelsang's sharply anti-capitalistic attitude. He argued that capitalism was not incompatible with Christianity. He recommended that poverty and other negative consequences of the system should be healed or ameliorated by social policy measures. Schindler was succeeded by Ignaz Seipel, whose thinking was firmly rooted in scholastic theology, but who nonetheless followed Schindler's

---

[6]See also Frambach and Eissrich (2015, 78ff).

liberal-Catholic orientation. Seipel was minister of social affairs in the Habsburg monarchy's last government. He was the personal mentor of Knoll who served him as private secretary in the year before his death.

3.2 Knoll Between the Two Currents

It appears not an easy task to find out what are the consequences of Knoll's interpretation of the history of Catholic social doctrine and of *Rerum novarum*. If Knoll denied that the Church had a mission with respect to specific arrangements of economic and social systems, this was probably not easy to accept for the major part of the hierarchy, although he could claim support from several renowned theologians, e.g. Johannes Messner[7] in Austria, Heinrich Pesch in Germany. He did not hesitate to describe the opportunistic attitude of the Church with respect to social and economic issues over the course of many centuries, while interpreting this flexibility as higher wisdom and prudent restraint. He became much more critical in this respect later (see the next section).

Emotionally, and with respect to substantial issues of the Social Question, Knoll appears to have been closer to Vogelsang's orientation than to the liberal-Catholic social thinkers. For Knoll, Vogelsang is "the great awakener of the social ideal in Austria and in Germany" (Knoll 1932, 91), and he also approves of Vogelsang basic idea of repealing the difference between capital and labour (95). But Knoll also leaves no doubt that Vogelsang's claim that the medieval feudal system of society based on fundamental principles of "natural law" was the true representation of a Christian social order, is untenable (14).

Moreover, Vogelsang's Christian fundamentalism was not only an example of "false pretension of Catholic social doctrine". Knoll was also aware that even apart from such an untenable claim it was wholly unrealistic to change the economic and social order in such a radical way. Hence, he accepted Seipel's liberal position that the Church basically accepted the capitalist order. On the other hand, he praised *Rerum novarum* for having rejected the non-interventionist position of liberal solidarism by postulating a moral obligation of the state to intervene in order to correct the most outrageous abuses of capitalism (226) On the whole, Knoll appears to have been basically in agreement with *Rerum novarum*'s equidistance to both orientations of Catholic social thought. The encyclical had not decided in favour of one side, but it had set limits for either side (224).

Knoll somehow aimed at a synthesis between Vogelsang's radicalism and liberal realism. He thought that workers could be elevated from their proletarian status of non-ownership by means of general employee participation schemes which could be implemented by social policy legislation within the existing economy. Given that the Social-democratic party was sharply opposed to this idea, Knoll pinned his hopes on the concept of corporate state and on the Catholic labour movement.[8]

[7]See the quote from Messner in Knoll (1932, 13).

[8]On the Catholic labour movement in Austria see Pelinka (1972).

When the fascist government established the *Ständestaat* (corporate state) after having crashed the socialist uprising in February 1934, Knoll served the regime as administrator of the *Vorwärts-Verlag* and its newspapers which had been expropriated from the outlawed Social-democrats. Together with like-minded Catholic social thinkers (Ernst-Karl Winter, Josef Dobretsberger) he had to realize soon that the authoritarian governments of Chancellors Engelbert Dollfuß and Kurt Schuschnigg were not at all prepared to grant any autonomous scope of manoeuvre to the Catholic workers movement (*Katholische Arbeiterbewegung*) which had been put in charge of the institutions of labour. The Chamber of Labour and the newly formed trade union organization always remained subjected to strict political control of the authoritarian government. But Knoll remained loyal to the regime until its demise in 1938, defending the idea of corporatism even for some time after 1945 (Pelinka 1977).

3.3 Knoll's Left Turn: Katholische Kirche und Scholastisches Naturrecht (1962)

In his last book of 1962 Knoll took more or less the same position towards Catholic social doctrine: that scholastic natural law did not provide a basis for the Church to decide about concrete issues of social and economic order, and that its basic sentences such as *suum cuique* were devoid of content. Therefore, scholastic natural law is not a social program, but only a "minimal program to guard against excesses in the social sphere" (Knoll 1962, 24). Only individualistic natural law which is the product of Enlightenment can give guidance with respect to political and social questions (14). Only individualistic natural law can flesh out the concept of political and economic freedom which has no meaning for from a theological point of view.

What is new in Knoll's last book is the author's sharply critical position towards the misuse of scholastic natural law by the hierarchy as apology of existing social conditions by confirming their compatibility with natural law, and towards the clerical hierarchy for upholding false pretensions of Catholic social doctrine in order to hedge its social and political privileges.

By upholding the pretension of competence in political and social issues, the hierarchy has sanctified extremely unequal societies and suppressive political structures against oppositional movements, mostly standing on the side of the ruling class, or on the side of the wealthy, and thereby defended its own wealth and the benefits it provided to the clergy. There are many examples where the Church even justified outrageous abuses which offended the morals of the minimal social program. When the Church has condemned class struggle in the 19th century (and also in *Rerum novarum*), it was fully aware that it gave support to the wealthy against the wretched (52). Only when social conditions had become untenable and public opinion or political power relationships had changed, was the Church prepared to adjust its social doctrine accordingly. Therefore, encyclicals always come late, mostly too late, which does not only apply to *Rerum novarum* but to *Quadragesimo anno* (1931) and to *Mater et magistra* (1961) as well. This also demonstrates that the Church does not have a social mission. Knoll even ridicules the hierarchy's claim for social competence when he predicted that the next social encyclical due in 1971 would equally praise private ownership, the welfare state, and also accept major elements of the Communist economic system (62–63)—always by referring to the same eternal principles of natural law.

For the individual, this means that Catholic men and women willingly had to accept his/her social rank. Knoll quotes the Swiss theologian Otto Karrer who even wrote that the proper attitude of Christian was "resignation" (81). By requesting social obedience from its believers, the Church also re-enforced and protected the interests of the clerical hierarchy vis á vis the laymen. To break through the false pretensions of the Church and its clergy, Knoll calls for a different conception of Christendom. Whereas, according to the official Catholic doctrine the order of the clergy is superior to the order of the laymen, giving the former the decisive voice not only in spiritual matters, but also in worldly matters, Knoll calls for a "dualism of the two orders, which are equal organs of the kingdom of God" (20). Intuitively speaking, not the circle, with the clergy as central point, is the true representation of Christianity, but the ellipsis with its two focal points, with the focus on the lay with respect to wordly issues (20).

In his contribution to the book *Kirche und Zukunft* of 1963 Knoll heavily criticized the entitlement of "integral Catholicism" to supreme authority not only in the sacral sphere, but also in the secular world, which had been renewed by Pope Pius X with his slogan "*Omnia instaurare in Christo*" (Daim et al. 1963, 74). If this claim was out of touch with reality, it was still upheld by the Church with respect to the Catholic lay movement to which it denied autonomy. Knoll opposed "integral Catholicism", emphasizing the independence of the Catholic lay movement vis á vis the clerical hierarchy.

Knoll's claim for an equal position of Catholic lays with respect to questions of social and economic order had a strong "anti-clerical touch",[9] of course not in the sense that he was against clergy in itself, but against the pretentious claim of the Church hierarchy to have the last word in the debate about Catholic social doctrine. It would appear as a logical consequence to call for an end of Papal social encyclicals. Why Knoll did not draw this conclusion remains an open question.

[9]In an obituary written in 1964 Peter Diem wrote: "Knoll was an anti-clerical Catholic"—not in the sense that he was against clergy in itself, but against the pretentious claims of many clerics.

4 Concluding Remarks

In his last book Knoll speaks of „the tragedy of the Vogelsang School" (Knoll 1962, 56–57). Its representatives' belief that they were propagating the true social doctrine of the Church was not confirmed by *Rerum novarum*. But the Vogelsang School was equally misled by claiming the competence of the Church for approval for a social program of this kind. At the same time, Knoll was convinced that "the Vogelsang system had progressively gained relevance in view of the development of social policy legislation after 1945". Moreover, he thought that there were indications for economic and social trends which pointed towards a "transformation of capitalism" (*Umbruch des Kapitalismus*), to which no objections were raised in the encyclical *Mater et magistra* of Pope John XXIII (58).

There is continuity of Knoll's sympathy for essential elements of the social and economic programme of the Vogelsang School from his book of 1932 to *Katholische Kirche und scholastisches Naturrecht* thirty years later,[10] with the reservations against the false pretensions of Catholic social doctrine. During the 1930s Knoll also actively supported the idea of a Corporate State. This idea was approved of as a "middle way" between capitalism and socialism by Pope Pius XI by the encyclical *Quadragesimo anno*. In reality, this implied political support for anti-democratic, authoritarian fascism which had been established in Italy by Mussolini, who actively supported the anti-democratic endeavours of the Christian-social party in Austria. When fascist dictatorship was established in Austria after the uprising of the Social-democrats in 1934, Knoll served the authoritarian regime in important functions. Apparently he hoped for a more democratic version of corporatism with free elections in the representative bodies of the corporate constitution.

With its decidedly anti-clerical orientation, Knoll's attack on the false pretensions of Scholastic natural law and his challenge of the clergy provoked heavy reactions from the hierarchy and in print media owned by the Church.[11] From the clerical side his criticism of official Catholic opportunism was called "outrageous", although Knoll had carefully documented that in reality the Church had often not only tolerated, but explicitly endorsed acts of suppression and violence by Catholic governments. On the political side, he was charged with propagating the Communist and Socialist agenda. When his 1962 book was out of print after a few months, Knoll's enemies even succeeded to thwart a second printing by the same publisher.

But within a few years after Knoll's death, a remarkable change in the *Zeitgeist* had taken place, by which Catholic ways of thinking were deeply affected. Liberal virtues like freedom of speech became increasingly accepted in Catholic circles, the

---

[10]I could not find passages in Knoll's writings where he distanced himself from Vogelsang's assaults against Enlightenment philosophy and civil liberties.

[11]Examples are taken from Ernst Topitsch's introduction to the 2nd edition of Knoll's book (Knoll 1968, 12f).

hierarchy became more tolerant. It amounts to a rehabilitation of Knoll's position when, in the 1970s the archbishop of Vienna declared that there was no such thing as "Christian politics", but only "politics based on Christian responsibility".

References

Daim W, Heer F, Knoll A (1963) Kirche und Zukunft. Europa Verlag, Vienna

Diamant A (1965) Die österreichischen Katholiken und die Erste Republik, Verlag der Wiener Volksbuchhandlung, Wien s.a., translation of "Austrian catholics and the First Republic: democracy, capitalism and the social order, 1918–1934". Princeton University Press, Princeton, NJ, p 1960

Diem P (1964) Nachruf auf Professor August Maria Knoll, Jan 1964. http://austriaforum.org/af/Wissenssammlungen/Essays/Religion/Nachruf_Knoll

Frambach H, Eissrich D (2015) Der dritte Weg der Päpste. UVK Verlagsgesellschaft, Konstanz Munich

Fuchs A (1949) Geistige Strömungen in Österreich 1867–1918. Globus Verlag, Vienna (new edn in 1984)

Klopp W (ed) (1894/1932) Die sozialen Lehren des Freiherrn Karl von Vogelsang. Grundzüge einer katholischen Gesellschafts- und Volkswirtschaftslehre nach Vogelsangs Schriften, Vienna

Knoll A (1932) Der soziale Gedanke im modernen Katholizismus Von der Romantik bis Rerum Novarum; Reinhold-Verlag, Vienna, Leipzig

Knoll A (1962) Katholische Kirche und scholastisches Naturrecht. Europa Verlag, Vienna

Knoll A (1968) Katholische Kirche und scholastisches Naturrecht, second edition, with a preface by Ernst Topitsch. Luchterhand-Verlag, Neuwied and Berlin

Pelinka A (1972) Stand oder Klasse? Die Christliche Arbeiterbewegung Österreichs 1933–1938. Europa Verlag, Vienna

Pelinka A (1977) August Maria Knoll, in: Neue Österreichische Biographie ab 1915. Große Österreicher Band XIX, Vienna

125 Years *Rerum novarum*—The Theological Perspective

Peter Schallenberg

1 The Man—Created to Receive God's Love

125 years ago, Pope Leo XIII published his encyclical letter *Rerum novarum*[1] which marks the beginning of dealing with the social question in the Catholic Church. One background of this issue for the Catholic Church was the famine in Ireland in 1846/47. Important questions in Ireland were the right of ownership and the freedom of association. In the background stand the questions of decent life for the workers and the natural rights of man. Pope Leo XIII refers to this in his encyclical letter and strengthens the idea that there are natural rights of man, in general independent of faith and church. After the school of Salamanca, which introduced rights for the indigenous people in Africa and America, individual rights were mentioned in the catholic tradition for the first time. They build the anthropological background of the social question. Besides the impression of the Irish famine the Pope was influenced by the American bishops, who cooperates with the knights of labour and feel religious reservations not that important in the situation when the poor workers needed help. In the United States the poor workers were mostly catholic due to the fact, that they were immigrants from Ireland, Italy and Germany (Schratz 2011, 48–51).

So the social question was highly important for the church, because workers were the basis of the Catholic Church in the USA still in the 20th century: "It became preeminently the church of laborer and city dweller, of ghetto and slum, and kept that image until the post World War II flight to the suburbs" (Hennesey 1981, 175; Schratz 2011, 51). By that the interest of the Pope and the curia for the

[1]German Text Edition see Leo XIII (1891).

P. Schallenberg (✉)
Theological Faculty, University of Paderborn, Germany
Center for Catholic Social Sciences, Mönchengladbach, Germany
e-mail: c.krauss@ksz.de; schallenberg@ksz.de

J. Backhaus et al. (eds.), *On the Economic Significance of the Catholic Social Doctrine*, The European Heritage in Economics and the Social Sciences 19, DOI 10.1007/978-3-319-52545-7_7

social question was evoked. Not the argument with Marx and Engels but with Henry George and the worker priest Edward McGlynn were central for the evolution of social teaching in the 19th century (Arnold 2011, 258). The question of the right of coalition was first discussed about the Knights of Labour, which were found in the USA in the 1830s. The knights dealt with the exploitation of the workers and were organized as a brotherhood according to the Freemason. This provoked the intervention of Sanctum Offizium, because Pope Leo XII forbid in 1825 this kind of organization with excommunicatio latae sententiae for his catholic members. But in the 1840s the US-American bishops reached a modus vivendi with the knights of labour and a kind of toleration by the church, which was fixed by the Baltimore council in 1866. Because it was seen by the church that the knights of labour, influenced by the catholic Henry George wanted in the first place help the workers. In these circumstances the idea of the natural law came again in the theological discussion. The core idea of this is that every man has dignity because of this nature. Nature is necessary to receive God's mercy as a person. You cannot neglect the natural condition of man as a basis also for a Christian anthropology. But Christian anthropology goes further and stresses, that man is creation of God and as ruler of the world responsible of the creation. Man is participating in creation by his ratio. This anthropology is important for social teaching of the church as it is established in *Rerum novarum.* Its biblical dimension is expressed in psalm 8: "What is man that you are mindful of him, and the son of man that you care for him?" Here the question of man is expressed and related to the idea of responsibility of man to fulfill God's will of all-bracing love. This is relevant in *Rerum novarum* by the mentioned responsibility to organize the working conditions and societal life. Leo XIII, denies not only the actual socialism of his time but also the idea of Ernst Bloch in his book "the principal of hope" (Bloch 1985), that every problem will be solved in the future, when the world as a whole has been turned into an socialist state: In the contrary the Pope stresses the responsibility of every person, to make God's love visible in the world and account to God for his life. This thought builds a strong tradition in Catholic Social teaching to this day, as it is also the core issue of the encyclical letter *Caritas in veritate* (Beretta et al. 2009; Cordes 2009, 324–332; Kruip 2009, 388–392; Küppers 2009, 419–427; Nothelle-Wildfeuer 2009, 3–9, written by Pope Benedikt XVI. on June 29th 2009. This encyclical is not only about social issues but a survey of catholic theology of history and anthropology explicitly on Augustinian priming. That means, economic and social policies and politics in general are viewed from a metaphysical point of view. Politics and economy are not only dealing with the adequate in the current situation but with the good for the life for every human being. The core question is: how can Christian love influence political and economical structures, how can mercy influence structural questions of justice? This question is not only reflected in both encyclical mentioned, but was a core question in the theology of Joseph Ratzinger and so Benedikt XVI. Is there a clear path from the Augustinian inwardness of human conscience to inner and outer justice in state and economy? For it is a strong confidence in catholic theology, that all systems in the world (and politics and economy are such systems producing aims as justice and solidarity) should conduct the human as God's image with an immortal soul to God and his eternal love. The moral frame of reference is important for this. "On this subject the Church's social doctrine can make a specific contribution, since it is based on man's creation "in the image of God" (Gen 1:27), a datum which gives rise to the inviolable dignity of the human person and the transcendent value of natural moral norms."[2] This was expressed in former times perfectly in the first question of Catholic Catechism: "What for is man on earth? Man is on earth to serve God, to love him and by that come to heaven." That is continued by: "The desire to God is written in the man's heart, because men is created by and for God. "The central point of this spirituality is Love. So the Catechism of 1993 starts the first chapter "The life of man—to know and love God" with the words: "God, infinitely perfect and blessed in himself, in a plan of sheer goodness freely created man to make him share in his own blessed life. For this reason, at every time and in every place, God draws close to man". When this is correct and should be true, it is the best for every man to get the gift of endless love. The human being has a right for this love which can of course only be demanded of God, but of no court on earth. Then it is decisive that every man can find this love at least partially in his live and become so God's image (imago dei) (Pieper 2014). At the same time the way of virtue can be called Love which is explained broadly in the revelation of the New Testament and developed as an ethical system by the fathers of the church. Pleased through another person be allowed to acknowledge the happiness of the own life: this is exactly what is meant by the idea of creation as gift and offering of the own life. Here nature is thought completed and opened in the space of mercy. Nature and its randomness is interpreted as creation and divine necessity.

As mentioned above, man with his ratio is a specific issue in the world, because he can plan the future and overlook more than just the present. This is the starting point of natural law. As Joseph Ratzinger stresses: In modern times the only still existing idea of the natural law are the human rights, which come to man just because he is member of humanity (Ratzinger 2005, 35). By this you can also see the core issue of the encyclical *Caritas in veritate*: development. Not any development, but development in progress on the vocation of man by God to eternal life.

2 The Duties of Theological and Secular Institutions

For that in many social encyclicals as in *Rerum novarum* and *Caritas in veritate*, the background of institutions is mentioned as vocation and person, love and justice, truth and gift, freedom and ratio. So the basis of societal life is in question: what is the last meaning of our economic and social frame/order? Why do such orders and systems exist? From the point of view of Catholic social teaching the answer is clear: all societal systems and institutions, may they be theological (visible church with visible sacraments) or secular (state, laws and visible separation of powers)

[2] Caritas in veritate, no. 45.

should support the man's vocation to receive love and to give love. This serves from the Christian perspective as instrument to reach the aim of man, which is not to accumulate material quantities but to enjoy spiritual qualities, according to the Augustinian "frui" in contradiction to "uti", which expresses only the useful aspect of basic commodities.[3] Everything is serving to fulfill man's vocation, to receive spiritual gifts of which love is the most important. As it is mentioned in *Caritas in veritate* love is the best truth about man, over which nothing bigger and better can be thought, to use and slightly modify a word of Anselm of Canterbury.[4] *Caritas in veritate* is in fact the principal and core issue of Christian anthropology and the social teaching of the church. Justice (and also social justice), which is a central question of social teaching, is the first and necessary, but not sufficient step of realizing love, which is only partially possible outside the paradise. I cannot give a gift to a person, when I didn't give him before the things he has a right to (see *Caritas in veritate*, no. 6). First the basic needs must be fulfilled to give the chance of surviving to man. But remaining on the level of basic goods estranges man from his vocation of receive and give love. As Pope John Paul II said in his social encyclical *Centesimus annus*, one hundred years after *Rerum novarum*, this evokes an alienation of man by losing his meaning of life.[5] This is accelerated extremely in every day's consumption, when artificial needs are fulfilled, which distract man of this core issue on earth and does not help man to a true experience of this person or personality (see *Centesimus annus* no. 43). In the view of Christian anthropology it is the most important issue of state as welfare state and state founded on the rule of law, to prevent this development. To explain it by the parable of the Samaritan: it is the state's duty to prevent man of laying in the street, hurt by alienation which makes it necessary to wait for the helping Samaritan. Just the opposite: man should participate in the creation of a civilization of love, which is close to the civitas Dei of Augustine.[6] Here it is important to remember the duality of civitas Dei and civitas terrena by Augustine: the civitas terrena is secularized and statutorily regulated just to ensure the fulfillment of the basic needs of man. The civitas Dei means the good life of bliss. The state secures the base for peaceful und tolerant living together, i.e. law and justice. The civitas Dei is not simply congruent with the visible church but can be found in the forum internum in the eternal soul which has to decide between "uti" and "frui", i.e. between egocentric utility and give and receive of selfless love. This choice can be judged in the forum externum. The difference between the spiritual quality and the quantity of life is a cornerstone of European metaphysics and anthropology as it is mentioned in Plato's Gorgias: "Better suffer injustice than commit it." When just surviving is replacing good and meaningful life, the ethical consent is lost. This happens more and more in western

[3]See Benedikt XVI (2009).

[4]See Anselm of Canterbury (2005, 21). "Et quidem credimus te esse aliquid quo nihil maius cogitari possit".

[5]See Johannes Paul (1991).

[6]See Augustinus (2007).

postmodern society by relinquishing the metaphysical question and ban religion strictly in privacy.

3 The Eschatological Dimension of Social Ethics

The parable of the Samaritan in the gospel of Luke implicitly shows that love is more than justice although love assumes justice. That also means God's mercy assumes man's nature and is going to make it perfect. "Gratia non destruit sed supponit et perfecit naturam".[7] Man's redemption by God's mercy make it possible for man to recognition and realization of real love in the inner attitude of faith (to God's revelation in the church and the sacraments) and hope (on fulfillment of the personal pursuit of happiness). Thus Hans Urs von Balthasar mentioned that life according to nature is only a life with fulfillment of basic needs, but a Christian life is life in plenty and so life with thanks to God: Eucharist (von Balthasar 1960, 179). Such a life is incarnated in Christ and is revealed to man by the sacraments. So it creates the second nature of man. Because the state is able to prevent man of being robbed or alienated but cannot prevent man of losing the meaning of personal life. The welfare state is grounded on fundaments which it cannot guarantee by itself: the personal gifted and received love, which it only can make possible and hope for it. This is "the logic of give and forgive", which is certificated in the prologue of John's Gospel as the beginning of the whole creation and so being the nature of God, who creates by the logic of love man.

Of course this logic cannot deliver economic rules directly: there is no direct line from God's existence to rules for the market, this would be a naturalistic and economistic wrong conclusion. But the rules of the market and its mathematical basis are only one side of the medal of economy. Social ethics will just concentrate on human capital; man as person in the economic system. That was also meant in the encyclical *Rerum novarum*, where no ideology, whether capitalism nor socialism is in favor, but man's dignity as God's creature. In the economic sphere the church has not technical solutions to offer, because it misses specialized competence. But it is the church's duty and competence to judge what helps concretely man's dignity and is promoting the common good, which is not only the best possible of most people but the absolute best for every person.

How should this be possible in a world that is missing the metaphysical perspective and feels completed in pure materialism? So social ethics has always to keep in mind the eschatological view. The just development of the person is the core issue of social ethics.

This issue is in danger by two historical philosophical traditions: the one of Jean-Jacques Rousseau and the one of Auguste Comte. While Comte sets absolutely on technical development and progress, Rousseau's philosophy is the return

[7]For the background see Goertz (2010, 221–243).

to nature of mankind. Both ideas split progress and development from moral judgment and so from man's responsibility. Theologically expressed it means: to see progress only in measurable steps of forum externum does not match with human person in Christian understanding because man possesses an eternal soul. Man is not only a mechanistic machine. Although man is oriented to the good out of nature—for the catholic teaching also after the original sin—without the revelation and the knowing of God the good becomes more and more unclear materially. Although by nature the man owns the pursuit of happiness, without faith the good tends to be mixed up with the pleasant or the just technical right. The frankness for the supernatural gift of love may exist in man by nature, but without faith it may fail. Between the natural state of Rousseau and the original state of Christianity there may be formal similarities. Also for Rousseau the original sin is the use of the ratio, but he expects human and finite redemption, not redemption by God or sacrament. His idea is autonomy against theological heteronomy. Rousseau agrees with Christian faith in the idea of the original good nature of man. As Ernst Cassirer mentioned the man is good of nature as long as the nature does not express itself by natural impulses but is open to reach the idea of freedom, because the difference between human beings and all other beings is its perfectibility (Cassirer 2012, 45).

4 Reciprocity of Personal Freedom and Social Justice

The encyclical *Caritas in veritate* culminates in the small sentence: "God is the guaranty of true development of man" (*Caritas in veritate* no. 29). Behind this background the encyclical is in favor of social market economy as an institution that makes encounters of men possible. The social market economy is the third way between pure capitalism and socialism already mentioned in *Rerum novarum*. This shows the long and strong tradition of the ideas of *Rerum novarum* although it is always conformed to actual challenges. That market of encounter is impeded, when enterprises feel answerable only to investors and shareholders but forget the common good of society. For banks, which are necessary for modern economy, this is valid in a special way. The aim of the institution of social market economy is retributive justice and solidarity with actual living and also with coming generations. This is also the deeper meaning of acting as entrepreneur: it is not the meaning of accumulating profits but to create jobs, gaining profits by that and enabling others to gain profits. Only with that the development of a civilization of love is possible, as it is aimed in Catholic social teaching from *Rerum novarum* to *Caritas in veritate* and beyond. This civilization should enable man to live a globally successful life. Here you can see the difference of an Augustian natural law and the scholastically natural law. In the tradition of Augustine mean is understood as a person who is free and has the right of progress to reach the fulfillment of his personal aim while the scholastically view only gives the right to a special and individual being. Man has the right to develop himself to recognize his inner meaning. So in the Christian anthropology you need a legal system who stresses the personal freedom of man. This could be found in the social market economy, when iustitia socialis, as all-round social justice, is implemented by an institutional caritas. Social justice as participative equity with the elements of participation and contribution aims at surmounting social exclusion and missing participation and can be understood as social love, i.e. caritas. Inclusion, not exclusion is the societal program of Catholic social teaching. Participatory equity in this understanding includes solidarity and at the same time subsidiarity, which means responsibility of those able to take it. This is ethically required to fulfill the ideas of Christian anthropology. An Ordoliberalism means that exactly as personal freedom is embedded in strong just order in this kind of liberalism. And Ordoliberalism is the background of social market economy.

5 Promoting Human Freedom to the Good

The human freedom must be understood as well as freedom of thinking. As in *Caritas in veritate* mentioned the world seems to be ill, because "thoughts are missing".[8] Thoughts are the decisive point, because when you think something you open the possibility to act according to the thought. So thoughts are important for the decision to act just to fulfill your basic needs or to act in aiming at the life in all-round love and happiness as it describes God's plan with mankind. Thoughts are by this important for moral freedom because you can choose between these two opportunities. But although man decides in favor of the good he must be understood as a creature of deficiency. Man as God's creation, called to give and receive love is also limited by his natural capacity to fail and, in theological language, to sin. To sin means to live as if God does not exist, to eliminate him from day to day life, to doubt of the own necessity of existence and to feel dispensable as individual. Against that the freedom to the good must be promoted, although it can fail. God's good thought was the creation of man and his destination to eternal life. If you leave that anthropological base of economy and social ethics, economic and social acting is reduced to technocratic pragmatism, because the last meaning of life is missed. Of course as mentioned in *Rerum novarum* as a reaction of the situation of the poor workers in the USA, catholic social teaching has its duty in helping improving the situation of the poor. But the background of his duty is man's creation as image of God with his own dignity. So it is important to introduce that Christian anthropology also in the public sphere and the legal order of a society. So far there is no difference between the challenge of Catholic social teaching at the time of *Rerum novarum* and today. The anthropology is the background of catholic social teaching to all times. Its promotion is still necessary in a democratic state founded on the rule of law. This is the distinguished challenge and duty of the church.

[8]See caritas in veritate no. 53, citing the encyclical populorum progression of Paul VI, no. 85.

References

Anselm von Canterbury (2005) Proslogion. Lateinisch/Deutsch. Reclam, Stuttgart

Arnold C (2011) Die amerikanische Dimension der sozialen Frage und die Entstehung von Rerum novarum. Rezension zu Schratz, Sabine (2011): Das Gift des alten Europa und die Arbeiter der neuen Welt. Zum amerikanischen Hintergrund der Enzyklika Rerum novarum (1891). Paderborn. In: Jahrbuch für Christliche Sozialwissenschaften 52 (2011), pp 257–262

Augustinus (2007) De civitate Dei. dtv, Munich

Benedikt XVI (2009) Caritas in veritate. Verlautbarungen des Apostolischen Stuhls, Nr. 186, herausgegeben vom Sekretariat der Deutschen Bischofkonferenz. Libreria Editrice Vaticana, Bonn

Beretta S et al (2009) Amore e verità. Commento e guida alla lettura dell´Enciclica „Caritas in veritate“ di Benedetto XVI. Milano

Bloch E (1985) Das Prinzip Hoffnung. Suhrkamp, Frankfurt

Cassirer E (2012) Über Rousseau. Suhrkamp, Berlin

Cordes PJ (2009) Kirchliche Soziallehre und Offenbarung. Zur Enzyklika „Caritas in veritate“. In: Die Neue Ordnung 63:324–332

Goertz S (2010) Gratia supponit naturam. Theologische Lektüren, praktische Implikationen und interdisziplinäre Anschlussmöglichkeiten eines Axioms. In: Ottmar John; Magnus Striet (Eds.): „...und nichts Menschliches ist mir fremd“. Theologische Grenzgänge. Pustet, Regensburg, pp 221–243

Hennesey JJ (1981) American Catholics. A history of the roman Catholic community in the United States. Oxford University Press, New York/Oxford

Johannes Paul II (1991) Centesimus annus. In: Texte zur katholischen Soziallehre. Die sozialen Rundschreiben der Päpste und andere kirchliche Dokumente. Bundesverband der Katholischen Arbeitnehmer-Bewegung Deutschlands - KAB, Kevelaer, pp 689–764

Kruip G (2009) Entwicklung und Wahrheit. Die Sozialenzyklika Benedikts XVI. ermöglicht viele Lesarten. In: Herder Korrespondenz 63:388–392

Küppers A (2009) Jenseits von Angebot und Nachfrage. Die Enzyklika „Caritas in veritate“ und die Wirtschaftskrise. In: Internationale Katholische Zeitschrift Communio 39:419–427

Leo XIII (1891) Rerum Novarum. In: Texte zur katholischen Soziallehre. Die sozialen Rundschreiben der Päpste und andere kirchliche Dokumente. Bundesverband der Katholischen Arbeitnehmer-Bewegung Deutschlands - KAB, Kevelaer, pp 1–40

Nothelle-Wildfeuer U (2009) Liebe und Wahrheit, Gerechtigkeit und Gemeinwohl als Leitlinien von Entwicklung. In: AMOS International 3:3–9

Pieper J (2014) Über die Liebe. Kösel, Munich

Ratzinger J (2005) Was die Welt zusammenhält. Vorpolitische moralische Grundlagen eines freiheitlichen Staates. In: Idem: Werte in Zeiten des Umbruchs, Herder, Freiburg, pp 28–40

Schratz S (2011) Das Gift des alten Europa und die Arbeiter der neuen Welt. Zum amerikanischen Hintergrund der Enzyklika Rerum novarum (1891). Ferdinand Schöningh, Paderborn

von Balthasar HU (1960) Merkmale des Christlichen. In: Idem: Verbum Caro. Skizzen zur Theologie I. Johannes Verlag, Einsiedeln

Dr. Johannes Antonius Veraart: A Catholic Economist on *Rerum Novarum*

Robert W.J. Jansen

> *Science does not prescribe the direction of social phenomena, but social phenomena prescribe the directions of science. Every time again it is the main sin of Economics to have forgotten this Aristotelian-Thomist wisdom.*
>
> J.A. Veraart, public lecture, 8 January 1940, 3.

1 Introduction

Up to the first half of the nineteenth century Catholics faced political discrimination in the Netherlands. The Constitution of 1848 enabled them to improve their positions in society. Catholics organized themselves in trade unions, employer organizations and political interest groups in order to pursue their interests. Catholic politicians even succeeded to participate in every cabinet from 1918 up to 1994 (Verhagen 2015, 9). Dutch Catholics adored and obeyed their popes in the nineteenth century. They did not question papal authority. In particular Pope Leo XIII (1878–1903) contributed to their emancipation with his encyclicals, in particular *Rerum Novarum* in 1891. This encyclical on the rights and duties of capital and labour influenced many politicians and scholars and became a source of discussions among Catholics (Verhagen 2015, 32). To investigate the impact of *Rerum Novarum* on economics and industrial organization I restrict myself to catholic politician and economist professor Dr. Johannes Antonius Veraart (1886–1955). He was a productive and assertive scholar committed to labour and parliamentary democracy in the first half of the twentieth century. Although almost neglected the

The author accepts sole responsibility for statements of fact and opinions expressed in this essay.

R.W.J. Jansen (✉)
Investigator Collective Labour Agreements, Ministry of Social Affairs and Employment, The Hague, The Netherlands
e-mail: R.W.J.Jansen@tele2.nl

J. Backhaus et al. (eds.), *On the Economic Significance of the Catholic Social Doctrine*, The European Heritage in Economics and the Social Sciences 19, DOI 10.1007/978-3-319-52545-7_8

literature considered him as the *auctor intellectualis* of the Dutch variant of industrial organization or corporatism (in Dutch known as *Publiekrechtelijke Bedrijfsorganisatie*, abbreviated as PBO). The purpose of my essay is to answer the following questions:

- What were his educational and political backgrounds?
- What were his economic approach and ethics? In particular what was his relationship with German economics?
- How did he interpret the encyclical *Rerum Novarum*?
- What was his influence as a politician and economist?

To answer these questions I investigated amongst others his academic and political writings. In particular I studied his doctoral dissertation *Wages* (Dutch title *Arbeidsloon*) which he defended in 1910. Further I consulted literature about the political history of catholicism in the Netherlands.

I also had the opportunity to consult the Veraart collection at the National Archive in The Hague. Additionally I read relevant parts of the digitalized Aalberse diaries deposited at the Huygens Institute for the History of the Netherlands. My essay ends with a brief consideration of the relevance of *Rerum Novarum* in the 21st century.

2 Background

Johannes Antonius Veraart was born in Amsterdam, where he attended the Sint Ignatiuscollege, a catholic grammar school. His parents belonged to the catholic middle class. To determine the impact of *Rerum Novarum* on Veraart it is necessary to be acquainted with his educational career and political involvement. See Appendix 1 for a short timeline of his career.

2.1 Education

At the age of eighteen Veraart enrolled the Faculty of Law at the University of Amsterdam. Here, he developed a special interest in the emerging academic discipline of economics. His professors included Willem Treub (Radical Liberal politician and economist, 1858–1931), David van Embden (Liberal economist, 1873–1923), Antonius Struycken (Government Theory, 1891–1941) and Joannes Theodorus de Groot (Philosophy, 1848–1922). The latter taught him Thomism and Neothomism (For reasons of readability the term Thomism will be used below to refer to both closely related philosophies). Thomism evolved into the philosophical foundation of Political Catholicism in the nineteenth century. Having its origins in the writings of Saint Thomas Aquinas (1225–1275) this philosophy provided a vision of the world created and sustained by God's divine purpose (Rogier and de Rooy 1998, 626; Conway 1996, 9, 14). Van Embden lectured Veraart introductory economics from a perspective of philosophy of science (discussing the concepts of *causality* and *predictability*) and supervised his doctoral dissertation *Arbeidsloon.*[1]

After defending his dissertation an intellectual friendship evolved with priest professor Dr. Joseph Theodorus Beijsens (1864–1945) the *nestor* of Dutch Thomism and follower of pope Leo XIII. Both men exchanged letters and discussed about economics and ethics. In his contribution to the journal *Studia Catholica* in honour of Beijsens' Golden Jubilee Veraart emphasized the importance of the jubilee for modern economics and public law. Beijsens rejected the utilitarian assumption of economic individualism claiming that individuals maximize their welfare, instead he adhered to the Aristotelian-Thomist approach of dualism. This approach assumed the complementarity of the individual and the society which had its origin in a divine order. In line with this dualist approach labour and capital were considered mutually dependent and their agreement resulted in *the beauty of good order.*[2] In his contribution Veraart remarked that John Maynard Keynes (1883–1946) and Young Americans—*Roosevelt's braintrust*—were good examples of the acceptance of dualism (Veraart 1937, 422–427).

2.2 Politics

The emancipation enabled catholic scholars to compete for professorships. These appointments involved the minister of the Interior and the boards of the universities (in Dutch *Colleges van Curatoren*).

In 1915 catholic economists competed for a professorship at the University of Leiden. This competition was not without mutual criticism and slander. The main competitor of Veraart was the catholic politician and lawyer Dr. Piet Aalberse (1871–1948). In his diaries Aalberse described Veraart as an *old liberal* and accused him of denigrating catholic economists such as the German Jesuit Heinrich Pesch (1854–1926) who was the author of the widely respected *Lehrbuch der Nationalökonomie* (1905–23). Liberal prime minister and minister of Interior Cort van der Linden (1846–1935) was actively involved in this appointment procedure. Neither Aalberse nor Veraart obtained the professorship but the Liberal economist Durk van Blom (1877–1938).[3]

[1]National Archive, Collection Veraart, 1904–1955, no. inventory 2.21.306, no. 50.

[2]Objective of Aristotelian-Thomist philosophy is to satisfy individual and societal needs at a reasonable level. National Archive, Collection Veraart, 1904–1955, no. inventory 2.21.306, no. 697 and 1176; Leo XIII (1891), par. 19.

[3]Gribling (1961, 289) remarked that public disappointment about not appointing Aalberse constituted a sign of the necessity to establish a catholic university. In 1923 the Catholic University of Nijmegen was established. This university started with a faculty of law and a faculty of humanities but did not have a faculty of economics.

Prime minister Cort van der Linden appointed Aalberse as professor of economics at the University of Delft in 1916. Remarkably Veraart ranked first and Aalberse third on the proposal of the board.[4] Three years later he succeeded his competitor who became minister of Labour in the cabinets Ruys de Beerenbrouck I and II.[5] Finally, Veraart became *rector magnificus* of the Technical University of Delft in September 1939. His academic career showed an extraordinary number of books, articles, public lectures, privatissima and speeches expressing his economic ideas and political opinions.

Veraart joined the *Rooms Katholieke Staatspartij* (*Roman Catholic State Party*, abbreviated as RKSP) with the intention to change its conservative attitude. From 1925 up to 1929 he represented the RKSP as a member of parliament. He favoured the adoption of *a catholic democratic thought* and frequently criticized his party for supporting the economic policies of the cabinet. His efforts were unsuccessful. In 1933 he left the RKSP to found with others the *Katholieke Democratische Bond* (abbreviated as KDB) after a merger the *Katholieke Democratische Partij* (abbreviated as KDP). As chairman Veraart propagated a *brave* economic policy entailing a national recovery plan to combat unemployment. To implement this policy social democrats, democratic calvinists and KDP had to cooperate. Veraart described in various publications his worries about the crisis of parliamentary democracy. In particular he considered extra-parliamentary cabinets as a threat to parliamentary democracy (Veraart 1929, 195; Beekman 1935, 482–492).[6] In 1939 he returned to the RKS.[7]

Veraart expressed the opinion that the state should take care of the wellbeing of its citizens in every society. The state was always a Culture State and a Welfare State. Only the sovereign state possessed the means no other power could use. Its sovereignty must be used on behalf of the welfare. So it was understood in the past but not anymore since 1800 (Veraart 1931a, 38). He considered the mass unemployment of the thirties a national scandal and blamed prime minister Hendrikus Colijn (1869–1944). He worried about the demoralizing effect of lasting

[4]Dominican priest Bernardus Constant Molkenboer (1878–1948) a specialist in Vondel studies congratulated Aalberse with a small poem: "*Cort voelt Goddank wat waard is. Een Roomse kop die niet veraard is*". Huygens Institute, Collection Aalberse, diary 13 June 1916. See also: Collection Aalberse, diary 8 June 1915, 2 August 1915, 31 March 1916, 10 May 1916; Gribling (1961), 292.

[5]Huygens Institute, Collection Aalberse, diary 10 February 1919; Gribling (1961), 287–288.

[6]Between 1913 and 1940 the Netherlands had four extra-parliamentary cabinets. These cabinets included the cabinet Cort van der Linden, 1913 up to 1918, the cabinet De Geer I, 1926 up to 1929; the cabinet Ruys de Beerenbrouck III, 1926 up to 1929; and the cabinet Colijn V lasted to two days in 1939.

[7]National Archive, Collection Veraart, 1905–1955, archive inventory no. 2.21.306, no. 177 and no. 554.

unemployment and feared violent outbursts (1938, 8, 15, 20).[8] In his public lecture of January 1940 he made a positive remark about the policies of the French minister of Finance Paul Reynaud (1878–1966) and rejected Dutch economic policy of budgetary cuts.[9] He argued that the national fund of means of production (in Dutch *nationaal fonds van voortbrengingsmiddelen*) was reduced considerably and not extended where necessary. Reynaud instead pursued a policy to stimulate investment and production (Veraart 1940, 16; Kuisel 1983, 125–127).[10]

During the Second World War Veraart stayed in London where he advised cabinet-in-exile Gerbrandy about economic policies. He became the personal economic advisor of prime minister Pieter Sjoerds Gerbrandy (1885–1961) in 1942 (Schmiermann 1990, 135). The latter dismissed him immediately after he published a critical article in the weekly *Vrij Nederland Londen* in 1944. Veraart had criticized the governmental ideas to restrict the role of parliament after the war.[11] In London he maintained and extended his academic network including amongst others the Aquinas Society, the Catholic Social Guild, the Union Culturelle des Pays Bas de l' Europe Occidentale, the Newman Association, the London International Assembly and the Bavarian Circle.[12] This network offered him an audience to exchange his thoughts about economics, democracy and industrial organization after the war.

3 Economic Approach and Ethics

At the beginning of the twentieth century Dutch economists studied the writings of foreign economists. They made acquaintance with the writings of German speaking economists and moral philosophers such as Gustav von Schmoller (1838–1917),

[8]Veraart was not the only catholic scholar concerned about unemployment and its threat to democracy. A similar concern had the well-known French Thomist philosopher Jacques Maritain (1882–1973). Maritain feared that impoverishment of the labouring class would prevent capitalist societies to realize the ideal of democracy (Hittinger 2002, 17, 61, 63). Veraart (1931b, 255) must have been familiar with Maritain, because he mentioned him in a critical discussion of the French author and poet *Léon Bloy* (1846–1917). His Ph.D. candidate Tillmann Fehmers (1935, 17, 19, 79) confirmed this familiarity in his dissertation about the Taylor-system. Tillmann Fehmers discussed extensively Maritain's philosophy about human behaviour and responsibility manoeuvring between individualism and collectivism.

[9]In 1922 Veraart argued that an increase in public debt was acceptable in case of preventing famine during wartime, reducing a shortage of houses and supporting the unemployed. He legitimated this increase of public debt with a cost-benefit analysis. See: Veraart (1922, 545–546).

[10]Reynaud spoke about a "guided economy within the framework of liberty", see: Kuisel (1983, 127).

[11]Title of this article *Het Constitutioneel Vraagstuk*. See: Parlement en Politiek, Mr. J.A. Veraart, www.parlement.com, accessed on 16 December 2015; Fasseur (2014), 351; National Archive, Collection Veraart, 1905–1955, archive inventory no. 2.21.306, no. 850.

[12]National Archive, Collection Veraart, 1904–1955, archive inventory 2.21.306, no. 40. The Bavarian Circle invited him for a meeting with the theme *Ein foederalistisches Deutschland und Europa*.

Adolph Wagner (1835–1917), Eugen von Philippovich (1858–1917), Victor Cathrein (1845–1931), Heinrich Pesch (1854–1926) and Karl von Vogelsang (1818–1890). Veraart's doctoral dissertation can be considered as an example of this acquaintance.[13] However, the choice of wages as subject of his dissertation should be seen in connection with the attention *Rerum Novarum* paid to wages. He defended that academic disagreement about the concept of wage had its origins in differences of opinion about the object and principles of economics (Veraart 1910, 1–2).

3.1 Object and Principles

Object of economics was the process of caring for mankind with scarce means of satisfaction. To study this process Veraart distinguished between a realist approach and an ethical approach. He adopted this distinction from Wagner and Philippovich (Veraart 1910, 6, 1921, 7–8).

The realist approach consisted of a descriptive and a theoretical approach. The descriptive approach focussed on collecting facts about the economy. The theoretical approach included an empirical investigation and a pure theoretical investigation. The former investigated economic phenomena like wages as a special case of prices in a context of causality. The latter studied special economic phenomena from a general theoretical perspective. To put it differently, this type of investigation applied general pricing theory to wages (wages did not differ from ordinary prices) (Veraart 1910, 8, 50–51).

Veraart (1910, 17) pointed out that the pure theoretical approach had not be confused with a hypothetical-theoretical approach based on *the principle of economic individualism* (in German *Oekonomisches Prinzip*/*Prinzip des Optimums*). He rejected this principle of optimal satisfaction of individual needs in favour of a society that coordinated and organized the social-economic forces (Veraart 1938, 21). This rejection showed his Thomist background. His public lecture of January 1940 about the realist school reminded the audience that the main sin of economics was to have forgotten the Aristotelian-Thomist wisdom that social phenomena determine the development of economics and not otherwise.[14] Too easily economists imposed either their own system of thought or their political passions on social phenomena. As examples he mentioned Karl Kautsky (1854–1938), Leon Walras (1834–1910) and Joseph Schumpeter (1883–1950) (Veraart 1940, 2–3,

---

[13] Veraart (1940, 24) referred to the sceptical reception of Marshall's Principles of Economics by the Dutch mathematician professor W.H.L. Janssen van Raay (1862–1937).

[14] Veraart (1940, 9, 27, 1947, 11–12, 27) approximated the rise of the realist school around 1910. He referred to Cassel, Keynes, Marshall and Pigou. He rejected the attempt to transform economics into an exact science. Irreducible human behaviour was an important factor in economic data. The danger existed to reveal a causality between economic phenomena that turned out to be a fatal error—due to irreducible human behaviour. To put it differently an investigation could reveal a false causal relationship.

5–6). Economists using the hypothetical-theoretical approach argued that Veraart was wrong. They explained their approach with the argument that either the necessary facts were missing or the causality among the phenomena was not yet observed (van Buttingha Wichers 1912, 215). The ethical approach applied ethical principles to evaluate the process of care. In the chapter on ethical-economic principles Veraart (1910, 7, 160–169) discussed the writings of the German moral philosophers Cathrein (1845–1931), Pesch (1854–1926) and Vogelsang (1818–1890). For this purpose he formulated four ethical-economic principles not based on catholic morality:

(a) First principle: Society had the duty to ensure that as many as possible members enjoyed an *eubiotic* life and existence. The adjective *eubiotic* should be understood as the art of living healthily and happily, and the prevention of diseases (Veraart 1910, 149–151, 1947, 69). Contemporary terminology would probably choose the word *wellbeing*.
(b) Second principle: Coercive and voluntary human efforts had to be in such a balanced relationship that a healthy life could be achieved for as many as possible members of society. This relationship determined the extent of using limited means of satisfaction and implied either direct public production or regulation of the free production (Veraart 1910, 152–153).
(c) Third principle: The choice of objectives subordinate to the main objective of a healthy life and existence required an evaluation of their pros and cons. Empirical-theoretical knowledge, common sense or both should be used in this evaluation (Veraart 1910, 157–158).
(d) Fourth principle: Objectives should be achieved at the lowest costs possible (in German economics known as *Prinzip des kleinsten Mittels*). This meant that evaluation of the pros and cons of a means of satisfaction (in contemporary terminology *a policy instrument*) had to be based on empirical-theoretical knowledge, common sense or both (Veraart 1910, p 159–160).[15]

Certainly aware of the dominance of value-free science Veraart warned that both approaches should not be confused. The realist approach allowed the investigation of the effectiveness of measures to achieve given objectives but did not discuss the social desirability or ethics of these objectives. To solve the controversy about ethical and non-ethical economics he introduced a subjective and an objective effective critical approach to evaluate objectives. This approach did not fall back on the ethical economics of Wagner, Pesch and Spann (Veraart 1921, 1, 7–8, 1947, 23; Cobbenhagen 1935, 430–431, Kolnaar and Meulendijks 1998, 2).[16]

---

[15]These principles show resemblance with Aristotelian thought. Aristotle discussed the choice of objectives and means within the state to achieve happiness. See: Aristoteles, Politica, Historische Uitgeverij, Groningen, 298–299.

[16]The subjective effective critical approach evaluated the effectiveness of human action in terms of the objective(s) set either individually or collectively. The objective effective critical approach evaluated the effectiveness of human action in terms of reasonable satisfaction of reasonable human needs (Cobbenhagen 1935, 430).

Veraart spent many efforts in disseminating his views about economics, industrial organization and democracy. Despite these efforts he succeeded to pursue with his doctoral students a realist research agenda of his own. These students, mainly graduated engineers from Delft, applied modern empirical and statistical-mathematical techniques within his field of interests. They investigated subjects such as government expenditures and business cycles (Baars 1937), measuring labour productivity in various industrial branches (Van der Schalk 1938), and pricing of urban building ground (Pet 1940).

3.2 Wage

Veraart (1910, 28) subscribed to a subjective theory of value to determine prices and wages. Subjects expressed the value of the available means of satisfaction (consumer goods, services, factors of production) with their preparedness to pay or to accept an amount of money in a range between a minimum and a maximum amount. These means of satisfaction had either *user value*, *productive value* or *exchange value*. The mechanism of determining prices did not differ from the determination of wages. Both resulted from an exchange between a demanding subject and a supplying subject involving subjective and objective factors. The subjective factors included maximum and minimum valuation, individual power and market policy, and government intervention. The available quantities and compositions of the means of satisfaction constituted the objective factors (Veraart 1910, 68–69, 1947, 75–76).

Veraart structured his discussion of wages with a distinction between a realist and an ethical approach. In both approaches he discussed the role of the subjective and objective factors. Within the realist approach his pure-theoretical investigation addressed the determination of the wage level on the labour market. The preparedness of the owner to pay for a quantity of labour determined the maximum wage the labourer received. The labourer determined the minimum wage for the quantity of labour supplied to the owner. The resulting wage level depended on the power of the subjects (the capability to make the other accept a certain distance from the minimum or maximum wage) and the market policies (the readiness to use power) of both parties. Power and market policies made the wage level shift either into the direction of the minimum or maximum wage. Ethical considerations explained state intervention in the process of exchange. This intervention directly or indirectly set the wage level. Examples of direct intervention were minimum wages and immigration policies. Indirect interventions included education and regulation of the number of competitors. Veraart restricted his empirical investigation to industrial labourers, servants and civil servants in Europe (Veraart 1910, 68–69, 72–75, 110–111). He did not present any wage statistics about these groups.

Veraart criticized the ethical economists for setting wages either equal to the produced value or to the needs. From his perspective the preparedness of the owner to pay labour determined a wage that probably could not satisfy all needs of the labourer. For this reason, he developed his own ethical theory of wages and labour policy to achieve an eubiotic life and existence. Achieving this objective under conditions of market competition required minimum wages, maximum prices and protectionism. In case trade unions succeeded in demanding a wage equal to an exchange value based on the subjective sacrifice of the labourer or on increasing prices than state intervention was legitimate in the interest of other members and labourers in society (Veraart 1910, 172–173, 181, 189, 190–191).

To ensure the eubiotic objective the state should pursue a labour policy that was either part of an economic policy or part of an industrial organization of society. The last paragraphs of Veraart's dissertation outlined an idea about a legal organization of economy that avoided to his opinion authoritarian regulation. The main contours of this legal organization or primitive corporatist structure included:

(a) Decentralization and local regulation of the economy monitored by the national legislature.
(b) Professional organizations should be established under public law. Their boards had to cooperate with local authorities. After some time these boards should take over the major part of implementing and monitoring social and economic policy.
(c) International conferences about economic policies to protect the legal organization of the economy. International agreement was necessary. To give an example, a change in economic relations (the introduction of a minimum wage or the organization of production in the interest of an eubiotic life and existence) would be impossible in case of competition from countries with low labour costs or speculative production (Veraart 1910, 192–193).

Beijsens encouraged Veraart to elaborate these contours in favour of a new economic society. These contours became the foundations of his future career. Being an economic consultant to the printing branch enabled him to experiment with his ideas in practice. Proudly, he described his involvement in the conclusion of the collective agreement in the Dutch printing trade that introduced novelties such as a right to labour, no dismissal of labourers without valid reason, and labour courts of employers and labourers. This agreement lasted from 1914 up to 1919.[17]

Veraart publicly defended that a decent wage policy could not be introduced without industrial democracy.[18] In 1947 he discussed the concept of reasonable wage in terms of real wage. A fund of available consumer goods and durables constituted an objective limit on real wage. The extend of this fund was variable in history. Thus real wage was in his view not always a reasonable wage guaranteeing an eubiotic life. He expected the adoption of an industrial organization under public law to complete the process of industrial organization. In combination with a

[17]National Archive, Collection Veraart, 1905–1955, archive inventory no. 2.21.306, inventory no. 664; Veraart 1947, 29–32.

[18]Amersfoortsch Dagblad/De Eemlander, De conjunctuur-werkloosheid, Praeadviezen der heeren Wibaut en Veraart, 18 oktober 1932, 4.

National Economic Plan this completion would elevate the (non-universal) theory of pricing to a new stadium in the Netherlands. The determination of real and reasonable wages had to be seen from this perspective (Veraart 1947, 83, 90–92).

4 Rerum Novarum

Pope Leo XIII intended to resist the spirit of revolutionary change with his encyclical *Rerum Novarum*. To resist revolutionary change the determination of wages played a crucial role. Here, Leo XIII could draw from the philosophy of Thomism that considered the determination of wages as a special case of *just prices*. The labourer provided his labour to the owner at an agreed wage. Decisive for the right wage level was the hierarchical position in society. A labourer earned a just wage if the wage was in accordance with his position in society (Schinzinger 1988, 24–25). *Rerum novarum* provided that owners gave everyone what was just. Exercising pressure upon labourers for the sake of gain was condemned by all laws, human and divine (Rerum Novarum 1891, par. 20). A sufficient wage enabled the labourer not only to support himself and his family but also offered him the opportunity to save (Rerum Novarum 1891, par. 46).

The social message of *Rerum novarum* caused controversy within the Dutch *Roman Catholic State Party*. The conservative current thought that the encyclical vindicated the demands of the rising labour movement (Roes 2004, 71). In 1896 catholic parliamentarians wrote a program referring to various encyclicals. As far as social policy was involved they referred to *Rerum Novarum*. They considered social questions as moral questions to be answered in the spirit of Christianity. Religion, family and private property constituted the foundations of society. The state should use its authority to protect these foundations (Oud 1990, 162; Rerum Novarum 1891, par. 8, 9, 13).

Repeatedly Veraart argued that the ideas in this encyclical were not original. In the nineteenth century priests formulated most of its ideas, for instance the British cardinal Henry Edward Manning (1808–1892) and the German bishop Wilhelm von Ketteler (1811–1877).[19] In 1931 he reminded the readers of the journal *Roeping* about a misunderstanding of *Rerum novarum*. Some groups thought that the publication of this encyclical indicated the exhaustion of the catholic economic program in a modern society. For this reason they scrutinized social reforms against the text of *Rerum novarum*. In case of dissimilarities the reasonableness and legitimacy of the reforms were doubted. Veraart rejected this view. *Rerum novarum* was in his view a historical document and had to be seen as *a child of its time*. Its ideas about humanity and human values were eternal but the application on

[19]National Archive, Collection Veraart, 1904–1955, archive inventory no. 2.21.306, no. 697, 702 and 846. Veraart also referred to the Italian economist Guiseppe Toniolo (1845–1918) who was a Thomist. Publications mentioned him as one of the inspirers of *Rerum novarum*. See: Faucci (2014, 119).

capitalism was of a temporary nature. The encyclical contained no in-depth analysis of capitalism like the analysis of the German economist Werner Sombart (1863–1941). The papal analysis restricted itself to the problems of labour but did not investigate the social maladies of a profit oriented *Wirtschaft*. Maladies that catholicism as a world power could not accept. In 1891 Political Catholicism was according to Veraart not so well developed in comparison to Marxism. However after the revolution of 1917 Russian society did not evolve as predicted by the *Communist Manifes*t and *Das Kapital*.[20]

In the course of time Political Catholicism came to possess the required organizations to build an entirely new social and economic order with the support of the state. Pope Leo XIII could not have known about the rise of powerful trade unions and collective labour agreements. Capitalism committed its *perverse* crimes in the thirties of the 20th century (Veraart 1931a, 32–34).

In 1941 the British *Catholic Social Guild* invited Veraart to give a series of lectures about *Rerum novarum* which he accepted. He did not change his view about the encyclical. Again he emphasized the historical character of the encyclical but he was more positive about the encyclical *Quadragesimo anno* published by pope Pius XI in 1931. He told his audience that *Quadragesimo anno* was up against the system of capitalism and gave the outlines for a better social economic order. In his opinion *Rerum novarum* did not go that far. It only tackled the slavery into which modern labour had been brought by the power of a ruthless liberal system.[21] Two years later Veraart outlined his view about corporatism during a series of lectures held at the invitation of the *Newman Association*. He proposed to establish bodies under public law which were responsible for labour legislation and collective labour agreements. Rather important, he mentioned decentralization, democracy and independent organizations of labourers and employers as characteristics distinguishing corporatism from corporate state planning of fascism and national socialism.[22]

The importance Veraart attached to *Quadragesimo anno* was also revealed in his review of Peter Drucker's *The End of Economic Man*. He considered this study about the origins of fascism and national socialism as a failure (Veraart 1942, 2, 4–6). Austrian-American economics had influenced the author and his economic man continued the ethics of economic individualism. In particular Drucker (1939/2009, 40) wrote that economic freedom failed to establish equality and destroyed the belief in capitalism as a social system in spite of material blessings. This emphasis on equality misjudged in Veraart's view the evolution of capitalism into the direction of a reasonable provision of human needs. The majority of the population did not demand equality but asked a sufficient income to satisfy their reasonable

---

[20]Veraart was a board member of the *Society to study the planned economy in the Sovjet Union* (in Dutch *Vereeniging tot bestudeering van de planhuishouding in de Sovjet Unie*). National Archive, Collection Veraart, 1905–1955, archive inventory no. 2.21.306, no. 556.

[21]National Archive, Collection Veraart, 1905–1955, archive inventory no. 2.21.306, no. 702.

[22]National Archive, Collection Veraart, 1905–1955, archive inventory no. 2.21.306, no. 664.

needs. Further, Veraart remarked that Drucker reduced the importance of christian and catholic social movements. After his "interesting" discussion of the attempts of the catholic church to reform Drucker should have discussed the encyclical *Quadragesimo anno*, because this document outlined a new order without revolution. To Veraart's disappointment he did not even refer to this encyclical.[23]

5 Influence

As a member of parliament Veraart did not eschew to vote against the position of his catholic delegation in parliament. He was one of two catholic parliamentarians who voted against the reduction of death duties in 1926. One year later he voted as only member of the delegation against the decrease of the income tax because the tax revenues were needed to solve social problems.[24]

His voting behaviour should be considered from the perspective of his realist and ethical approaches to economics that included an anticyclical fiscal policy to combat unemployment respectively an attempt to achieve the objective of improving the living conditions of mankind to a reasonable level.

Thomism inspired Political Catholicism to develop the idea of corporatism. This idea had two interpretations. The first interpretation was that of an alternative political organization of the state. The second interpretation entailed a different structure for society. The first interpretation remained for a long time a minority current within the RKSP and emerged as a distinctive trend in the thirties (Luykx 1996, 231). Veraart adhered to this interpretation. He propagated with conviction the idea of corporatism since the defence of his dissertation. His corporatism introduced an economic order of cooperating enterprises in an economic sector together with relevant trade unions in order to achieve mutual benefits. To realize corporatism he followed two steps. The first step focussed on collective bargaining agreements in economic branches. The existence of these agreements proved the preparedness of trade unions and employers to see their branch as a social-economic unit. The second step entailed agreements about labour conditions in councils with representatives of labour and capital. These councils had to be responsible for managing productive activities. This expressed harmony between labour and capital. In the future social legislation could be entrusted to these councils and restrain the role of the state (Windmuller and de Galan 1979, 66–67).

Veraart admitted that without appropriate measures consumers could be damaged. To prevent negative consequences he proposed a national council of

[23]National Archive, Collection Veraart, 1905–1955, archive inventory no. 2.21.306, no. 907. The review is titled *Een mislukt boek* (1942).

[24]Parlement en Politiek, Mr. J.A. Veraart, www.parlement.com, accessed on 16 December 2015.

consumers with a right to appeal against policies hurting their interests. He expressed the view that the state should give these regulatory councils an appropriate legal status and authority. He thought that initially employees and employers could easily introduce these councils in voluntary agreement (Veraart 1921, 144; Windmuller and de Galan 1979, 66–67).

Between 1919 and 1921 an experimental system of joint industrial councils was established on a private basis among catholics with the intention to establish a public system of such councils in the future. The experiment failed because of the reluctance of catholic employers and the radicalism of Veraart. The latter wanted the councils to have immediate responsibility for many economic matters (Luykx 1996, 237). His ideas about the joint industrial councils worried the RKS In parliament minister Aalberse criticized Veraart for disturbing and confusing the RKSP with his ideas.[25] Aalberse rejected a top down public regulation of economic and social life. The rise of industrial councils should be the result of a natural process of cooperating persons according to Christian principles. The legislator had to guide, to supplement and to monitor this process.[26]

In London Veraart contributed to an undated affidavit about the structure of the economic order of the post war Netherlands. The organization of this decentralized economic order had to be based on industrial and professional councils to withstand the assumptions of the Manchester School. These councils with representatives of labour and capital monitored markets, regulated prices and investigated financial administrations. Solidarity between groups characterized this order and labourers received a wage for the time they were either able or not to work. Their wage had to satisfy the reasonable needs at a reasonable level. He envisioned that the contradictions between labour and capital would disappear. The interest of the latter became subject to the general interest.[27]

The first post war cabinets continued the discussion of restructuring the economic order. Veraart's corporatist ideas competed with the social democratic ideas about planning and order. Labour minister of economic affairs Vos (1903–1972) reconciled both ideas in 1945. After several years of intense ideological debates an industrial organisation under public law with limited authority and a bureau for economic policy analysis were established. The industrial organisation under public law included a Social and Economic Council, voluntary industrial and commodity boards (van Zanden and Griffiths 1989, pp 205–209). Veraart was appointed crown member of the Social and Economic Council of the Netherlands in 1950. Up to 1955 he felt very strongly about solidarity, dignity and responsibility (National Archive 2005, 11).

---

[25]Huygens Institute, Collection Aalberse, diary 31 March 1921.

[26]Eerste Kamer, 33ste Vergadering, 30 maart 1921, pp 756–757.

[27]National Archive, Collection Veraart, 1905–1955, archive inventory no. 2.21.306, no. 576.

6 Conclusion

The encyclical *Rerum novarum* had a very modest impact on economists, economics and industrial organization in the Netherlands. However, the catholic economist Veraart was an exception. Today many *mainstream* economists will consider him as a complicated economist due to his use of difficult terminology for concepts and his Thomism. His dissertation showed that he had a good knowledge of German economic literature. The distinction he made between a realist and an ethical approach to economics was of major importance to his academic and political development. Veraart inherited this distinction from the German economist Wagner and the Austrian economist Philippovich.

Veraart presented his own interpretation of *Rerum novarum*. In the twenties and thirties his political influence to introduce corporatism was very limited because of the resistance within the catholic elite. In London he lectured about corporatism at the invitation of catholic non-profit organizations and advised cabinet-in-exile Gerbrandy. After 1945 his ideas about corporatism gained influence. The Netherlands adopted corporatist decision-making with the establishment of the Social and Economic Council, and the voluntary industrial and commodity boards in 1950. The government made him a member of this council because of his expertise. However, corporatism suffered from polarization between trade unions and employer organizations. A major change was the implementation of the Labour Foundation recommendation to introduce dispensation procedures allowing employers (and their employees) to request exemptions from collective labour agreements in 1996. The minister of Social Affairs and Employment obtained the authority to decide whether or not employers could be exempted after an official evaluation of the legal requirements. In January 2015 cabinet Rutte II abolished the commodity and industrial boards because of lack of democratic legitimization and duties impeding new market entrants.[28]

Is *Rerum novarum* relevant in the 21st century? Not according to Veraart who considered this encyclical as *a child of its time*, because the current economies have changed in comparison to those of the past century. Today, capitalism has no real intellectual competitors and gives leeway to unbridled market forces. The consequences of these forces ask for heterodox ideas and precise observations of social and economic phenomena.

Veraart behaved very much like an early modern heterodox economist confronted with emerging mainstream economics. A small number of economists criticise mainstream economics for not having predicted the economic crisis of 2008. This was due to an obsession with rationalism, profit maximization and market equilibrium. A new approach requires attention for changing regulations and institutions. Veraart had a similar criticism as his rejection of the assumption of

[28]Tweede Kamer, vergaderjaar 2013–2014, 33910, no. 3, 3.

economic individualism showed. He distinguished himself from the current critical economists with his thoughts about corporatism as an alternative institution to capitalism and totalitarian economic models. For this reason, Veraart deserves a biography. And last but not least for his defence of parliamentary democracy.

Appendix 1: Short Timeline Professional Career Veraart

1904–1908	Student of Law, University of Amsterdam
1910	Doctoral dissertation Arbeidsloon (Ph.D.)
1919–1940	Member Provincial Council Zuid Holland
1919–1955	Professor of Economics, University of Delft
1925	Member of Roman Catholic State Party (Dutch abbreviation RKSP)
1925–1929	Member Second Chamber of Parliament representing the *RKSP*
1932	Ended membership of *RKSP* because of the board's rejection of proposals to restrain the consequences of the economic crisis
1933	Established Catholic Democratic Association (Dutch abbreviation *KDB*)
1939	Again member of *RKSP*
1939–1940	Appointed Rector Magnificus University of Delft
1940–1944	Advisor economic policy to cabinet Gerbrandy in London
1942	Personal economic advisor of prime minister Gerbrandy
1944	Dismissed by cabinet Gerbrandy
1950–1955	Appointed crown member of the Social and Economic Council of the Netherlands

Source: Parlement en Politiek, Mr. J.A. Veraart, www.parlement.com.

Archives

Huygens Institute for the History of the Netherlands, Collection Aalberse, The Hague
National Archive, Collection Veraart, 1905–1955, archive inventory number 2.21.306, The Hague
National Archive (2005) Inventaris van het archief van Joannes Antonius Veraart (levensjaren 1866–1955) over de Jaren 1904–1955, The Hague, 11

References

Amersfoortsch Dagblad/De Eemlander, De conjunctuur-werkloosheid, Praeadviezen der heeren Wibaut en Veraart, 18 oktober 1932, 4
Aristoteles, Politica, Historische Uitgeverij, Groningen, pp 298–299
Baars A (1937) Onderzoek naar de mogelijkheid tot beinvloeding der conjunctuurbeweging door kapitaaluitgaven der overheid en door andere overheidsmaatregelen. De Erven F. Bohn nv, Haarlem

Beekman EHM (1935) Veraart en de politiek. Roeping 7(13):482–492
Cobbenhagen MJH (1935) Prof. Dr. Veraart als economist. Roeping 7(13):430–431
Conway M (1996) Introduction. In: Buchanan T, Conway M (eds) Political Catholicism in Europe 1918–1965. Clarendon Press, Oxford
Drucker P (2009) The end of economic man. The origins of totalitarianism. Transaction Publisher, New Brunswick (USA)
Eerste Kamer, 33ste Vergadering, 30 maart 1921, pp 756–757
Fasseur C (2014) Eigen meester, niemands knecht. Het leven van Pieter Sjoerds Gerbrandy. Uitgeverij Balans, Amsterdam
Faucci R (2014) A history of Italian economic thought. Routledge, London
Gribling J (1961) J.M. Aalberse 1871–1948. Uitgeverij De Lanteern, Utrecht
Hittinger JP (2002) Liberty, wisdom and grace. Lexington Books, Lanham
Kolnaar HJJ, Meulendijks PJFG (1998) The economist M.J.H. Cobbenhagen. In: WJ Samuels (ed) European economists of the early 20th century, vol 1, 2
Kuisel RF (1983) Capitalism and the state in modern France. Cambridge University Press, Cambridge
Leo XIII (1891) Rerum novarum. Encyclical of pope Leo XIII on capital and labor, www.vatican.va
Luykx P (1996) The Netherlands. In: Buchanan T, Conway M (eds) Political Catholicism in Europe 1918–1965. Clarendon Press, Oxford
Oud J (1990) Staatkundige vormgeving in Nederland, deel I, 1840–1940. Van Gorcum, Assen
Parlement en Politiek, Mr. J.A. Veraart, www.parlement.com. Accessed on 16 Dec 2015
Pet JC (1940) Prijs en waarde van stedelijke bouwgrond, Nijgh en Van Ditmar nv, Rotterdam
Roes J (2004) A historical detour: The Roman Catholic State Party in the Netherlands. In: Kaiser W, Wohnout H (eds) Political Catholicism in Europe, vol I. Routledge, London
Rogier LJ, de Rooy N (1998) In vrijheid herboren, N.V. Uitgeversmij Pax, The Hague
Schinzinger F (1988) Vorläufer der Nationalökonomie. In: Issing O (ed) Geschichte der Nationalökonomie. Verlag Vahlen, Munich
Schmiermann S (1990) Prof. Dr. J.A. Veraart (1886–1955) Een recalcitrant katholiek democraat. In: Jaarboek van het Katholiek Documentatiecentrum
Tillmann Fehmers P (1935) Kerngedachten uit de interne bedrijfsefficiëntie. NV Technische Boekhandel en Drukkerij J, Waltman, Delft
Tweede Kamer, vergaderjaar 2013–2014, 33910, no. 3
van Buttingha Wichers CG (1912) Nieuwe uitgaven, Mr. J.A. Veeraart, Arbeidsloon. De Economist 61(1):215–220
van der Schalk FJC (1938) De wiskundig-statistische analyse van de arbeidsproductiviteit en haar praktische toepassing op eenige bedrijfstakken en ondernemingen in Nederland. De Erven F, Bohn nv, Haarlem
van Zanden J, Griffith RT (1989) Economische geschiedenis van Nederland in de 20e eeuw. Uitgeverij Het Spectrum, Utrecht
Veraart JA (1910) Arbeidsloon, proefschrift. Schröder, Amsterdam
Veraart JA (1921) Beginselen der economische bedrijfsorganisatie. NV Uitgevers Maatschappij, Bussum
Veraart JA (1922) Economische wetenschap en sociale politiek. In: Sociale voorzorg
Veraart JA (1929) Opstellen over politiek. Melchior, Amersfoort
Veraart JA (1931a) Kapitalisme en katholicisme. In: Roeping 1(10):32–34
Veraart JA (1931b) De school van Léon Bloy. Roeping 4(10):255
Veraart J A (1937) Beijsens en de economie. In: Studia Catholica, pp 422–427
Veraart J A (1938) Bestrijding van de blijvende werkloosheid. Overdruk, Economisch Technisch Tijdschrift, no. 1 tot en met 4
Veraart JA (1940) De realistische school in de economie, rede 8 januari 1940. Waltman, Delft

Veraart JA (1947) Beginselen der publiekrechtelijke bedrijfsorganisatie. Uitgeverij Paul Brand, Bussum
Verhagen F (2015) Toen de Katholieken Nederland veroverden. Boom, Amsterdam
Windmuller JP, de Galan C (1979) Arbeidsverhoudingen in Nederland, deel 1. Uitgeverij Het Spectrum, Utrecht

The Roman Connection: From *Rerum Novarum* to Corporatism in the Netherlands

Andries Nentjes

1 Introduction

In the encyclical *Rerum Novarum* of 1891, the Catholic church made a stand against socialism and against liberalism. Against socialism for its belief in class struggle and call for abolition of private property. Against liberal capitalism for its destructive individualism and the deep poverty of many workers. The encyclical calls for a return to Christian morals and cooperation between labour and capital instead of class struggle. The recommendations to improve the position of workers, made in the encyclical, could be fitted into the existing legislation of European capitalist societies without breaking up the market economic system. However, the end of the nineteenth century also saw the beginning of Political Catholicism. More radical than the Pope, its proponents hoped to end class struggle through fundamental reform of the market economy. They envisaged a society and state in which labour and capital would cooperate peacefully in self-governing vocational associations: the corporative state.

Although by now almost forgotten, the corporative state was in the first decades of the twentieth century an ideal, worth to pursue for many men and women, deeply unhappy with the existing economic system, but wary of Socialist and Communist blueprints for a better world. In some European countries Corporatism did even get a try: Italy (1922–1945), Portugal (1933–1974) and Austria (1934–1945) (https://nl.wikipedia.org/wiki/Corporatisme).

This chapter tells the story of Corporatism in the Netherlands; very much an effort to find a political form for the call for the end of class struggle in *Rerum novarum*. The key figure in the story is the Catholic Dutch economist Johannes Antonius Veraart (1886–1955). In the years between 1910 and 1950 he developed a blueprint of a corporatist economic system, called Statutory Organisation of

A. Nentjes (✉)
Economics and Public Finance, University of Groningen, Groningen, The Netherlands
e-mail: a.nentjes@online.nl

J. Backhaus et al. (eds.), *On the Economic Significance of the Catholic Social Doctrine*, The European Heritage in Economics and the Social Sciences 19, DOI 10.1007/978-3-319-52545-7_9

Business. In guild like organisations, named Business-ships, employers and workers of a branch of industry take together the major economic decisions, geared to the common good of the sector. Socialists picked up some of Veraart's ideas and the Social-Democrat Labour Party came with a proposal in which Business-ships function as organisations of decentralized state control of business. In defence of his Catholic Corporatism Veraart did not fear the confrontation, but also took over some elements of the Socialist scheme.

After the Second World War the general belief in the Netherlands was the days of old school liberalism were over. The economy was to be rebuilt by a "roman-red" coalition government; so Catholics and Socialists had to overcome their old controversies and present a common view on the post-war economic order. We shall see how in the interaction between pre-war economic beliefs and the new experience of fast economic recovery a consensus grew on the way to go. In particular we will look at the position given to and adaptations made in the Statutory Organisation of Business.

2 Two Encyclicals on the Condition of the Working Class

In industrializing Europe the last decades of the nineteenth century were the era of "the social question". Growing awareness of the poverty of large parts of the working population in the fast growing urban agglomerations fuelled the public discussion on the question who was to be blame for the evil and what could be done to remedy the misery. In 1891 Pope Leo XIII had the courage to state the position of the Catholic Church in the encyclical *Rerum novarum*. Forty years later, in 1931, Pope Pius IX published *Quadragesimo anno*, a sequel in which the same questions were addressed. The next two sub-sections focus on how critical the two encyclicals are of the existing market economic system and what they say about corporatist arrangements.

2.1 Rerum Novarum

Rerum novarum is the first encyclical of the Catholic Church on social-economic issues (Frambach and Eissrich 2016). In front of all other questions stands the wretched condition of the majority of the working class. The words on who is to blame are hard and bitter: They commemorate how "the ancient working men's guilds were abolished in the last century, and no other protective organization took their place. Public institutions and the laws set aside the ancient religion. Hence, by degrees it has come to pass that working men have been surrendered, isolated and helpless to the hard heartedness of employers and the greed of unchecked competition". … "To this must be added that the hiring of labor and the conduct of trade are concentrated in the hands of comparatively few; so that a small number of very rich men have been able to lay upon the teeming masses of the labouring poor a yoke little better than that of slavery itself" (art. 3).

The focus on the exploitation of labour gives the argument has a strong Marxian flavour. Yet there is a crucial difference. The papal bull rejects with force Marx's dogma that "class is naturally hostile to class, and that the wealthy and the working men are intended by nature to live in mutual conflict". Instead the fault is found in the transformations law makers have made in the existing legal framework, to create the conditions under which a market economy can function; in the same act they undermined Christian ethics. Those two intertwined developments are identified as the decisive forces that have led to the deplorable social situation. So, the distorted relation between the two classes is a result of the political process. However, the natural order is that the two classes live in harmony: "Each needs the other: capital cannot do without labor, nor labor without capital." (art. 19).

The message of *Rerum novarum* is that a natural order that has been severely damaged by human actions in the past can be remedied; but in no other way than "by a return to Christian life and Christian institutions" (art. 27). "Foremost because religion draws the rich and the working class together, by reminding each of its duties to the other, and especially of the obligations of justice" (art. 19). It is a call for cooperation that transcends social-economic classes.

In the reflections on remedies, the papal bull deals comprehensively with the moral base in articles 20–30. Thereafter follow in articles 31–62 the public measures, legislation and private actions that can bring material improvements in the condition of the labour class. The State has to play a role in this matter (art. 31–47). First of all the ruler should serve the common good, to the benefit of every class (art. 32). It implies the duty "to act with strict justice towards each and every class alike" (art. 33). The plea for equal treatment is supported with the practical argument that the more the general laws of the country are to the benefit of the working class, "the less need there will be to seek for special means to relieve them" (art. 32).

In an encyclical "on the condition of the working classes" one can expect a long passage on the task of the State in the domain of labour relations. Strikes of work do occur, and the encyclical does not repudiate them (art. 39). However, the state should counter with public measures the grave inconvenience a strike may cause (art. 39), and laws should prevent the disturbance of the public peace by violence and disorder (art. 36, 39). The working man has rights in which he should be protected by the State; first of all the interest of his soul (art. 40), that means freedom of religion, and cessation from work on Sundays and certain holy days (art. 41). In material things State regulation may be required: to prevent abuse of workers (art. 36), to restrain overdue long working times (art. 41, 42), and to protect women and children (art. 42). Wages should be sufficient to support "a frugal and well-behaved wage-earner" (art. 45); basically a plea for a legal minimum wage. Worried not to give the State a too strong arm in social-economic matters, the encyclical recommends an intermediate level of societies or boards to address them; the State being appealed for its sanction and protection, should circumstances require (art. 45). Working people should be encouraged to obtain property; however, apart from avoiding excessive taxation, the policies to do so remain undefined (art. 47).

The last part of the encyclical gives guidelines for private associations (art. 48–63). Employers and workmen may of themselves effect much by means of associations and organisations that afford aid to those in distress (art. 48). Associations that do exist, bring together either workmen alone, or workmen and employers. It is for the first time that the Catholic Church gives its blessing to such organisations (Wiarda and Sharpe 1996, 37). Both types are welcomed, but evident is a preference for the mixed type associations, which will "draw the two classes more closely together" (art. 48). They cannot be prohibited by public authority. However, the encyclical warns to stay away from societies "managed on principles ill - according to Christianity and the public well-being" (art. 54). Meant are trade unions adhering to socialist and communist ideologies. Christian working men do better to form associations among themselves. There are only hints as to what their tasks could be; the most specific recommendation is to create a fund to help members in need due to accident, illness, old age and distress (art. 58). No mention is made that a trade union can operate as a party on the labour market in negotiating with employers on wages and other labour conditions. Above all, the Christian trade union is an institution to create and strengthen solidarity within and between classes, to emancipate workmen in Christian sense that is social betterment with chief attention to the duties of religion and morality (art. 57). It brings the reader back to the call of *Rerum novarum* "to re-establish Christian morals, apart from which all the plans and devices of the wisest will prove of little avail." (art. 62).

In essence *Rerum novarum* is a call for a return to Christian life. The complementary demand for a return to Christian institutions is made specific in a list of steps to be taken, which is very much a survey of work that was already in progress and could be fitted into the existing legislation of European capitalist societies without causing economic upheaval. In the Netherlands, for example, trade unions were legal in 1891, the year *Rerum novarum* was published. The guilds had been formally terminated in 1798 and definitively in 1818. It had made an end to their authority under public law. There were, however, never placed legal restraints on the right of workers and of employers to associate. Due to the late start of the industrial revolution in the Netherlands, the first association with features of a "modern" trade union was formed, relatively late, in 1866, by Amsterdam book printers. It had a mutual support fund and send requests with demands for higher wages to employers (Brugmans 1929, 265). Although strikes had been forbidden in the Netherlands by the *Code Pénal* art. 414–416, Brugmans (1929, 254–255) did find no evidence that the law actually had prevented strikes from occurring. So, the law of 1872, which undid the crime status of striking, had only symbolic significance. Excesses in the context of strikes, such as threats and molestation, remained criminal offences (Brugmans 1929, pp. 254–258). In the last three decades of the nineteenth century, trade unions came into existence: the first ones were on a non-religious base, usually with a socialist or communist orientation, then came the orthodox Protestant unions (Werkman 2007, 25–29) and at last those on a Catholic base (Sprenger 1970). The events demonstrate that for the Netherlands the recommendation made in *Rerum novarum* are very much an historical account of what had happened.

Rerum novarum is certainly not a plea for a Corporatist society. And that was not because of a lack of knowledge or indifference. In the second half of the nineteenth century aversion of Liberal individualism went hand in hand with ideas of how social cohesion could be restored. Corporatist notions were part and parcel of that discussion. To stay well informed Pope Leo XIII had formed a commission, which in 1884 had provided him with the definition of Corporatism as a "system of social organization that has at its base the grouping of men according to the community of their natural interests and social functions, and as true and proper organs of the state they direct and coordinate labor and capital in matters of common interest" (quoted from Wiarda and Sharpe 1996, 35). An early and crisp description of what in the twentieth century would become known as Corporatist State. The only passages in *Rerum novarum* that could be interpreted as a hint in that direction are the reference in art. 3 to the guilds' functioning as a protective organisation for workmen and the recommendation in art. 45 of an intermediate level of societies or boards to address issues in the domain of labour relations; the State being appealed for its sanction and protection, should circumstances require. Labelling this a call for corporatism is too farfetched.[1]

2.2 *Quadragesimo Anno*

The vision on the social question that inspired the encyclical of 1891 was shared by many European catholic thinkers. They did not face the restrictions that withhold the Head of the Catholic Church from demanding deep political-economic reforms, and were free to let their thoughts roam on how a good and just Christian society would look like. Schumpeter (1954: 764, 765) even speaks of Political Catholicism. By the end of the nineteenth century it came with something that was new, "namely, a definite scheme of social organization that, making use of the existing elements of groupwise co-operation, visualized a society - and a state - operating by means of self-governing vocational associations within a framework of ethical concepts"; and he adds: "This is the 'corporative' state adumbrated in the encyclical *Quadragesimo anno* (1931)". The encyclical appeared on the occasion of the fortieth anniversary of *Rerum novarum*. Let us see whether *Quadragesimo anno* indeed is in support of the corporative state.

Similar to *Rerum novarum* the encyclical *Quadragesimo anno* calls for the correction of morals and next to that for reform of institutions (art. 77). But in its reflections on reform on institutions *Quadragesimo anno* is far more specific. Clearly so in its reference to the past: "The overthrow and near extinction of that rich social life which was once highly developed through associations of various kinds" has changed the role of the State. Since there remain virtually only

[1]Some observers see this differently; such as Fortuyn (1980: 1), who claims that *Rerum novarum* wants State intervention to occur in a corporative ordered society.

individuals and the State, and with a structure of social governance lost, the State has taken over all the burdens which the wrecked associations once bore, and has been overwhelmed and crushed by almost infinite tasks and duties (art. 78). However, it is a "disturbance of right order to assign to a greater and higher association what lesser and subordinate organizations can do" (art. 79). The more perfectly a graduated order is kept between the various associations, in observance of the principle of "subsidiary function", the more prosperous the condition of the state will be (art. 80). Different from today's definition of subsidiarity as a broad, leading principle in the quest for an optimum between political centralisation and decentralisation in the EU, the encyclical *Quadragesimo anno* sees subsidiarity as a guiding principle for reorganization of the market economy. The argumentation starts with the observation that the existing human society is founded on classes with divergent aims and therefore inclined to enmity and strife (art. 82). It separates men into two divisions, as into battle lines and turns the labour market almost into a battlefield. The cure is a society where industries and professions are constituted as well-ordered members of the social body. In those groups, men will have their place, not according to position in the labour market, but according to the social functions each performs (art. 82). *Quadragesimo anno* sees it as natural to civil society that those who are in the same industry or profession form guilds or associations, which basically are self-governing organizations (art. 83). They create the conditions where employers and employees collaborate in production and cooperate amicably (art. 84).

The argument leads to the open recommendation that the social policy of the state must devote itself to the re-establishment of self-governing organisations based on type of industry and profession, in which the interests common to that industry or profession should hold first place (art. 82, 83, 85). Although not mentioned explicitly, it is evident the encyclical sees this as a policy preferable to direct State intervention in the labour market. Schumpeter reads the above passage in *Quadragesimo anno* as a rough outline of a Corporatist State. And that with good reasons. But it is a sketch that leaves a lot of space for filling it in with further organisational details. In Sect. 3 we will see how this was done in the Netherlands in a Catholic corporatist blueprint that appeared a decade before *Quadragesimo anno* and still had political clout in the first years after the Second World War.

3 Dutch Corporatism in the Interwar Period

The vision on the social question that inspired the encyclical of 1891 and the new ideas brought forward by the thinkers representing Political Catholicism, were well received in the Netherlands, with 35% of the population Catholic and taking it serious in a country with a Protestant majority. It was a climate in which a Dutch brand of Corporatism could germinate and grow. The key figure is Johannes Antonius Veraart (1886–1955). In the decades between 1910 and 1950 he unfolded, defended and improved his Catholic blueprint of an economic order with salient

Corporatist characteristics. In the process, he came in collision with socialists who had picked up his idea of creating a Business-ship per branch of industry, but had given it a socialist twist. On his turn Veraart took over some of their ideas on the coordination of Business-ships. We shall investigate in this section whether this was a development towards convergence of the Catholic and socialist conception of the ideal economic system.

3.1 The Catholic Blueprint for Corporatism in the Netherlands

In 1914 young Veraart became involved in an effort to reconstruct the ailing book printing industry: competition between firms was murderous and wages low compared to salaries for similar work elsewhere. The Dutch labour market was developing towards a structure in which labourers and their employers in a sector each had formed their own organisation and had started to engage in negotiations on collective labour contracts. In 1909 the practice, still very much an experiment, had been made legal under civil law (Werkman 2007, 50). Veraart managed to give the contract a highly innovative extension. In exchange for good labour conditions, rules concerning the rights of workers, arbitration and a system of firm jurisdiction, the trade unions accepted to support actively the agreements the employers in the book printing industry had made among them on product prices, on conditions of supply and on entry into the industry (Werkman 2007, 52; Dullaart 1984, 33–35). In hindsight this was a voluntary engagement that had pronounced features of sector corporatism. Key economic variables had been pinned down by collective agreement among those active in the industry. Coordination through the market had been set aside. Yet, one major component of full corporatism was still lacking: the authority to enforce the commitments under public law. Although the scheme was short lived, one could view it as a bode of what the future might have in store. It certainly expressed the ongoing change in the political economic mood, and the search for an alternative for nineteenth century "unregulated", individualist capitalism. During the inter-bellum a discussion on corporatist structural reforms went on in the Netherlands "to a degree the outsider can hardly imagine" (Windmuller et al. 1985, 69). Among Catholics, but also among Protestant labourers, united in their own trade union, as Werkman (2007) has shown.

Veraart was for three decades the great advocate of a conversion of the then existing market economy into a Corporatist economic system. He sees is as the next stage in what today we would call an evolutionary development. It is evident, he writes in *The Principles of Organisation of Business* (1921a), that the days of perfect competition and fully free exchange may have been a fair representation of the real world in the first half of the nineteenth century, but it is evident those days are over. What one sees, is that competition has been and still is making place for "organisation". In the late nineteenth century trade unions have been formed, and trade union leaders have shown a growing willingness to engage in negotiations for a collective wage contract. Employers from their side also formed associations and have responded to workers' initiatives. Collective labour contracts have been concluded and their number is increasing. What we also see, is instead of competition among firms, a coming together of firms in the same branch of industry, to agree on the quality of their products, how to calculate the cost, to decide on prices and conditions of delivery. Veraart is extremely negative about perfect competition, praised so highly by "the Austrian school". He had seen it coming down to cut-throat competition between firms, which too often did lead to disastrously low wages, hand in hand with extremely low incomes for employers. In modern terminology, "a race to the bottom". So it is a good thing that this world of perfect competition is on the way out. However, Veraart also warns that growing organisation of workers on the labour market, of firms on their product markets, and also the collective labour agreement between employees and employers is not without dangers when each group only goes for its own private interest. Too high wages lead to the downfall of weaker firms and consequently also to unemployment; too high product prices result in lower output and too low consumption. There apparently is a task for the government here. Not by thwarting the ongoing self-organisation in business, but by leading it into the appropriate direction through structural reforms, based on a broad political consensus among the various political groups in Dutch society. In 1921 Veraart foresees a political solution with all the traits of corporatism. The workers and firms in a branch of industry are brought together in a "'corporation" or "business" We shall stick to the term business-ship, which later on came into general use. The business-ships should get authority under public law. Its General Board, with an equal number of representatives of employers and of employees, plus three representatives of the general interest (which form the Executive Committee, appointed by the Minister), makes regulations, enforceable under public law, which bind the workers, employers and owners of the firms in the business. The regulations will concern: (1) the wage of labour and other labour conditions in the sector, (2) product prices, but only maxima and minima, and conditions the product should meet, (3) the taxes to be paid by the participants to finance the expenditure of the organisation. The General Board carries out the jurisdiction regarding its regulations, based on complaints filed by members of the Business-ships. To protect the interests of consumers, Consumer Councils can be installed that can bring in objections against drafts of regulations of the General Board of Business-ships. A Supervisory Council will oversee the functioning of the General Board.

Veraart insists that a Business-ship with authority under public law should only be introduced in a branch of production where self-organisation has attained sufficient maturity; with trade unions of workers and associations of employers and firms in place, and where voluntary cooperation under private law has come from the ground. The requirement reflects Veraart's hopeful expectation of an evolutionary development towards the new corporatist economic order. It's coming of age will bring incisive changes in how the economy functions. In the first place in the labour market. The collective labour agreement inherited from the past will be void. The talks between employers and employees in the General Board of the Business-ship will result in regulations regarding wages and other labour conditions, binding for all in the Business-ships. If it is detected that an individual labour contract does not comply with the regulation, employer and employee pay a fine. In the product market the regulations restrict the scope for competition between suppliers. But there remains scope for individual entrepreneurship A firm is not forbidden to go for maximum firm profits. It can choose its price between the margins imposed by the regulation and bring down costs by improved efficiency and by innovation; badly run firms can go bankrupt, entry of new firms remains possible.[2] Veraart thinks innovation incentives of individual firms will not suffer and technical progress that leads to better products and lower costs will go on. One can have his doubts about that in an organisational structure designed to suppress the "vagaries" of competition.

In the three decades that followed after 1921, Veraart went on to improve his corporatist blueprint. In the process he benefitted from proposals from and discussion with social democrats.

3.2 *Socialists on Statutory Organisation of Business*

The Social Democrat Labour Party had ending the private property of the means of production as a major objective. The report on socialisation (*Het Socialisatievraagstuk*, 1920) is an update. Socialisation will proceed in stages, depending on the degree of concentration of firms in the various branches of industry. Under Capitalism the advantages of large-scale production are not fully used; socialisation therefore offers the possibility to raise productivity and improve the standard of living (see also Dullaart 1984, 76). Socialisation should not take the form of giving firms into the hands of its workers; it will lead to furthering of the workers' group interest to the detriment of the consumer. Firms should come under the control of the state, with each firm, or group of firms resorting under a ministry. The report of 1920 leaves, however, the Board of a nationalised firm considerable freedom to make its own decisions. The workers will receive a form of codetermination by choosing their representatives in a Council that monitors labour conditions, safety measures and performance standards. At the national level a General Economic Council will be formed that replaces Parliament in matters of business.

Three years later follows a report on codetermination of workers (*Bedrijfsorganisatie en Medezeggenschap*, 1923). It is written by a commission on behalf of the Socialist Trade Union and the Social Democrat Labour Party and focuses on the present situation, where the socialisation of means of production has not yet taken place. Veraart (1921a) had done the suggestion that his statutory organisation of business might be acceptable for socialists as a preliminary

[2]The information on scope for individual entrepreneurship comes from Veraart (1947).

objective for the time being. The 1923 report did indeed propose to bring firms together in Business-ships in those branches of industry where concentration of firms is insufficient to make them suitable for socialisation. Next to that the report recommends participation of workers in the decision making of the Board of a firm, with the argument it will serve as a training ground for workers, who in the socialist future will have to run factories. Similar to Veraart's scheme the Business-ship will be governed by a General Board in which representatives of employers, employees and the community have a seat. Different from Veraart, the representatives of the community, that is to say the Executive Committee, appointed by the Minister, can never be overruled by employers and employees. Evidently, the construction is in an additional safety to prevent that the employers and employees in the Board of a Business-ship let the interests of their groups prevail.

The wage and other labour conditions are not fixed by the regulations of the Board of the Business-ships, but will remain the outcome of negotiations between representatives of employers and employees (read trade unions), laid down in a collective labour contract for the branch of industry. Whereas in Veraart's Catholic version, regulation of wages by the Board of the Business-ship, which implies a ban on strikes, will end class struggle, socialists see Statutory Organisation of Business as a transition stage to full socialisation; so on the labour market the class struggle goes on (Dullaart 1984, 75).

Nationally, at the top of SOB there will be a Central Economic Council in which representatives of employers, of employees, and representatives of the general interest, in the person of members of Parliament, will have equality of seats. The Council's major task is monitoring and approving the regulations drafted by the Boards of Business-ships; next to that it advises the government. In Veraart (1921a) supervision is a task spread over Supervisory Councils; one per Business-ship or group of Business-ships.

In the nineteen thirties the political-economic sentiment in Europe differs from the twenties. The Great Depression stimulated the rise and spread of the notion of economic planning. Were Nazi Germany and the Soviet Union with its Five Year Plans not exemplary of what economic planning could achieve? Could the planning technique not as well be applied in a democratic society, to counter the chaos and inefficiency of uncontrolled capitalism? The new hope is reflected in the name "The Plan for Labour" (*Het Plan van de Arbeid*, 1935). The report brought out by a commission from the Socialist Trade Union and Social Democrat Labour Party, intended to offer a perspective, not only for socialists, but also for enlightened non-socialists. It comes with a two-pronged approach of the persistent economic depression: public works and ordering of production. We focus on ordering, as summarized by Nentjes and Postma (1972). The tendency towards overproduction, inherent to unordered capitalism, makes it necessary to give the General Economic Council (GEC) the status of "super body in the economic domain" in a system of top-down planning. To prevent undue expansion, GEC uses its national regulatory powers to decide on the investment in production capacity, assisted by a Central Business Cycle Bureau, which makes prognoses of the future need for output capacity. Branches of industry that are not socialised, are organized in

Business-ships. The Board of a Business-ship allocates the allowed investment in output capacity to the firms in its sector. In this way the Business-ships capacitate the GEC to control output capacity while preserving the advantages of decentralization.

Compared to Veraart's Catholic scheme of 1921 the Socialist Plan of 1935 reduces the autonomy of Business-ships by bringing them under the aegis of the GEC. At the same time their tasks are enlarged by receiving the authority to decide on closure and entry of firms and on rationalisation of production, taken away from the firms. In peculiar contrast, wages and other labour conditions are left outside the planning system. They remain the outcome of negotiations on the collective labour contract between trade unions and employers' associations.

3.3 Towards a Roman-Red Understanding on a Corporatist State?

In Veraart's 1921 publication the General Boards of the Business-ships are practically autonomous in their decisions; no mention is made that coordination of sectors might be a problem. The Socialist report of 1923 had criticised Veraart 1921 for not safeguarding the general interest and foresaw "a struggle on life and death between the various business-ships" that would leave "standing alongside an army of unemployed in the midst of a society impoverished by expensive and scarce production" (*Bedrijfsorganisatie en Medezeggenschap*, 1923, 31). However, the Socialists missed here that already before the publication of their report Veraart (1921b) had brought forward the idea of an Economic Council (Dullaart 1984, 46–47); possibly picked up from the socialisation report (S.D.A. 1920). In his last book (*De beginselen van de publieke bedrijfsorganisatie*, 1947) it appears under the name Social-Economic Council. In 1947 Veraart even embraces economic planning, originally brought forward in the Socialist Plan for Labour of 1935. The book of 1947 gives the definitive form of Veraart's conception of Statutory Organisation of Business. He is in agreement with Socialists that ultimately it is task of the State to take responsibility for "a reasonable provision in reasonable needs of all" (Veraart 1947, 105). With regard to the organisation of business, the national government has to delegate that responsibility to the Social Economic Council (SEC), which monitors the Business-ships and has the authority to annul regulations of lower bodies that run counter the general interest. The potential problem of an imbalance between the sector plans of the various Business-ships will be solved through the coordination of plans by the SEC. The information needed for the task is contained in the National Economic Plan. Wages and prices will be important components of the Plan. Despite his support for an Economic Plan, which he even calls "the keystone of the Statutory Organisation of Business", Veraart (1947) persists that the sector plans come up from below, brought forward by the Boards of the Business-ships. Top-down planning and control, as the Socialists want it, would stifle the initiative of the social groups. Just because business takes planning in its own hands, will it be possible to push back the intervention of the state in economic life. Veraart (1947) seems to assume that the price information given in the National Economic Plan will result in sort of optimal coordination of the decisions made by the Business-ships and only by exception make it necessary for the SEC to intervene.

Despite the difference in opinion on top-down versus bottom-up planning, it is clear that in the course of time Veraart and his socialist opponents had been converging in their views on how to save the Dutch economy from the market system: the socialists had accepted the guild like system of Business-ships and Veraart had welcomed Economic Planning. But was that enough for a political compromise between the socialist and Catholic Party? And what exactly was the position of Veraart? There is no doubt that in the first years after the Second World War his Corporatist blueprint was widely supported by wage dependent workers; not only by those organised the Catholic trade unions, but in the Protestant trade unions as well (Werkman 2007). The vulnerable spot was his relation with the Catholic Party. Veraart had not been successful in his efforts to get broader open political acceptation of Corporatism. As Rob Jansen mentions in Chap. Introduction, there was too much resistance of the Catholic political elite.

Whether the rapprochement in the views on Statutory Organisation of Business could lead to political cooperation on that issue between Catholics and socialists also depended on the relations between political parties in the Netherlands. Until deep in the nineteen thirties the Labour Party was seen by the other major Parties as too radical and therefore not fit as a coalition partner. The political isolation ended only after the Party had distanced itself from the dogma of class struggle, had stopped to vote against the defence budget out of principle and accepted the constitutional monarchy. The Nazi-German invasion in May 1940 and the occupation that followed also brought political opponents closer together. The five years' experience of standing together against the common enemy softened the strong political differences and promoted even an illusion of political unity.

The war years also brought the full transition to a centrally controlled economy: direct regulation of output per sector, wage and price controls and rationing of consumption. It came with restrictions of individual liberty, harsh sanctions and unprecedented scarcity. Not an experience to feed warm feelings for the controlled economy. Yet, after the liberation in May 1945, it was undisputed that in the existing state of economic emergency the government had no other option than to continue the direct controls of production, wages, prices and rationing of consumption.

But what had to come next, after the period of overwhelming scarcity? Hein Vos, the author of the section on SOB in the Socialists' Plan for Labour of 1935, had distilled from the "underground" discussions during the war years "the general conviction that after the war the statutory organisation of business would be necessary on all counts" (*Voorontwerp van Wet op de Publieke Bedrijfsorganisatie*, 1945). His opponent of the interwar years, Veraart claimed: "After the Second Wold War, the idea of statutory organisation of business has won, as with one stroke, among the competing social reforms, which until 1940 had so much attention in our country" (Veraart 1947, 145). Two men with no doubt about the road to go in building up a new economic order. But in which way: the Catholic, or the Socialist direction? Or perhaps a compromise on a common road?

4 After the War: Consensus Through Dilution

In the provisional Dutch government, installed in 1945 before elections, the Socialists had a strong position. They could take the lead and Hein Vos became the Minister who had to deliver the legal base for the future economic order with the Drafts of Law for two closely connected issues: Statutory Organisation of Business and Economic Planning.

4.1 Economic Planning

The most urgent of the two was economic planning. In June 1945 the Prime Minister stated that "reparation and building up of the Netherlands' production capacity can only be done effectively on the basis of a general social-economic-financial plan. Such a plan has to be designed by a scientific Bureau appointed by the Council of Ministers" (Schermerhorn 1945). In September 1945 the Central Plan Bureau, under director Jan Tinbergen, started its work. The Draft of Law, in which the tasks of the Central Plan Bureau are delineated, followed in spring 1946. Parliament was informed that the National Welfare Plan will be of help to coordinate the policies of the involved Ministries. Next to macro-economic figures the Plan will state the targets for production, prices and investments per sector. The implementation of the tasks will be carried out by bodies of Statutory Business Organisation that will be created. The Draft of Law on Business-ships had been submitted to Parliament in Fall 1945.

In the campaigns that preceded the first elections after the war, held in 1946, the pre-war dividing lines between political parties did show up again. The Catholic People's Party got the most seats in Parliament. In the Catholic-socialism coalition government, formed after the election, Vos was degraded to Minister of Transport; from now on two Ministers from the Catholic Party, successively Huysmans and van den Brink, were to bend Vos' Drafts of Law into Catholic direction. Not necessarily the direction Veraart wanted to go; the two Ministers had views more in line with the political strongmen within the Catholic Party. In the defence of the *Draft of Law on the Central Plan Bureau* Minister Huysmans argued that planning should not be top down, but has to come up from below, that is from the business bodies that make plans for their own sector. A National Economic Plan is necessary as a source of information and help in coordinating the sector plans for the Economic Council that has the supervision of the business organisations for the branches of industry. The Central Economic Plan, drafted by the Central Plan Bureau, should be conceived as "writing the history of the future", in which corrective government interventions are only included in so far they are needed. By bringing in this changed interpretation of economic planning, the Minister did appease the opponents of Vos' original draft, which had unfolded the vision of a top-down planned and controlled economy. Actually, Huysman's interpretation of economic planning is very much in line with the view in Veraart (1947). The *Law on the Central Plan Bureau* was accepted by Parliament in Spring 1947.

4.2 Statutory Organisation of Business

Coming to political agreement on the Statutory Organisation of Business took many more years. In the *Draft of Law on Business-ships*, submitted in 1945 by Minister Hein Vos, the national government decides on the targets per sector for production, prices and investments, stated in the Central Plan. The task of implementing them is delegated to the Business-ships. Each Business-ship is placed directly under the Ministry responsible for the sector. So, the Business-ships are sheer organisational entities to carry out the sector policies of the government. A Commissar appointed by the Minister presides the Board of the Business-ships. He has the authority to submit decisions of the Board to the Minister for suspension or annulment. The *Draft of Law* by Vos is straightforwardly state socialist. It has no place for a General Economic Council, as had been proposed in the *Plan for Labour* of 1935. Instead, the organisational structure set out in the *Draft* is a copy of the State bureaucratic Business-ships for Food Provision, in place during the years of German occupation, which were basically a continuation of the Dutch Agricultural Crisis Organisations set up in the Great Depression (de Jongh 1945).

The draft did not get the public reception Vos had hoped for. Trade unions as well as employers' organisations were highly critical. In particular they were against the Commissar with his far reaching authority (Wermuth 1997, 101). After the elections of Spring 1946, the new, Catholic Minister submitted in 1948 a new draft of law on Statutory Organisation of Business to parliament. It has a Social Economic Council (SEC) in which workers, employers and experts nominated by the government have an equal share in seats. Although subsidiary to the supervising SEC, the Business-ships are autonomous statutory bodies that make their own binding decisions for the domain of economic life they have been created for. And in the Board of the Business-ship there will not sit a representative of society. After a long period of discussions the draft passed parliament in the fall of late 1949, to come in force as law on January 1, 1950.

Up to this point, it looks as if the Catholic corporatist view, worded in Veraart 1947, had won. But that is not the whole story, which actually took a remarkable turn. Whether the Dutch economy would indeed go the corporatist way, that is to say to what extent the regulations made by the Boards of Business-ships would take over the coordination through markets, depended on the authority with regard to regulating wages, prices, production and investment, granted to the boards. And here minister van den Brink made a U-turn on the road mapped out by Veraart. Yes, the law granted the boards of the Business-ships strong autonomy; however, simultaneously the domain where they have a task was shrunk drastically. Excluded from their regulations are: wages, prices and decisions on starting, expansion or closing down of firms. Further, the regulations should not obstruct healthy competition. In practice, van den Brink and successive ministers after him have indeed been restrictive in the tasks handed over to the Business-ships that came into being. It left them with decision powers far too constrained to fulfil the tasks envisaged by advocates such as Veraart. The original idea that the public bodies should regulate wages and prices, still defended by the Catholic authors Groeneveld (1945/46) and Veraart (1947), was out. Instead of replacing the market economy, the regulations of the Business-ships would have to help the market economy to function adequately. From their beginning on in 1950, it must have been evident for the attentive observer that Business-ships would not become the focal bodies of a Corporatist economy. The Catholic party, which never had openly embraced corporatism, had in fact distanced itself from the corporatist ordered society.

What about the Social Democrats? Socialists of type Hein Vos could still cherish the hope that the text of the law was only a formal framework, which could be filled with a plan socialist content when the opportunity would come (Vos 1952). More relevant is that by 1950 most socialists had lost their belief in the centrally planned economy as the appropriate way to direct business activities towards the general interest (Verloren van Themaat 1958). The major economic objectives—full employment, economic growth, balance of payments equilibrium, price stability and a fair distribution of income—can be achieved with more general measures.

4.3 Statutory Organisation of Business Embedded in a Market Economy

By the end of the nineteen forties production capacity had been rebuilt; ransoming the consumption of essential goods was terminated and the direct control of prices and sector output was ended. The option to lay the task in the hands of the Business-ships under supervision of the SEC was not used.

In a meeting of the Dutch Association for Economics in 1947, Jan Tinbergen, the highly respected director of the Central Plan Bureau, co-author of the Plan for Labour in 1935 and Nobel Laureate 1969, had given his view on the place and role of direct controls and markets in the years to come. The government can use global measures in the domain of expenditures and taxes to tune the total demand for output to production capacity. Within a framework of global measures the price mechanism can fulfil its task efficiently. Specific controls can be withdrawn as soon as production has recovered so far that the non-rationed demand for goods can be met without causing too big price shocks. Competition is "an in many cases valuable institute for bringing order" (Tinbergen, 1947).

The after-war experience of rapid economic growth, rising incomes, full employment and the first beginnings of the welfare state, was totally different from the "poverty amidst of plenty" in the nineteen thirties. It did restore the public trust in the performance of the market economy. Next to that the Keynesian and Tinbergian notion that macro-economic policy can be used to keep the economy on an even keel, if necessary, transpired to a broader public. The Catholic Party and the Labour Party found each other in the understanding that the coordination of business decisions could better be left to the market. For SOB there was only a place in a watered-down version, stripped from the authority to control markets; a far cry of the Corporatist and Socialist blueprints thought up in the interwar years.

Once set in place, the organisational structure of SOB was built up over the next decade and a half. About fifty Business-ships came into being, mainly in agriculture and the crafts, but none in manufacturing. In a cartoon published in 1954 one sees parents and a nurse, with a worried look in their eyes, staring down at a rather monstrous baby in a cradle with the letters SOB on the blanket. The caption: "It is and remains an ugly thing" (see Hazenbosch 2014). Over the decades the negative sentiment intensified, hand in hand with slow but steady decline in functions. The development towards the integrated market of the European Union was a major influence. Regulations made in Brussels diminished the national regulatory playground for the Business-ships. Employers had never been in love with SOB and trade unions were defiantly protecting their competences in the domain of labour conditions. The way downwards ended with the dissolution of SOB in 2014. Tasks worth to be continued were transferred to the Ministry of Economic affairs. The only component of Dutch Corporatism to survive, is the Social Economic Council. Representing the views of employers, employees and politically connected experts, the Council advises the national government on major economic issues.

5 Conclusion

In 1947 Veraart may have thought that by integrating a Social Economic Council and a National Economic Plan into his Statutory Organisation of Business he had come close to a system also acceptable for socialists as a practical solution for a society where full socialisation of the means of production is out of reach. Just after the Second World War there was a general feeling that the days of old school liberalism were over. Both sides seemed to agree that the market economy had to make place for an economy steered by regulations. On the surface, it looked as if the question whether regulation had to be the Catholic way bottom-up, or the socialist way top-down, was the last problem to be solved.

The law on Statutory Organisation of Business of 1950 did indeed establish a political peace. But not thanks to the convergence of minds on issues that had separated Catholics and socialists in the interwar period. The agreement on SOB was only possible because on both sides the old beliefs had gone. In the years of fast economic recovery after 1945 the market economy was bringing prosperity for everyone. The first steps towards a welfare state complementary to the market system lifted the position of the most vulnerable and fed the hope for more fairness in society. Not the political climate to make a break and start with an untested regulatory economy, designed by men of a former generation to meet economic problems that were no longer there.

SOB 1950 combined a watered down version of "socialist" economic planning with a watered down variety of "Catholic" corporatism. A structure designed to leave the market economy in place. In hindsight one can judge that SOB 1950 functioned as a mask, to hide that in fact the old corporatist and socialist designs for the economy had been thrown out of the window. One can also see SOB 1950 as a political peace offer, of which the burning took sixty four years.

The end of SOB came in 2014; almost hundred twenty five years after *Rerum Novarum*. That was not because the ideals of a peaceful and just economic order, upheld in the encyclical, had gone. No, Dutch society had found a better way towards its realisation than corporatism. In the century after the encyclical *Rerum Novarum* the corporatist economy had come to naught. The same can be said of the socialist controlled economy. Once seen by many as leading to a golden economic future, both roads turned out to be political dead-end alleys.

References

Brugmans IJ (1929) De arbeidende klasse in Nederland in de 19e eeuw (1813–1870). tweede druk, Martinus Nijhoff, Amsterdam

de Jongh JF (1945) De organen der sociaal-economische ordening. Amsterdam

Dullaart MHJ (1984) Regeling of vrijheid, Nederlands economisch denken tussen de wereldoorlogen. Ph.D., Erasmus Universiteit, Rotterdam

Fortuyn P (1980) Sociaal-economische politiek in Nederland 1945–1949. Ph.D., Rijksuniversiteit Groningen, Groningen

Frambach H and Eissrich (2016) Der dritte Weg der Päpste; die Wirtschafstideen des Vatikans. UVK, Konstanz und München

Groeneveld GW (1945/46) P.B.O. en prijspolitiek, Maandschrift Economie 10

Hazenbosch P (2014) Een stille dood of het einde van de PBO, www.vakbondshistorie.nl

Nentjes A, Postma JKT (1972) Besturen of bijsturen? Herstel en vernieuwing van de Nederlandse economie (1945–1950). In: de Haan H, Kuipers SK, Postma JKT (eds) Mens en Keuze. Opstellen aangeboden aan Prof. Drs. S. Korteweg ter gelegenheid van de voltooiing van zijn zeventigste levensjaar, B.V. Noord-Hollandsche Uitgeversmaatschappij, Amsterdam

Quadrogesimo Anno (1931)

Rerum Novarum (1891)

Schermerhorn W (1945) Herstel en vernieuwing, Speech of the minister-president on June 27, 1945. Text edition, Groningen

Schumpeter JA (1954) History of economic analysis. George Allen & Unwin Ltd, London

S.D.A.P. (1920) Het Socialisatievraagstuk. Amsterdam

S.D.A.P. (1923) Bedrijfsorganisatie en Medezeggenschap Rapport uitgebracht door de commissie ingesteld door N.V.V. en S.D.A., Amsterdam

S.D.A.P. (1935) Het plan van de arbeid. Rapport van de commissie uit N.V.V en S.D.A., N.V. De Arbeiderspers, Amsterdam

Sprenger J (1970) De geschiedenis van de roomskatholieke arbeidersbeweging 1888–1914, www.vakbondhistorie.nl

Tinbergen J (1947) Preadvies voor de Vereniging voor Staathuishoudkunde

Veraart JA (1921a) De beginselen der bedrijfsorganisatie. Bussum

Veraart JA (1921b) Preadvies voor de Vereniging voor Staathuishoudkunde

Veraart JA (1947) De beginselen der publiekrechtelijke bedrijfsorganisatie. Bussum

Verloren van Themaat P (1958) De P.B.O. opnieuw beschouwd, Socialisme en Democratie

Vos H (1952) Vijf jaren volkshuishouding. In: Ruygers G (ed) Socialisme in de branding. Arbeiderspers, Amsterdam

Werkman PE (2007) Laat uw doel hervorming zijn! Facetten van de geschiedenis van het Christelijk Nationaal Vakverbond in Nederland (1909–1959). Uitgeverij Verloren, Hilversum

Wiarda HJ, Sharpe ME (1996) Corporatism and comparative politics: the other great ISM. Armonk, New York

Windmuller JP et al (1985) Arbeidsverhoudingen in Nederland. Aula pocket

Wermuth E (1997) De publiekrechtelijke bedrijfsorganisatie. In: Balkenende J et al (eds) Vertrouwen in de economie: het debat. van Gorkum, Assen

The Justice and the Economics of *Rerum novarum* on Land

Nicolaus Tideman

1 Introduction

Leo XIII's (1891) encyclical *Rerum novarum* set the framework for Catholic discussion of economic justice for many subsequent decades. The encyclical had its genesis, according to Misner (1991), in drafts by at least two clerics other than Leo, which Leo integrated into the final version. Thus the encyclical has some elements of inconsistency that might be expected of a document written by a committee. While Leo was fully responsible for the final draft, I will treat the encyclical as the product of Church officials working together rather than that of a single individual.

I take the primary purposes of the document to be to criticize socialism and to specify the Church's position on appropriate paths for alleviating poverty, in the context of European ferment. As Nuesse (1985) explains, the encyclical was intended only tangentially to be a swipe at Henry George. Nevertheless, the encyclical's argument against socialism has a strong anti-Georgist slant, and a concern for the justice of private property in land plays a central role in the encyclical. Thus it is interesting to evaluate the argument that *Rerum novarum* makes about land, from the perspectives of justice and economics.

I argue that justice and economics confirm that, as George (1891) suggested, *Rerum novarum* is weak as a theory of justice and also weak as economics. I speculate on the causes of these weaknesses. In Sect. 2 I offer my understanding of the perspective of the authors of *Rerum novarum*. Section 3 provides textual analysis. Section 4 is a general commentary.

Nicolaus Tideman indebted to Florenz Plassmann for helpful suggestions.

N. Tideman (✉)
Department of Economics, Virginia Polytechnic Institute
and State University, Blacksburg, VA, USA
e-mail: ntideman@vt.edu

J. Backhaus et al. (eds.), *On the Economic Significance of the Catholic Social Doctrine*, The European Heritage in Economics and the Social Sciences 19, DOI 10.1007/978-3-319-52545-7_10

2 The Perspective of *Rerum Novarum*

The main target of *Rerum novarum* is socialism. Socialism was gaining influence in Europe in the late 19th century, and the Church hierarchy wanted to deliver the message that socialism is wrong. To deliver a credible message that socialism is wrong, the Church needed a theory of how the wretched conditions of workers could properly be alleviated through means other than socialism. The theory propounded in *Rerum novarum* is that the wretched conditions of workers are caused by employers who ask too much and pay to little (§3), and that the cure is for employers to be more generous (§20), for governments to regulate wages and working conditions (§33), and for the creation of mutual aid societies (§48). Unions are mentioned as if they were only mutual aid societies and had no role in negotiating wages (§49–51). Strikes are rejected (§52). George was not mentioned, and was referred to only obliquely (§10; Nuesse 1985, 245).

George had argued that the way to alleviate poverty was to collect the rent of land publicly and abolish all other taxes. George makes a distinction between capital (the product of human effort) and land (the product of nature) that was made neither by the socialists nor by *Rerum novarum*.

There are several possible reasons why capital and land are not distinguished in *Rerum novarum*:

A. The authors may have been using mental frameworks that did not allow for the distinction.
B. The authors may have understood the possibility of the distinction but thought that such a distinction would make no difference.
C. The authors may have understood the possibility of the distinction and felt that it would weaken their argument to acknowledge the possibility.

My reading of *Rerum novarum* suggests a version of C with touches of A and B. I believe that the authors of *Rerum novarum* thought that public collection of the full rent of land and public ownership of all of the means of production were equally wrong and abhorrent, even if they could be distinguished. Distinguishing them would not have improved their argument, and they may have wanted to gain the advantage of allowing capital and land to be conflated in the minds of their readers.

3 Textual Analysis

Paragraphs 4 and 5 of *Rerum novarum* take on socialism:

> 4. To remedy these wrongs the socialists, working on the poor man's envy of the rich, are striving to do away with private property, and contend that individual possessions should become the common property of all, to be administered by the State or by municipal bodies. They are, moreover, emphatically unjust, for they would rob the lawful possessor, distort the functions of the State, and create utter confusion in the community.

> 5. It is surely undeniable that, when a man engages in remunerative labor, the impelling reason and motive of his work is to obtain property, and thereafter to hold it as his very own. … Thus, if he lives sparingly, saves money, and, for greater security, invests his savings in land, the land, in such case, is only his wages under another form; and, consequently, a working man's little estate thus purchased should be as completely at his full disposal as are the wages he receives for his labor.

One might wonder why, to attack socialism, which is associated with public ownership of factories, the authors use an example involving ownership of land. I surmise that the reason is that the authors were seeking an example with which workers could identify. The typical worker would not aspire to own a factory but might be presumed to aspire to own a plot of land.

The essence of the argument is that if a person "invests his savings in land, the land, in such case, is only his wages under another form; and, consequently, a working man's little estate thus purchased should be as completely at his full disposal as are the wages he receives for his labor."

The limitation of this argument can be seen by considering an alternative example in which the frugal worker, for greater security, invests his savings in a slave. Would the authors contend that the slave "is only his wages under another form"? Presumably, they would not. They would say that it was not possible to own another human being, so the worker had dissipated his savings rather than transformed his wages to another form. One can invest only in that which can be owned. Paying for a thing is not sufficient to make an unownable thing owned. The authors of *Rerum novarum* knew this, and eventually they offered an attempt at a defense of ownership of land.

In §6 we find the beginning of a defense of land ownership:

> It is the mind, or reason, which is the predominant element in us who are human creatures; it is this which renders a human being human, and distinguishes him essentially from the brute. And on this very account—that man alone among the animal creation is endowed with reason—it must be within his right to possess things not merely for temporary and momentary use, as other living things do, but to have and to hold them in stable and permanent possession; he must have not only things that perish in the use, but those also which, though they have been reduced into use, continue for further use in after time.

The logic here is weak. It does not follow logically from the fact that humans have minds that humans must have the right to possess things. Still, part of what the authors contend can be defended on economic grounds. And indeed, one finds such a defense in the writings of Thomas Aquinas. In *Summa Theologica* II II 66, 2, Aquinas (2015 [1485]) says,

> Two things are competent to man in respect of exterior things. One is the power to procure and dispense them, and in this regard it is lawful for man to possess property. Moreover this is necessary to human life for three reasons. First because every man is more careful to procure what is for himself alone than that which is common to many or to all: since each one would shirk the labor and leave to another that which concerns the community, as happens where there is a great number of servants. Secondly, because human affairs are conducted in more orderly fashion if each man is charged with taking care of some particular thing himself, whereas there would be confusion if everyone had to look after any one thing indeterminately. Thirdly, because a more peaceful state is ensured to man if each

> one is contented with his own. Hence it is to be observed that quarrels arise more frequently where there is no division of the things possessed.
>
> The second thing that is competent to man with regard to external things is their use. In this respect man ought to possess external things, not as his own, but as common, so that, to wit, he is ready to communicate them to others in their need. Hence the Apostle says in the last chapter of First Timothy, "Charge the rich of this world to give easily, to communicate to others."

The first paragraph is essentially the economic argument for private property. One can imagine a society of perfect universal compassion, which would have no need for private ownership because everyone would always use every available thing in the way that would achieve the greatest human happiness. However, human societies that lack perfect universal compassion need extended private possession of things, because that is what makes investment individually rational. Humans who are not completely compassionate benefit greatly from institutions of enduring possession.

The second paragraph introduces the seemingly contradictory idea that "man ought to possess external things, not as his own, but as common." Aquinas probably had in mind Aristotle, who wrote in *Politics* (Book II, Part V):

Property should be in a certain sense common, but, as a general rule, private; for, when everyone has a distinct interest, men will not complain of one another, and they will make more progress, because everyone will be attending to his own business. And yet by reason of goodness, and in respect of use, "Friends", as the proverb says, "will have all things common." … It is clearly better that property should be private, but the use of it common; and the special business of the legislator is to create in men this benevolent disposition.

From a Christian perspective, being in charge of wealth is more like an assignment that an entitlement. Its defense is its social usefulness.

Even though Aquinas defends private property in terms of its social usefulness, he does not defend the exclusive possession of property by the rich. This can be seen from the way that Aquinas (2015 [1485]) treats an objection to private property, in *Summa Theologica* II II 66, 2:

> ***Objection 2***: Further, Basil in expounding the words of the rich man quoted above, says: "The rich who deem as their own property the common goods they have seized upon, are like to those who by going beforehand to the play prevent others from coming, and appropriate to themselves what is intended for common use." Now it would be unlawful to prevent others from obtaining possession of common goods. Therefore it is unlawful to appropriate to oneself what belongs to the community.
>
> ***Reply to Objection 2***: A man would not act unlawfully if by going beforehand to the play he prepared the way for others: but he acts unlawfully if by so doing he hinders others from going. In like manner a rich man does not act unlawfully if he anticipates someone in taking possession of something which at first was common property, and gives others a share: but he sins if he excludes others indiscriminately from using it.

The reference in Basil's objection to "the common goods [the rich] have seized upon" makes sense as a reference to common land that the rich have privatized. Aquinas's reply to the objection does not allow for absolute private property. He says, "[A] rich man does not act unlawfully if he anticipates someone in taking possession of something which at first was common property, and gives others a share." In other words, it is just to appropriate that which is common if you understand that when people come along who have none, you need to share with them. The authors of *Rerum* do not recognize this.

They might respond, "How is it possible to have the stable and permanent possession that is necessary for economic efficiency if you must always stand ready to share with yet another landless person who may come along?" The answer to this question was provided by Henry George. It is possible to have the efficiency of extended private possession of land without private appropriation of all of the return to land and other natural opportunities. Landlords and mortgage holders regularly appropriate all or nearly all of the rent of land while someone else occupies the residual claimant role and has the extended private possession that makes investment rational. Thus it would be possible for governments to collect what the landlords and mortgage holders now get, without interfering with the efficiency of extended private possession.

The defense of private ownership of land continues in §8 of *Rerum novarum*:

> 8. The fact that God has given the earth for the use and enjoyment of the whole human race can in no way be a bar to the owning of private property. For God has granted the earth to mankind in general, not in the sense that all without distinction can deal with it as they like, but rather that no part of it was assigned to any one in particular, and that the limits of private possession have been left to be fixed by man's own industry, and by the laws of individual races. Moreover, the earth, even though apportioned among private owners, ceases not thereby to minister to the needs of all, inasmuch as there is not one who does not sustain life from what the land produces. Those who do not possess the soil contribute their labor; hence, it may truly be said that all human subsistence is derived either from labor on one's own land, or from some toil, some calling, which is paid for either in the produce of the land itself, or in that which is exchanged for what the land brings forth.

In other words, the authors are saying, "God has given the earth for the use and enjoyment of the whole human race," and the way that those who possess no land receive their shares of the opportunities that the earth offers is by working for the landlords. That is a very strained interpretation of "God has given the earth for the use and enjoyment of the whole human race." A much more plausible interpretation of "God has given the earth for the use and enjoyment of the whole human race" is that humanity ought to share the rent from the earth's opportunities equally.

Next we have in §9 a pseudo-Lockean defense of property:

> [W]hen man thus turns the activity of his mind and the strength of his body toward procuring the fruits of nature, by such act he makes his own that portion of nature's field which he cultivates—that portion on which he leaves, as it were, the impress of his personality; and it cannot but be just that he should possess that portion as his very own, and have a right to hold it without any one being justified in violating that right.

This is at least somewhat Lockean because it is reminiscent of Locke's statement, "Whatsoever, then, he removes out of the state that Nature hath provided and left it in, he hath mixed his labor with it, and joined to it something that is his own, and thereby makes it his property." (Locke 2016 [1689], §26). However, Locke goes on to add his proviso, "at least where there is enough, and as good left in common for others." (Locke 2016 [1689], §26). In other words, Locke understands that the validity of the principle that a person owns what he improves from nature is conditional on natural opportunities not being scarce. The corresponding principle for the case when natural opportunities are scarce is that a person has a respectable claim to the value added by his efforts. The statement in the encyclical does not offer any indication of acceptance of such a proviso. Thus it is pseudo-Lockean rather than actually Lockean. Without a Lockean proviso, the principle of ownership by improvement is unjust because it implies that there will be none for those who come later, and it is inefficient because it induces people to waste effort being the first to improve natural opportunities, so that they can be the owners of them.

The idea that effort makes land one's own can be further criticized on the ground that if Leo XIII and his colleagues really believed this, then they ought to endorse the idea that when a tenant improves land leased from a landlord, the tenant ought to become the owner of the land that had belonged to the landlord. I am confident that they would not have endorsed this use of the principle they propose. Thus they do not really believe the stated principle.

In (§10) we arrive at the passage that was intended to be a criticism of George's ideas:

> 10. So strong and convincing are these arguments that it seems amazing that some should now be setting up anew certain obsolete opinions in opposition to what is here laid down. They assert that it is right for private persons to have the use of the soil and its various fruits, but that it is unjust for anyone to possess outright either the land on which he has built or the estate which he has brought under cultivation. But those who deny these rights do not perceive that they are defrauding man of what his own labor has produced. For the soil which is tilled and cultivated with toil and skill utterly changes its condition; it was wild before, now it is fruitful; was barren, but now brings forth in abundance. That which has thus altered and improved the land becomes so truly part of itself as to be in great measure indistinguishable and inseparable from it. Is it just that the fruit of a man's own sweat and labor should be possessed and enjoyed by anyone else? As effects follow their cause, so is it just and right that the results of labor should belong to those who have bestowed their labor.

The way that we know that the "some" of the first sentence is a reference to Henry George is that this is reported in "a footnote in an unusually complete account of the drafting of the encyclical that is based upon the manuscripts of the drafts and the detailed notes kept at the time by the private secretary of Pope Leo."[1] The sentences that follow the first represent a profound misstatement of George's proposal. George was very clear that his proposal was for a tax on the value that land would have if it had not been improved. He would leave all of the value added by human effort untaxed. The authors might possibly grant that this is what George proposed and still object on the ground (in the quotation above) that "That which has thus altered and improved the land becomes so truly part of itself as to be in great measure

[1]These words appear in Nuesse (1985), 245. The footnote that follows reads, "Giovanni Antonazzi, ed., L'Enciclica "Rerum Novarum" Testo Authentico e Redazioni Preparatorie dai Documenti Originali (Rome: Edizione di Storia e Letteratura, 1957), 93n. For a summary and comment, see [Moody (1961)], pp. 75–79."

indistinguishable and inseparable from it." They could be saying, in other words, "Sure the improver has a claim only to the value added by his improvement, but there is no way to separate the value of the land from the value of the improvement, so you need to grant that the improver owns the land as well as the improvement."

At a practical level, the possibility of separating the value of land from the value of the improvements is shown by the assessment procedures under the property tax in most places where there is a property tax. Assessors report the value of land and the value of improvements separately. Of course the procedures are imperfect. But such imperfection does not make it impossible as a practical matter to have a tax on land that exempts well-reasoned professional estimates of the value of improvements. Contrary to §10, it is not necessary to confiscate improvements in order to tax land.

Next, §11 buttresses the argument for private ownership of land with appeals to custom and to the Bible:

> 11. With reason, then, the common opinion of mankind, little affected by the few dissentients who have contended for the opposite view, has found in the careful study of nature, and in the laws of nature, the foundations of the division of property, and the practice of all ages has consecrated the principle of private ownership, as being pre-eminently in conformity with human nature, and as conducing in the most unmistakable manner to the peace and tranquility of human existence. The same principle is confirmed and enforced by the civil laws—laws which, so long as they are just, derive from the law of nature their binding force. The authority of the divine law adds its sanction, forbidding us in severest terms even to covet that which is another's: "Thou shalt not covet thy neighbor's wife; nor his house, nor his field, nor his man-servant, nor his maid-servant, nor his ox, nor his ass, nor anything that is his."

To these efforts to buttress the argument for private ownership of land, one can reply that sometimes it happens that customs are wrong and need to be changed. The quotation from the Old Testament treats servants as property. We came to recognize that servants cannot be property. Similarly, it ought to be conceded that it is imaginable that continuation of the unequal private appropriation of the rent of land is wrong and needs to be changed.

The idea that land ownership is supported by the quotation from the Old Testament is undermined in another way. The admonition not to covet one's neighbor's field occurs in the context of a division of land, as described in Joshua 13–19, that was intended to ensure that every Israelite except the Levites had land. (The Levites were supported by the tithe and were expected to not do any work that required land holdings.) Thus the commandment to not covet one's neighbor's field was not addressed to those who had no shares of land.

After §11 the encyclical discusses matters other than land, returning to land only in §46–47. In §45 there is an appeal for institutions that will ensure that market wages are not too low. In §46, the authors suggest that adequate wages will permit workingmen to save and buy land:

> 46. If a workman's wages be sufficient to enable him comfortably to support himself, his wife, and his children, he will find it easy, if he be a sensible man, to practice thrift, and he will not fail, by cutting down expenses, to put by some little savings and thus secure a

> modest source of income. Nature itself would urge him to this. We have seen that this great labor question cannot be solved save by assuming as a principle that private ownership must be held sacred and inviolable. The law, therefore, should favor ownership, and its policy should be to induce as many as possible of the people to become owners.

In other words, since it is essential that private ownership be held sacred, the law should induce workingmen to become property owners, so that they will support property ownership. The following paragraph elaborates the benefits that will follow:

> 47. Many excellent results will follow from this; and, first of all, property will certainly become more equitably divided. For, the result of civil change and revolution has been to divide cities into two classes separated by a wide chasm. On the one side there is the party which holds power because it holds wealth; which has in its grasp the whole of labor and trade; which manipulates for its own benefit and its own purposes all the sources of supply, and which is not without influence even in the administration of the commonwealth. On the other side there is the needy and powerless multitude, sick and sore in spirit and ever ready for disturbance. If working people can be encouraged to look forward to obtaining a share in the land, the consequence will be that the gulf between vast wealth and sheer poverty will be bridged over, and the respective classes will be brought nearer to one another.

The suggestion in the first sentence that "property will certainly become more equitably divided" is startling. It suggests that there was something inequitable about the division of property that prevailed. It would be surprising if Leo XIII and his colleagues were prepared to say this. The Latin in the encyclical is "primum certe aequior partitio bonorum."[2] The most direct translation would be "first, certainly, a more equal division of goods." But "aequior" can mean "more just" as well as "more equal."[3] So is not necessarily wrong to translate "primum certe aequior partitio bonorum" as "first of all, property will certainly become more equitably divided." However, in the context of the claim in the previous paragraph that "private ownership must be held sacred and inviolable," which suggests that ownership can never be unjust, it seems more plausible to translate the phrase in question as "first of all, wealth will certainly become more equally distributed." This is what follows with mathematical certainty when the poor save more.

The paragraph describes the rich as "the party which holds power because it holds wealth; which has in its grasp the whole of labor and trade; which manipulates for its own benefit and its own purposes all the sources of supply, and which is not without influence even in the administration of the commonwealth." This is a highly unflattering a description of the rich. The suggestion that buying land with their savings might persuade the poor to set aside their enmity for such powerful economic manipulators is unpersuasive. What is more plausible is that if people buy land, they will tend to become blind to the injustice of the inequality with which the gifts of nature are distributed. It is to be expected that a party that does not perceive such injustice will see that blindness as a good thing. If the poor buy land, they may

---

[2]https://w2.vatican.va/content/leo-xiii/la/encyclicals/documents/hf_l-xiii_enc_15051891_rerum-novarum.html.

[3]https://en.wiktionary.org/wiki/aequior.

still resent the power and manipulation of the rich, but they will not rail against the injustice of the unequal distribution of natural opportunities.

The paragraph goes on to name two other benefits of purchases of land by the poor:

> A further consequence will result in the great abundance of the fruits of the earth. Men always work harder and more readily when they work on that which belongs to them; nay, they learn to love the very soil that yields in response to the labor of their hands, not only food to eat, but an abundance of good things for themselves and those that are dear to them. That such a spirit of willing labor would add to the produce of the earth and to the wealth of the community is self-evident.

A response to this argument requires a more detailed specification of an alternative to the private appropriation of rent than has heretofore been presented. Assume that natural opportunities are to be shared equally and the returns to improvements are to be collected by those whose savings finance the improvements. Such a framework needs to account for the fact that the source of much of the rent of land is not nature but the provision of public infrastructure and public services. This component of the rent of land ought to be the income of the governments that provide the infrastructure and services. So my alternative to private collection of all rent includes assessors who are tasked with estimating the share of the rent of land that is due to public infrastructure and public services. This part of the rent of land goes to governments. The rest of the rent of land is divided equally among citizens. This means that if a person wishes to use a parcel of land with no public services and a rental value that is no greater than average, then that person's share of the rent of land will pay the tax on his parcel. He will pay no net land tax. Thus for a person who wants no public services and no more land, in terms of rental value, than everyone else can have, all the benefits of land belonging to those who work it will prevail. This benefit will be absent only for those who want public services or want to use more land than everyone else can use, and it is proper that they pay for these opportunities. Every user of land can have a title providing possession of indefinitely long duration, provided that a tax is paid for public services and for having more land than others can have. The benefits of being the owner of the land on which one works should apply as well to such an arrangement as to the arrangement proposed by the authors of the encyclical.

There is a third benefit of private ownership of land adduced in §47:

> And a third advantage would spring from this: men would cling to the country in which they were born, for no one would exchange his country for a foreign land if his own afforded him the means of living a decent and happy life.

This claim can be understood as motivated by the flood of emigration from Europe to America that was occurring in the 1890s. It is plausible that higher wages would reduce the rate of emigration from Europe. It is plausible that having title to land and confidence that one can receive the full benefits of improvements to one's land will further reduce the inclination to emigrate. It is reasonable to expect that sharing the rent of land equally among all citizens would do even more to lower the rate of emigration.

4 General Commentary

There are two fundamental difficulties with the treatment of land in *Rerum novarum*. First, *Rerum novarum* does not recognize that if "God has given the earth for the use and enjoyment of the whole human race" (*Rerum novarum*, §8), then just institutions must provide for the benefits of natural opportunities to be shared equally. Second, it does not distinguish between 1) public collection of the rent of land, and 2) socialism, which combines public collection of the rent of land with public ownership of capital. *Rerum novarum*, §46 says that the "great labor question cannot be solved save by assuming as a principle that private ownership must be held sacred and inviolable," but it does not distinguish between property in natural opportunities and property in the products of human effort. It presumes (§10) erroneously that the physical inseparability of land and capital makes them economically inseparable. *Rerum novarum* seems to have been written by authors who were striving to make the least implausible case for a position with respect to land that they knew was untenable. Its position on land should be rejected.

References

Aquinas T (2015 [1485]) Summa theologica. Xist Publishing

George H (2015 [1891]) The condition of labour: an open letter to Pope Leo XIII. Robert Schalkenbach Foundation

Leo XIII (1891) Rerum Novarum. Acta Leonis XIII, XI Available online at http://www.papalencyclicals.net/Leo13/l13rerum.htm and in Latin at https://w2.vatican.va/content/leo-xiii/la/encyclicals/documents/hf_l-xiii_enc_15051891_rerum-novarum.html

Locke J (2016 [1689]) Second treatise of government. Oxford University Press

Misner P (1991) The predecessors of Rerum Novarum within Catholicism. Rev Soc Econ 49(4):444–464

Moody JN (1961) Leo XIII and the social crisis. In: Gargan ET (ed) Leo XIII and the modern world. Sheed & Ward, New York

Nuesse CJ (1985) Henry George and "Rerum novarum". Am J Econ Sociol 44(2):241–254

Rerum novarum and Its Principle on the Just Taxation of Immovable Properties

Francesco Forte, Flavio Felice and Elton Beqiraj

1 Introduction. Historical Background and Plan of the Paper

Cardinal Vincenzo Gioacchino Pecci (1810–1903) raised to the pontifical seat in 1878 with the name of Leo XIII. He rejected his predecessor's refusal to undertake a reconciliation with the liberal culture, deciding to revive the dialogue with the contemporary world.[1] To this end, he pursued a new balance between faith and reason, between *new things* and tradition. On May 15, 1891, in the tenth year of his pontificate, Leo promulgated the first social encyclical letter. This document was titled RN, and has served as the "Magna Carta" of Catholic social thought.[2]

RN was published in a context of intense de-Christianisation. For example, the religious education had low levels of attendance. The Church seemed agonised, closed in itself and unable to coping with the social question deriving from the

[1]See the historical reconstruction of Catholic economic thought exposed by Almodovar and Texeira (2008, 62–87).

[2]As a matter of fact, *Rerum novarum* was published in Latin in instalments on the "Osservatore Romano", May 19, 20, 21 and the Italian translation only on the 23rd. The process of elaboration of the document has been deeply analysed by Misner (1991, 444–464).

F. Forte (✉) · E. Beqiraj
Department of Economics and Law, La Sapienza University of Rome, Rome, Italy
e-mail: micros.ricerche@vodafone.it

E. Beqiraj
e-mail: elton.beqiraj@gmail.com

F. Felice
Department of Humanistic, Social and Educational Sciences,
University of Molise, Campobasso, Italy
e-mail: felice@tocqueville-acton.org

J. Backhaus et al. (eds.), *On the Economic Significance of the Catholic Social Doctrine*, The European Heritage in Economics and the Social Sciences 19, DOI 10.1007/978-3-319-52545-7_11

second industrial revolution and the process of industrialisation and urbanisation of Europe.

In this context, the encyclical had a great twofold effect: attracting the attention of politicians and intellectuals worldwide and promoting the birth and the development of social movements.[3] The Catholics constituted associations of workers and entrepreneurs as well as cooperatives, rural banks and political parties.

We organize the first two parts of the paper as follows. The first[4] focuses on RN's theoretical background, whereas the second to the controversy between RN's and Henry George's property rights conceptions, with a special reference to the taxation of immovable property.

2 Theoretical Backgrounds of *Rerum novarum*[5]

2.1 The Precedents

Even if RN was the first encyclical letter prevalently dedicated to social-economic topics, it was not a "first work" because it had many connections to previous experiences in France, Germany, Great Britain and Italy. In France, from a practical point of view see, for example, the experience of the "Saint Joseph Society" for young manual workers (that was dissolved in 1830) and that of the "Saint Nicholas Society" that set up the first professional school in Paris. From a theoretical point of view, see Albano de Villeneuve-Bargemont's (1784–1850) 1834 work titled *Grand Triaté d'economie politique chrétienne*: *Économie politique chrétienne, ou recherches sur la nature et les causes du paupérisme en France et à l'étranger et sur les moyens de le soulager et de le prévenir.*[6] Here, he exposed the deep degradation of factories' workers and the possible remedies. On the other hand, Hughes-Félicité-Robert de Lamennais (182–1854), Jean-Baptiste Henri Lacordaire (1802–18619) and Charles Forbes Renè Count of Montalembert (1810–1870)[7] and

[3]The Italian experience was emblematic. In fact, the solution to the Roman question had brought Catholics to opt out of Catholic practical life. Indeed, *Rerum novarum* triggered civil involvement in political movements that peaked in 1919 with the foundation of the Italian People's Party by Sicilian priest don Luigi Sturzo.

[4]Contributed by Flavio Felice and Francesco Forte.

[5]See Charrier (2012).

[6]http://gallica.bnf.fr/ark:/12148/bpt6k86392c/f4.image.

[7]H.F.R. Lamennais and J.B.H. Lacordaire priests, philosophers and political activists in 1830 founded *L'Ami de l'Ordre*, precursor of *L'Avenir*, whose motto was "Dieu et la Liberté!" ("God and Liberty"). The Journal advocated an enlarged suffrage, separation of the Church and of the state, freedom of conscience, freedom of the press and of the instruction, new rights for the free associations and for the local administrations. The Journal criticized the "high industrialist barons who arbitrarily set wages". From 1835, Lacordaire delivered from the Notre Dame pulpit his famous "Conferences" that will turn him into a pioneer in the field of social doctrine. C.F.R. Count of Montalembert who was from 1835 member of the Chamber of the Peers, by right on inheritance

Frédéric Ozanam (1813–1853)[8] contributed to the debate according to a so-called "ultramontanist" perspective.

In Germany, a young priest, subsequently bishop, William Emanuel, baron von Ketteler (1811–1887), awakened Germany's social conscience with an anti-Marxist positive view of market economy, private property and free socially oriented associations.[9] In the United States, Cardinal James Gibbons (1834–1921) advocated the protection of labour and the promotion of the participation of Catholic workers to the labour unions. Gibbon had a key role in defending the private property rights from the sort of nationalisation of the Henry George's "land rent".[10] In the United Kingdom, Cardinal Henry Manning (1808–1922) advanced strong statements to defend the property rights. In Italy, Antonio Rosmini Serbati (1787–1855), Luigi Taparelli D'Azeglio (1793–1862) and Matteo Liberatore (1810–1892) discussed

---

(Footnote 7 continued)

was the main political and ideological supporter of the freedom of education principle of the Catholic liberal French Ultramontanism.

[8]F. Ozanam, founder of the Charity Association San Vincenzo De Paoli, during his period became professor of foreign literature at the Sorbonne University, for his researches on Dante, on the German middle literature and other contributions. He had aimed to demonstrate that the Catholic Church had been the most potent factor in civilizing the invading barbarians. According to him, the Catholic intellectuals of that epoch exerted a positive important role for the development of the modern culture. Friend of Lacordaire, he shared his ideas of freedom and democracy, concentrating on the social problem of poverty of the working class. He started a newspaper, *The New Era*, dedicated to securing justice for the poor and the working classes. Referring to the poor man as "the nation's priest", Ozanam said that the hunger and sweat of the poor formed a sacrifice that could redeem the people's humanity. "The problem that divides men and women in our day is … whether society will be only a great exploitation to the profit of the strongest or a consecration of each individual for the good of all and especially for the protection of the weak. There are a great many men and women who have too much and who wish to have more; a great many others do not have enough, have nothing, and are willing to take, if someone gives to them. Between these two classes of men, a confrontation is coming, and this menacing confrontation will be terrible: on the one side, the power of gold, on the other the power of despair. We must cast ourselves between these two enemy armies, if not to prevent, at least to deaden the shock. And our youth and our mediocrity does not make our role of mediators easier than our title of Christian makes us responsible".

[9]See in this symposium Eissrich (2016), "An economist view of the work of Wilhelm Emmanuel von Ketteler and its influence on the Encyclical Rerum novarum" and §1.2 below.

[10]According to US historian of the George Mason University Leonard Liggio the controversy between Cardinal Gibbon and Henry George catholic followers of his proposal of immovable property taxation of "land rent" was at the basis of the strong stand on the private property rights by "*Rerum novarum*". Liggio writes "Henry George's answer, or more precisely his dialogue with Leo XIII, in his *Open Letter*, was a continuation of a long debate between them, mainly through the hierarchy of North America's Catholic Church. This debate has been the background and cause of *Rerum novarum*" in and again: "To meet the American bishops' request of a public stand of Roman Catholic doctrine on private property in general, with specific reference to the works of Henry George, the Holy See presented the papal encyclical Rerum novarum". See Liggio (2003). See the paper in the Italian version, in Antiseri (2005, 496 and 519–520).

the topic from different perspectives. Let us thus consider five paramount figures: Rosmini, Ketteler, Manning, Taparelli D'Azeglio and Liberatore.[11]

2.2 *Antonio Rosmini Serbati*

Rosmini was born in Rovereto, which is a town situated in the Region of Trento then belonging to the Austrian Empire. He was a priest coming from a rich family, whose entire heritage he gave to charitable activities. He was educated in Domodossola, which is a town in Piedmont. Here, he founded a new religious order called *Istituto della Carità*. Rosmini was an eminent philosopher, jurist and political scientist. However, Pope Pius IX put Rosmini's main works on politics and on the political and economic constitution in the Index of forbidden publications. But Pope Leo XIII fully rehabilitated the orthodoxy of Rosmini liberal thought. In 2007, Pope Benedict XVI declared him blessed. In Rosmini's thought, which presents many similarities with that of Friedrich von Hayek and of Ordo,[12] the free human persons endowed with moral value are the central actors of the economy. They are not perfectly rational machines but human beings characterised by emotions, sentiments, ideals and values. In Rosmini's view, one can adequately understand human beings only through the analysis of their attempt of finding the truth. Somehow anticipating Hayekian assertions, Rosmini conceived knowledge as something imperfect, partial and unpredictable because human persons are essentially social, i.e. are by nature, *spiritually* "in society with God" and *empirically* in society with the other persons. As the person is "the first seat of freedom", property is the synonym of freedom itself. "Juridical freedom means nothing but the power that the person-proprietor has over his own thing, with which he can morally do what he pleases". Property represents an entirely *personal* principle, involving *consciousness*: "self" must exist before "his" can exist. In Rosmini's opinion, the act of *appropriation*, which is the human act of acquiring external ownership, is typical of the human person.

"Property—he writes in his philosophy of law—is a sphere around the person; in this sphere nobody else can enter". Thus, "property is the principle of derivation of any juridical right and duty". As humans are imperfect, their political societies cannot be "perfect" as Hayek will later point out. In Rosmini's opinion, the improvement of the spontaneous social order takes place by the free social actions of the person. However, a legal constitution has to regulate the spontaneous order. Its main task is that of assuring a *social justice* primarily based on liberty, property

[11]For an analysis of the natural law social economics movement see Sandonà (2013, 797–808).

[12]This presentation of A. Rosmini thought with particular regard to property rights owe much to Mingardi (2004, 63–97). With the bibliography of the works of Rosmini relevant for the theme of property rights. On the theme of the tax principles of Rosmini, see Hoevel (2007, 67–84). On the similarities of Rosmini philosophical, juridical and economic thought and those of Hayek and Ordo see Antiseri et al. (2011) on Rosmini in general see Muratore (2007).

rights and responsible labour. Consequently, the state is in function of the persons, who maintain their individuality even when they are associated in the intermediary bodies and in the whole society.

Rosmini Serbati (1996) maintains it is not true that property legitimation lies in the existence of civil society. On the contrary, the civil society is legitimate insofar as it does not harm the properties of the human people. Rosmini legitimates the original appropriation of things, differently from Locke, by considering the *purposefulness* of the action. Therefore, Rosmini takes a strong stand against the idea that private property rights (or any other right or duty) is the outcome of a social contract. The idea of an explicit consent given by all people at the beginning of civil society is an empty hypothesis and a vain pipedream. The idea of a tacit consent, capable of creating agreed rights, is also entirely imaginary. In fact, "Before appropriation, things must not be thought of belonging to everybody; in fact, they belong to no one". As the state is in function of the persons, such collective activities as education and social assistance should be, preferentially, in the private sector.

Then, Rosmini believes that the payment of taxes has an intimate tie with the free decision of people to participate and finance the society. However, justice would require taxes had to burden their beneficiaries. This means avoiding the mistake of "wrongly making citizens pay a tax of which they will never take advantage" or "making all pay for a few". People must know the benefit coming from a tax. The policymaker should assume citizens agree to pay taxes for having this benefit.

The taxes should not fall simply on capital but "on capital multiplied by work": that is on the citizens' capital and personal incomes. Therefore, the good taxes are, generally speaking, income taxes, following the principle that "all properties share the burden of the state in proportion to their income". However, the workers must be free from any tax, if we cannot assume that they earn more than what is necessary for their survival.

2.3 William Emanuel, Baron von Ketteler

Von Ketteler was born in Westphalia from an aristocratic family. After he became bishop of Main, he approached the labour question (Von Kettler 1864) according to an anti-Marxist perspective. Ketteler based his critique to Marx on previous serious studies he had made in Bavaria and Hesse (Novak 1984; Dougherty 1985; Janz 1998). Like Mark, Ketteler acknowledged the labour exploitation deriving from the free competition among the people migrating from the country to the town. However, differently from Marx, Ketteler did not support the class struggle, the abolition of the private property and the state bureaucratic centralisation of the process of decision-making. Ketteler identified the problem in the *abuse* of the private property: or a private property that does not is an instrument for the increase of productivity. Ketteler said, "Communism is a sin against nature" because it attacks the property right, which (a) is the only instrument to secure good management; (b) it alone can successfully respond to market conditions; and (c) private property is more likely to generate peace. By charity, man more fully participates in the divine nature. However, moral solutions are not enough. In an assembly of German bishops at Fulda, in September 1869, bishop Von Ketteler proposed these remedies: prohibition of child labour in factories; limitation of working hours in factories; separation of the sexes in works; legal regulation of working hours; obligation of caring for workmen not voluntarily unemployed; a law protecting and favouring cooperative associations of workers; state factory inspectors. In his book on the Labour Question and Christianity, he blames liberal free market economics with its unrestricted, unlimited competition for supply among workers for their misery, agreeing with Lasalle. In the same time, he expresses his reservations about guild and proposed charitable institutions for destitute workers, Christian family life and morals, true Christian education, and producers' cooperatives funded by wealthy Catholics.

Carl Marx read the book of Ketteler and reacted to it in a letter to Engels of 1868. Here, he defined Ketteler as a dog who flirts with the labour question when it suits to his purposes. In the unfinished book titled "Christianity and Social Democracy" Ketteler argues that many of the proposals of the Gotha Program of the German Social Democratic Party are justified. Stressing the need of state legislation against the exploitation of workers, he stressed the idea of a participation of the workers to the profits of the enterprises. One other end, he warns against the new slavery that would derive from "a working state" resulting from the property nationalization.

2.4 Edward Manning

Manning was an Anglican priest that converted to Catholicism in 1851. He became the Cardinal Archbishop of Westminster. In that position, he advocated for the workers' right to organise trade unions in order to improve their working conditions, such as the level of wages, the number of working hours and the quality of workplaces.

In his 1877 lecture titled "Dignity and Rights of Labour" originally held at the Leeds University, Manning quoted Adam Smith in support of his argument that "the property which every man has in his own labour is of all forms of property the most sacred and inviolable." However, differently from Smith, Manning concluded that whatever rights capital possesses, labour possesses in the same degree. In general, he highlighted the primacy of the moral natural law over economic dynamics (Lisska 2012, 745–786). As the material goods are constitutively at the service of humankind, they have to remain instruments for human development and not to become the final goals of human activity. A similar statement appeared in RN one year later. It is reasonable to assume that Manning had influence on that. In his analysis of the encyclical published in the *Dublin Review* in July 1891, he pointed the novelties of the new social and economic scenario; for example, to abolish guilds, without replacing them by different institution. In this way workers became isolated and defenceless in an unrestrained labour market competition. On the other hand, Manning did not deny the value of a properly regulated competition.

2.5 *Luigi Taparelli d'Azeglio*

Luigi Taparelli d'Azeglio,[13] from 1833 professor of Natural Law in Palermo was an admirer of the liberal catholic philosopher Antonio Rosmini (Gray 1920, 1–16). This is an important point in the interpretation of Taparelli D'Azeglio principles adopted in *Rerum novarum*, of "social justice", of subsidiarity and of "polyarchical" conception of Governments, from the local to the supranational ones, anticipating the theory of Club Governments, which owe much to Antonio Rosmini liberal philosophy and economics.[14]

Taparelli D'Azeglio, in his main work "Theoretical essay of a natural law based on facts",[15] applies to the social question a concept social justice, based on merits and responsibility (Burke 2010) tempered by charity adopted by *Rerum novarum*, much similar to that of the Rosmini.[16]

This principle of "social justice" do as follow the principle of polyarchy, as plurality of private and public authorities at various level, local, regional, national and multinational and that of "hypotaxis", which translated in Latin is

[13]See especially Antiseri (2010) and Heritier (2015, 1076–1078) Luigi Taparelli D'Azeglio (brother of the more known writer, painter and liberal patriot Massimo D'Azeglio, one of the main figure of the Italian Risorgimento) studied in Turin Seminar and entered in the Jesuit Company. Subsequently he was appointed Dean of the Roman College (now Gregorian University) and he reintroduced "Thomism" in the curriculum of the School.

[14]See Bher (2003, 99–115), writes "Taparelli argued, other than the most elemental ones—such as the family or simple partnerships—are always composed of other societies. The natural and just relationships between the myriad of associations that human beings tend to form, ranging from the family to the State and beyond, he groups under the heading of 'Hypotactic Right.' Relatively smaller societies are called 'deutarchie,' or 'secondary' while the relatively larger, relatively more perfect or autonomous, societies, epitomized in the nation State, are 'protarchie,' or 'primary' societies. Beyond the nation State there is the association, or brotherhood, of independent peoples, called the 'etnarchia.'"

[15]In Italian: *Saggio teoretico di diritto naturale appoggiato sul fatto.*

[16]Thomas Beher actually maintains that social Justice, according to Taparelli D'Azeglio, consists only formally Saint Thomas' concept of "a legal order and normative ideal within a society". In Taparelli D'Azeglio's view of society "individuals and their various associations are given the maximum range of liberty […] with a minimum of interference from superior authorities […] governed by the principles of conflicting rights, prudence, and, ultimately, of charity". See Bher (2013). The similarity with Rosmini theory above described, strictly liberal in the European political meaning of the word is evident.

subsidiarity[17] (Hypo is "sub" and "taxis" means "response" to a need). It was obvious for Nell Breuning, the extensors of the Encyclical "Quadragesimo Anno" of Pope Pius XI who had been a student of Matteo Liberatore (Burke 2010) and recommended, as fundamental, the book of Taparelli on the Natural Law, to adopt his "hypotaxis" principle, as "subsidiarity".[18] The concept of polyarchy in connection with subsidiarity is clearly present in *Rerum novarum*.

In 1860, Luigi Taparelli D'Azeglio in three long papers on the Jesuits Review "La Civiltà Cattolica", entitled "Freedom in economics",[19] presents the idea of a Christian economics based on the supremacy of "order" rather than interest. This "order", based on the facts of reality, is "the natural order" (an Ordo in the sense of Eucken Ordo theory). In the "Order" human individuals are "persons" with the natural duty of earning the life by labour in the late sense of the word, the natural rights to property to freely earn the fruits of that labour and the natural right to a social life forming own associations, as, primarily the family, with ownership of own immovable property.

"Leaving full freedom to the human passions, a regulatory center shall emerge, formed by the most powerful stock exchanges and from the most accredited banks which shall rule with their rods wage rates, sales, currencies, credit, and even the sort of empires, depending from the stock exchange players. Do you want to call this serfdom as economic freedom?".

Firmly opposed to private monopolies, Taparelli's doctrine was similarly against the omnipotent State. "In Catholic doctrine the State is ordered to the goodness of the person, in the heterodox view it is sacrificed to the goodness of the big State, rich, powerful, independent while most people shall be poor, abject, oppressed". The Unions of workers have an important role, as well as both the monopoly of the labour force by the Unions against the capitalists and of the capitalists against the workers are unacceptable.

---

[17]Bher (2003, 106), writes "The word *ipotattico* draws from the rules of Greek grammar, *hypotaxis*, which governs the modalities of coordination between clauses, specifically, the arrangement of inferior clauses within the functioning of the whole sentence. It was an excellent extension into the neologism *dritto ipotattico* to convey the rights of social groupings, within their just relationships, organized toward the common good. The principles he elaborates in this regard have found their place, though indirectly and imperfectly, in Catholic social doctrine, known as the "principle of subsidiarity," first explicitly used by Pius XI in the social encyclical, *Quadragesimo Anno*. Indeed, one may render the Greek *hypo taxis* directly in Latin as *sub sedeo*. The Latin expression *subsidia* applied, then, not just to mean "help", but in the first instance to auxiliary troops within the Roman legion, as they "sat below" ready in reserve to support the battle. The "help" in this context is from the bottom up, not from the top down, as the inferior and mediating groups all participate in achieving the common good of the more perfected association. While Taparelli uses the legion as an analogy for society in various contexts, the rights and obligations derived from the laws of subsidiarity vary according to a host of historical considerations and competing rights and obligations".

[18]See also Mc Kinely Brennan (2013).

[19]In Italian: "*La libertà in economia*", in "La Civiltà Cattolica", 1860, VIII, 33–53; 159–174; 414–433). Subsequently, translated in French, the papers have been collected in a volume titled *Essai sur les principes philosophiques de l'Économie politique*.

"One must obey to the free market principle only when economic freedom it is linked essentially with the moral order". This is the absolute necessary basis of any true social freedom: those who want to get freedom without law erect a building without foundations.

Law and Ethics must coincide. Thus, "the happiness of a society does not depend so much from the degree of political power of the mass of people (on which somebody insists so much!), but from the wisdom of the civil laws and from the right administration of justice: reasonably, indeed, because from the end one assesses the means".[20] In other words, political freedom of democracy is not necessary nor sufficient to a "good Government", but economic freedom is necessary to follow the laws of "Order".

As Paolo Heritier observes (Heritier 2010), the conception of Order of Taparelli D'Azeglio appears objectionable, and is now unacceptable, because a "rule liberalism" under a constitution, does imply democracy.[21] Obviously, also in Rosmini liberal theory democracy also essential. However, Rosmini refuses the majority rule and is in favor of a qualified majority, in which property rights have a role in order to avoid the possible exploitation of the property owners by a majority without properties. However, as Heritier maintains, Taparelli D'Azeglio appears a liberal thinker as for the freedom of the individuals in the market and civil life.

2.6 Matteo Liberatore

Matteo Liberatore was a Jesuit who cofound the review *La Civiltà Cattolica* in collaboration with his teacher Taparelli in 1850. Libertatore served as the ghost-writer of RN. As he wrote a book on the principles of economics, Liberatore's expertise was very useful in the writing of the encyclical letter because he clarified the interdependence between labour, capital and the private property right. As Alejandro Chaufen observes (Chafuen 2003, 247–268), Liberatore was a sort of anticipator of the Austrian school of economics. In fact, he maintained the private property rendered the workers the true owners of the fruits of their labour. In this way, they increased the sense of responsibility of their duties in the society and at home. In Liberatore's opinion, the respect of the private property principle secured peace and an abundant production as well as it helped the people to move away from poverty. In this perspective, Liberatore criticised the thesis according to which the private property right is a *jus gentium* because it could create some misunderstandings if one has not clear the fact that the *jus gentium* derives from the moral natural law. Thus, he argued that it was better to use an expression more easily understood, such as that of "natural right".

---

[20]The following quotations are from the papers of Taparelli on the economic freedom.

[21]It reflects the fears of Conservatives of that time that the extension of the voting rights to the masses and, more generally, to any other elector, in the area in which the kings had power, could erode the political status of the Church.

According to Liberatore, the state has the right to regulate but not abolish or limit the private property. Even if there was a consensus among all the nations, it would not possible to justify the abolition or substantial limitation of private property. An echo of Rosmini argumentation emerges here. According to Liberatore, the inheritance right and the property right go together, because the owners of the property also have the right over its fruits.

The governments (state, provinces and municipalities) could apply taxes for accomplishing their functions at the service of the community (see Liberatore 1889, Chap. 3, §3, Articles I, II, III, IV; Sturzo 1979). However, Liberatore conceived the legitimation of the taxes because of their relationship with the benefits that the public authorities provide to the taxpayers. He did not accept a distributive function of the taxes. Here again, there is an echo of Rosmini constitutional principles of just taxation.

As for the issue of the accumulation of much property, Liberatore's was that "those who do not put their happiness on things" or may strive for wealth. Besides helping them to have the comforts of life "which assuredly are not forbidden by any divine precept" and besides enabling them to the duty of providing for their children, the property of a wealth may be an instrument for the practice of many virtues, as the support of the needy persons, and collective private initiatives of social nature.

Anyway, Liberatore accepted that the state's intervention that was aimed at protecting the weak people. This did not mean that the state could monopolise the charitable activities. Liberatore firmly denied this monopoly because "it is not only an offense to the rights of the founders but they are also an atrocious affront to the poor that it pretends to protect. It harms them, not only because the state takes a large portion of what belongs to the poor to pay for its employee [...], but also because it dries the fountain of generosity. It takes away from the citizens the freedom of employing their own wealth in charitable activities, when they distrust the state and its bureaucrats" Finally, Liberatore was in favour to a minimum wage of the working activity, a regulation of the number of working hours (maximum ten a day) and the abolition of the under thirteen years old children's work.

3 Property Rights in *Rerum novarum* and the Controversy with Henry George[22]

3.1 The Debate in the US Catholic Community on Property Rights and Its Taxation Before the Rerum novarum, *as One of the Backgrounds of* Rerum novarum

According to Leonard Liggio,[23] the long debate in North American Catholic community was the background and the cause of *Rerum novarum*. Even if this

[22]This part is done by Felice and Forte.

[23]See Liggio, already quoted; De Rosa (1991).

proposition appears as an over statement, it opens a very important perspective on *Rerum novarum's* background and its present relevance.

The controversy between the American bishops and Henry George, leader of the political movement in favour of land's taxation, was very important for North American Catholics. In fact, the US bishops made frequent appeals for having several statements from the Holy See on the conception of the immovable property as an inviolable right. This position was on the opposite of Henry George's thesis.

Liggio noted the American bishops were increasingly interested to real estate purchase and management because they wanted to provide appropriate locations for the churches, schools and hospitals before the prices of land rose. The bishops were, therefore, in strict relations with savings banks and mortgage holders. They participated to "the struggles and the risks of acquiring land and income to support orphanages and schools: a story of capitalist heroism". The bishops thought Henry George's theory of taxation of land rent was wrong, because the assessment of the value of land fabricated or for fabrication depended on from the people's incomes and savings as well as those of the enterprises and the owners. Thus, the immovable property principle diffused a competitive market economy of the land for fabrication. In turns, this phenomenon had a positive impact for the generality of people.

However, Henry George's *Progress and Poverty* was gaining popularity in American Irish Catholic circles of workers, especially within the new wave of immigration. Edward McGlynn, who was a pastor of St. Stephen's Catholic Church, a well know speaker and social leader, promoted this economic view. On which, Cardinal Simeoni, who was the prefect of the congregation for the Propagation of the Faith, wrote to Cardinal McCloskey, Archbishop of New York; that McGlynn's statements were contrary to the teachings of the Church as they formed a socialist attack on the inviolability of the private property. Cardinal McCloskey gained Father McGlynn's agreement not to make further public addresses on the land tax. Nevertheless, McGlynn campaigned for Henry George's candidacy for mayor of New York in the fall of 1886. Archbishop Corrigan removed McGlynn from his pastorate of St. Stephen's Catholic church, by quoting from Leo XIII's encyclical letter *Quod apostolici muneris* (December, 1878). Here, Leo affirmed the violation of the right of private property is against the natural law.

Therefore, Corrigan's Pastoral Letter and the removal of Father McGlynn created a strong attention on this topic by the Holy See. In May 1887, the American Cardinal Gibbons discussed the Henry George position, visiting Henry Cardinal Manning, Archibishop of Westminster, in London. In this meeting, Gibbons and Manning opposed the idea of placing the writings of Henry George on the Index of Forbidden Books because that would give them the importance that they did not deserve and might lead to increased popularity of the books. Together with Bishop Corrigan, they pressed the Roman Curia until 1890 for a more public demonstration of the Catholic teaching on the right of the private property.

3.2 Rerum novarum *Strong Stand Against Discriminatory Taxes on Immovable Property*

Rerum novarum focused on the property rights, with a special reference to the immovable property. The document distinguishes the pertinence of this right to humans as social beings, contrasting with the animals. In fact, humans work in order to get the fruits of their labour not only by consuming them, as the animals do, but also to own and freely dispose of them. The private property is a right of every individual necessary to realise his/her own rightful aspirations to achieve independence, to form a family, to provide to his present and future needs and to those of his family as well as to accomplish social actions in the interest of the common good. An echo of Rosmini resounds in the text of *Rerum novarum* when it sates, "Man precedes the State, and possesses, prior to the formation of any State, the right of providing for the substance of his body. The law, therefore, should favour ownership, and its policy should be to induce as many people as possible to become owners".

Therefore, *Rerum novarum* condemned socialism in its broader meaning of collective property system (Ward 1968, 363–370). This economic view was against the natural justice, the principles of freedom and the common sense (Leo XIII 1891, n. 11). The encyclical also strongly criticized the injustices affecting the countries that undertake the path of free capitalist market system.[24] However, while it suggested reforming capitalism, it totally rejected socialism (Solari 2010, 87–113).

Leo XIII concluded the first chapter of *Rerum novarum* titled "*Socialism, a false remedy*" with a Rosminian statement *as* follows. "The main tenet of socialism, community of goods, must be utterly rejected, since it only injures those whom it would seem meant to benefit, is directly contrary to the natural rights of mankind, and would introduce confusion and disorder into the commonweal" (Leo XIII 1891, n. 14).

On the other hand, given the important benefits of diffusion of private properties, the State (in the late sense of the word) had to avoid to burden them by a differential taxation. The property right derives from nature, not from man; the State has the right to control its use in the interests of the common good alone, but by no means to absorb it yet. The State would therefore be unjust and cruel if under the name of taxation it deprives the private owner of more than is fair. Here, it is again easy to see that the encyclical actually followed the principles of just taxation of Antonio Rosmini, whose systematic treatment of them was likely the only available.

According to same author (see in particular Costa 2010, 235–262), the theory of the Encyclical of property rights as natural rights is contradictory because is founded on labour and not on occupation of land. It is inadvertently Lockean because it is justified the labour on the property, *which in itself belongs to everybody*. These authors argue that the Encyclical merely adopted a common sense idea

[24]In the Italian language, due to the influence exerted by Benedetto Croce, "economic liberalism" goes under the name of "Liberism".

of property, then popular. One may observe that it may be true that the conception of the Encyclical corresponds to common sense idea of property. Nevertheless, the Encyclical theory has good theoretical roots in the Roman law. In the tradition of the Roman law from Gaius to Justinianum, all natural goods are *res nullius* before their occupation.

Both Gaius and Justinianum' code defined them as *res nullius* because of the universal recognition of this principle. *Rerum novarum* did consider the private property as a law of nature for the humans, because it adopted the principle that property was a natural attribute of human individuals as *persons,* endowed with an intrinsic moral value differently from the mere animals. The encyclical also applied this principle to deny that labour was a commodity as well as to stand against the workers' exploitation. This is actually the theory of the private property rights of Antonio Rosmini who significantly influenced the *Rerum novarum's* framework, even if Matteo Liberatore had criticized Rosmini's theory because it would have implied a dangerous subjectivism. On the other hand, Pope Leo officially condemned forty propositions of Rosmini as contrary to the Church. In the *The Five wounds of the Church* Rosmini criticised the Vatican bureaucrat powers, in "A *Plan of a Constitution according to Social justice*" he proposed a Constitution Court, not the Church, as the supreme judge about the conformity of the state laws to justice. Leo XIII's critique to Rosmini had nothing to do with his conception of private property, which does not appear at all in contrast with that of Saint Thomas. Rather it represents a logical evolution of it.

3.3 Henry George Reaction to Rerum novarum *Propositions Against Discriminatory Taxes on Immovable Property*

Henry George argued that the *Rerum novarum's* strong position on the property right had been set forth to combat his proposal of a differential taxation of the rents of land.[25] However, he was partially wrong because *Rerum novarum* had asserted the need to respect the natural law of property rights without denying that when the property received a particular differential benefit from a public expenditure for it, there was a case for a special tax, to cover the cost of that expenditure. George was asserting not only that the tax on the rents of land should cover the costs of generating them by public expenditures. The tax should absorb the entire rent, making possible to exonerate the beneficiaries of other public expenditures from paying the costs of them.

[25]See on this theme Tideman (2016), "The Justice and economics of Rerum Novarum on Land" in this Symposium. This section of our paper has greatly benefited from the discussion with N. Tideman in the Symposium.

Henry George was unable to perceive the difference between taxes to pay the cost of the benefits of public services, distributed on all the beneficiaries in relation to the costs, and taxes that absorb all the benefits of some class of beneficiaries of public services exonerating the others. Thus, George replied to Leo XIII with an open letter. He expressed his consensus on *Rerum novarum's* statement that labour deserved its fruits not only with its remuneration but also with the full possession of the property right. At the same time, he communicated his strong dissent on the *Rerum novarum's* conclusion on property taxation because it would be contradictory. However, there was no contradiction because the *Rerum novarum's* principle of just taxation foresaw the possibility of taxing for covering the cost of the public services but did not admit a redistributive role of taxation. George wrongly confused Ricardian rents deriving from the fertility of the land or of the sea with urban rents deriving from the external economies of the development of the town and from public expenditures paid with fees (e.g. water supply). These last give a general benefit to resident, visitors and real estate owners. George assumed that these rents like those coming from the intrinsic fertility of the land were a gift by the nature. His reasoning, in the "Open letter to Leo XIII", run as follows.

"Being created individuals, with individual wants and powers, men are individually entitled to the use of their own powers and the enjoyment of the results. There thus arises, anterior to human law, and deriving its validity from the law of God, a right of private ownership in things produced by labour [...]. This right of property [...] originating in the right of the individual to himself, attaches to things produced by labour, but cannot attach to things created by God. Thus, if a man take a fish from the ocean he acquires a right of property in that fish, which exclusive right he may transfer by sale or gift. But he cannot obtain a similar right of property in the ocean, so that he may sell it or give it or forbid others to use it. [...]. Or, if he cultivate grain he acquires a right of property in the grain his labour brings forth. But he cannot obtain a similar right of property in the sun which ripened it or the soil on which it grew [...]. For a man who out of the proceeds of his labour is obliged to pay another man for the use of ocean or air or sunshine or soil, all of which are to men involved in the single term land, is in this deprived of his rightful property and thus robbed."

From this basic theorem, Henry George and his subsequent followers deducted the proposal of "leaving land in the private possession of individuals, with full liberty on their part to give, sell or bequeath it". It was useful to apply a tax that shall equal the annual value of the land itself, independently of the use made of it or the improvements on it.

George's thesis was taxing annually these unearned rents. In this way, one could abolish any other tax, and still he/she managed to provide the resources to the necessary public services. However, this ideas was wrong at that time because, as Henry George recognised, because of the population growth and the civilisation progress, it occurred the functions of the state increased. Consequently, there was the necessity of increasing revenues to finance this public expenditure.

In *Rerum novarum's* view- as noted above- the taxes had to cover the costs of public services. For *Rerum novarum* these costs, when of general character, as those mentioned by George, should be paid by every beneficiary in relation to their incomes, without any exclusion. In any event, Leo XIII did not change his proposition about the iron law of the respect of property right in the human order and about the damages that Government may do with discriminatory taxes on them (Schwarzman 1994).

But Henry George thesis about the tax on urban property "unearned" rent as a good tax is still actual, as it is often considered as a ground not only of specific taxes on the costs of specific public services to urban properties, but also a good reason for the taxation of urban property in addition to the general income taxation. In particular, OECD quarters and the European Union Commission have recently suggested that reducing taxes on labour and increasing the taxes on immovable property improves economic growth (Arnold 2008; Johansson et al. 2008; Arnold et al. 2011, 59–80; E.U. COMMISSION 2012, 4). Other researches seem reach conclusions that support the RN position (Summers 1981, 533; Kneller et al. 2009, 74, 171–190; Angelopulos et al. 2006, 1615–1660; Arnold et al. 2011; Arnold et al. 2011, but not significant Xing 2011).[26]

4 Econometric Research on Effects on Immovable Property Taxes on GD OECD Countries 1965–2013[27]

4.1 Econometric Research on the OECD Countries

In this third Part of the paper, we present an econometric research on the OECD countries. We have first considered all the 34 OECD countries,[28] then the 21 EU countries of OECD, then the 10 Eurozone countries plus Sweden[29] and—finally—the 6 Anglo Saxon (Anglos) countries.[30]

[26]Xing (2012, 379–382) finds that the shift to taxes on financial assets favors growth or is less damaging than income taxation or labor income taxation. A shift to immovable property damages growth.

[27]This Part has been done by Elton Beqiraj and Francesco Forte.

[28]The 34 OECD countries are Australia, Austria, Belgium, Canada, Chile, Check Republic, Denmark, Estonia, Finland, France, Germany, Greece, Hungary, Iceland, Ireland, Israel, Italy, Japan, Korea, Luxembourg, Mexico, Netherland, New Zeeland, Poland, Portugal, Slovakia, Slovenia, Spain, Sweden, Switzerland, Turkey, UK, USA, Norway.

[29]The 21 EU countries are Austria, Belgium, Check Republic, Denmark, Estonia, Finland, France, Germany, Greece, Hungary, Iceland, Ireland, Italy Luxembourg, Netherland, Poland, Portugal, Spain, Sweden, Switzerland, UK, Norway The 11 The Eurozone countries here considered are Austria, Belgium, Finland, France, Germany, Greece, Ireland, Italy Netherland, Portugal, Spain. We have not considered Luxembourg, because too small.

[30]The 6 Anglo countries are Australia, Canada, Ireland Israel, New Zealand, USA.

We have regressed, with different estimators,[31] GDP growth rates and revenue/GDP ratios of the immovable recurrent and not recurrent property taxes, combined with total tax burden, taxes on incomes and profits and capital gains, personal income taxes, profit and capital gain taxes, social security contributions, consumption taxes, from 1965 to 2013.

The results as for the OECD countries as a whole are represented in Tables 1, 2, 3, 4, 5 and 6.

Starting with Immovable property taxes as main independent variable and aggregate fiscal burden and an "Anglo" dummy as control variable, we note a negative relation between recurrent immovable property taxes and GDP with a coefficients from −0.33 to −0.87. The aggregate fiscal burden too has a negative coefficient with GD Anglo is significant, as the constant.

Considering, then Immovable property taxes combined with aggregate income profits and capital gains, the results—as for recurrent immovable property taxes, tax burden, Anglo, constant—are similar to those of Table 1. Income and profit taxes have a positive coefficient of about 0.1.

Let us now consider Immovable property taxes coupled with personal income taxes, while the other variables remain the same as before. The negative coefficient for the tax on immovable property is −0.931, with the estimator HT. The relation of the personal income tax with GDP is not significant.

Now we turn to Immovable property taxes combined with profit and capital gain taxes.

With estimator FE, the negative coefficient of recurrent immovable property taxes in the relation with GDP is now −1.4 for the estimator FE. Firm taxes have a tiny negative coefficient of −0.001 with GD.

Combining Immovable property taxes with social security contributions, we find a negative coefficient of the relation between recurrent immovable property taxes and GDP ranging from −0.356 with POLS to 1.2 with FE.

Social security contributions, too, have negative coefficients with GDP; but they range from 0.046 with POLS to 0.451 with HT and are smaller than for the recurrent immovable property taxes also with the other two estimators.

Finally, we combine Immovable property taxes with consumption taxes. The negative coefficients of recurrent immovable property taxes with GDP are much smaller than in the previous tables, while the consumption taxes have a positive coefficient with GDP of about 0.12–0.24.

To sum up, the relation of the recurrent immovable property taxes and GDP is always negative, with coefficients that may be >1 while the coefficient of the relation of the income, profit and capital gain taxes may be positive, even if with modest coefficient. The negative coefficient of profit and capital gain taxes is only

---

[31] 1. POLS = OLS (Ordinary Least Square) "Pooled" Estimator 2. POLSR = POLS (Ordinary Least Square Pooled Estimator Robust to Hetero-scedasticity) 3. FE = Fixed Effects Panel Estimator 4. RE = Random Panel Effects Estimator and 5. HT = Hausman–Taylor Estimator.

Table 1 Economic growth and immovable property taxes

	POLS	POLSR	FE	RE	HT
Rec. tax imm. pro. rate	−0.329*** (0.12)	−0.329*** (0.10)	−1.421*** (0.46)	−0.660*** (0.22)	−0.870*** (0.25)
Nonrec. tax imm. pro. rate	−0.111 (0.42)	−0.111 (0.25)	0.001 (0.33)	−0.060 (0.30)	0.007 (0.42)
Total tax rate	−0.049*** (0.01)	−0.049*** (0.01)	−0.103** (0.03)	−0.073*** (0.02)	−0.113*** (0.03)
Anglo	0.909*** (0.29)	0.909*** (0.28)		1.342** (0.53)	1.456* (0.79)
Constant	4.515*** (0.34)	4.515*** (0.38)	7.342*** (0.99)	5.559*** (0.60)	7.026*** (0.83)
N. obs	1198	1198	1198	1198	1198
R2	0.036	0.036	0.016	0.035	
Adj. R2	0.033				
R. MSE	2.87	2.87			
F	11.28	11.78	10.52		

*$p < 0.1$, **$p < 0.05$, ***$p < 0.01$

Table 2 Economic growth, immovable property, and personal income, capital gains taxes

	POLS	POLSR	FE	RE	HT
Rec. tax imm. pro. rate	−0.326*** (0.12)	−0.326*** (0.11)	−1.328*** (0.46)	−0.662*** (0.22)	−0.820*** (0.25)
Nonrec. tax imm. pro. rate	−0.113 (0.42)	−0.113 (0.25)	0.034 (0.36)	−0.049 (0.31)	0.056 (0.43)
Per.l inc., profit and ca gains taxes	−0.005 (0.02)	−0.005 (0.02)	0.082 (0.10)	0.026 0.05	0.109** 0.06
Total tax rate	−0.047*** (0.01)	−0.047*** (0.01)	−0.138** (0.06)	−0.084*** (0.03)	−0.164*** (0.04)
Anglo	0.920*** (0.29)	0.920*** (0.29)		1.263** (0.53)	1.005 (0.81)
Constant	4.500*** (0.34)	4.500*** (0.38)	7.480*** (1.07)	5.629*** (0.66)	7.489*** (0.82)
N. obs	1198	1198	1198	1198	1198
R2	0.037	0.037	0.018	0.035	
Adj. R2	0.032				
R. MSE	2.87	2.87			
F	9.03	9.41	8.05		

*$p < 0.1$, **$p < 0.05$, ***$p < 0.01$

Table 3 Economic growth, immovable property, and personal income taxes

	POLS	POLSR	FE	RE	HT
Rec. tax imm. pro. rate	−0.340*** (0.11)	−0.340*** (0.11)	−1.482*** (0.45)	−0.646*** (0.23)	−0.931*** (0.25)
Nonrec. tax imm. pro. rate	−0.099 (0.42)	−0.099 (0.24)	−0.029 (0.33)	−0.072 (0.30)	−0.010 (0.42)
Personal income taxes	−0.026 (0.03)	−0.026 (0.02)	−0.080 (0.10)	−0.021 0.04	−0.003 0.06
Total tax rate	−0.035** (0.01)	−0.035** (0.01)	−0.075* (0.04)	−0.061** (0.02)	−0.103*** (0.03)
Anglo	1.036*** (0.29)	1.036*** (0.29)		1.401*** (0.54)	1.550* (0.82)
Constant	4.258*** (0.39)	4.258*** (0.43)	7.250*** (1.06)	5.325*** (0.62)	6.800*** (0.85)
N. obs	1124	1124	1124	1124	1124
R2	0.035	0.035	0.011	0.034	
Adj. R2	0.031				
R. MSE	2.81	2.81			
F	8.21	8.79	7.15		

$^*p < 0.1$, $^{**}p < 0.05$, $^{***}p < 0.01$

Table 4 Economic growth, immovable property, and profit and capital gains taxes

	POLS	POLSR	FE	RE	HT
Rec. tax imm. pro. rate	−0.336*** (0.11)	−0.336*** (0.11)	−1.432*** (0.46)	−0.695*** (0.23)	−0.888*** (0.24)
Nonrec. tax imm. pro. rate	−0.117 (0.42)	−0.117 (0.25)	−0.017 (0.34)	−0.062 (0.30)	−0.012 (0.42)
Tax firm rate	−0.001 (0.00)	−0.001** (0.00)	−0.001*** (0.00)	−0.001*** (0.00)	0.001 (0.00)
Total tax rate	−0.05*** (0.01)	−0.05*** (0.01)	−0.094*** (0.03)	−0.072*** (0.02)	−0.102*** (0.03)
Anglo	0.897*** (0.29)	0.897*** (0.28)		1.392** (0.53)	1.513 (0.77)
Constant	4.606*** (0.36)	4.606*** (0.39)	7.132*** (0.81)	5.566*** (0.61)	6.684*** (0.84)
N. obs	1158	1158	1158	1158	1158
R2	0.038	0.038	0.015	0.037	
Adj. R2	0.034				
R. MSE	2.83	2.83			
F	9.17	11.33	12.55		

$^*p < 0.1$, $^{**}p < 0.05$, $^{***}p < 0.01$

Table 5 Economic growth, immovable property taxes, and social security contribution

	POLS	POLSR	FE	RE	HT
Rec. tax imm. pro. rate	−0.356*** (0.12)	−0.356*** (0.11)	−1.193*** (0.40)	−0.740*** (0.19)	−1.205*** (0.29)
Nonrec. tax imm. pro. rate	−0.138 (0.42)	−0.138 (0.25)	−0.245 (0.37)	−0.129 (0.32)	−0.228 (0.42)
Social sec. contribution	−0.046** (0.02)	−0.046** (0.02)	−0.581*** (0.131)	−0.141*** (0.05)	−0.451*** 0.08
Total tax rate	−0.035*** (0.01)	−0.035*** (0.01)	0.073 (0.05)	−0.028 (0.03)	−0.051 (0.04)
Anglo	0.773*** (0.30)	0.773*** (0.29)		0.897 (0.57)	0.151 (1.30)
Constant	4.474*** (0.34)	4.474*** (0.38)	6.239*** (1.17)	5.441*** (0.67)	6.057*** (0.89)
N. obs	1198	1198	1198	1198	1198
R2	0.040	0.040	0.02	0.036	
Adj. R2	0.036				
R. MSE	2.87	2.87			
F	9.86	10.48	10.81		

$*p < 0.1$, $**p < 0.05$, $***p < 0.01$

Table 6 Economic growth, immovable property, and consumption taxes

	POLS	POLSR	FE	RE	HT
Immovable property tax Rate	−0.029 (0.06)	−0.029 (0.02)	−0.029*** (0.00)	−0.031*** (0.00)	−0.024 (0.06)
Consumption tax rate	0.121*** (0.03)	0.121*** (0.03)	0.221** (0.09)	0.160*** (0.05)	0.241*** (0.07)
Total tax rate	−0.084*** (0.01)	−0.084*** (0.01)	−0.194*** (0.04)	−0.121*** (0.02)	−0.190*** (0.03)
Anglo	0.481** (0.23)	0.481** (0.22)		0.419 (0.31)	0.300 (0.57)
Constant	4.089*** (0.35)	4.089*** (0.38)	6.605*** (1.04)	4.909*** (0.59)	6.238*** (0.71)
N. obs	1198	1198	1198	1198	1198
R2	0.042	0.041	0.038	0.041	
Adj. R2	0.038				
R. MSE	2.86	2.86			
F	12.96	14.55	14.86		

$*p < 0.1$, $**p < 0.05$, $***p < 0.01$

0.001 while that of social security contribution is important, but much smaller than that of the recurrent taxes on immovable property with all estimators.

The consumption taxes relation to GDP have a positive coefficient with a value that may arrive to +0.24. Notice that here the recurrent taxes on immovable property have negative coefficients substantially lower than those when they are combined with income, profit and capital gain taxes, likely because in this case their effect is not influenced by the effects of the other direct taxes that may fall on immovable property.

4.2 *Immovable Property Taxes as Main Independent Variable of EU Member Countries Belonging to OECD*

Let us now consider the 21 countries member of EU that belong to OECD and begin with:

Immovable property taxes as main independent variable and the aggregate fiscal burden and as control variable (Table 7).

We find negative coefficient of the recurrent taxes on immovable property; that may arrive close to −0.9. Non-recurrent taxes on immovable property now may have a negative coefficient with GDP of −0.27.

Taking Immovable property taxes coupled with aggregate taxes on income, profits and capital gains, we get results similar to those of Table 2 both for recurrent and not recurrent taxes on immovable property, while the relation of the income, profit and capital gain taxes to GDP is not significant (Table 8).

Coupling Immovable property taxes and personal income taxes, we find, as in the previous table, a negative relations of the immovable property taxes to GDP

Table 7 Economic growth and immovable property taxes

	POLS	POLSR	FE	RE
Rec. tax imm. pro. rate	−0.166 (0.13)	−0.166 (0.11)	−0.894** (0.36)	−0.352*** (0.11)
Nonrec. tax imm. pro. rate	−0.234 (0.43)	−0.234 (0.18)	0.271** (0.11)	0.012 (0.14)
Total tax rate	−0.075*** (0.02)	−0.075*** (0.02)	−0.142*** (0.03)	−0.105*** (0.02)
Constant	5.450*** (0.56)	5.450*** (0.67)	8.390*** (1.22)	6.681*** (0.76)
N. obs	695	695	695	695
R2	0.04	0.04	0.03	0.04
Adj. R2	0.04			
R. MSE	2.78	2.78		
F	9.31	7.35	12.82	

$^{*}p < 0.1$, $^{**}p < 0.05$, $^{***}p < 0.01$

Table 8 Economic growth, immovable property, and personal income, profit, capital gains taxes

	POLS	POLSR	FE	RE
Rec. tax imm. pro. rate	−0.172 (0.13)	−0.172 (0.11)	−0.752* (0.40)	−0.355*** (0.10)
Nonrec. tax imm. pro. rate	−0.212 (0.42)	−0.212 (0.18)	0.324*** (0.11)	0.065 (0.14)
Per.l inc., profit and ca gains taxes	0.027 (0.03)	0.027 (0.03)	0.098 (0.10)	0.054 (0.04)
Total tax rate	−0.092*** (0.02)	−0.092*** (0.02)	−0.190*** (0.06)	−0.136*** (0.03)
Constant	5.710*** (0.63)	5.710*** (0.74)	8.802*** (1.33)	7.167*** (0.79)
N. obs	695	695	695	695
R2	0.04	0.04	0.04	0.04
Adj. R2	0.03			
R. MSE	2.78	2.78		
F	7.19	5.65	10.36	

$^{*}p < 0.1$, $^{**}p < 0.05$, $^{***}p < 0.01$

Table 9 Economic growth, immovable property, and personal income taxes

	POLS	POLSR	FE	RE
Rec. tax imm. pro. rate	−0.169 (0.13)	−0.169 (0.11)	−0.929** (0.40)	−0.396*** (0.13)
Nonrec. tax imm. pro. rate	−0.214 (0.42)	−0.214 (0.19)	0.239** (0.11)	0.078 (0.13)
Personal income taxes	0.022 (0.03)	0.022 (0.02)	−0.026 (0.13)	0.035 (0.03)
Total tax rate	−0.085*** (0.02)	−0.085*** (0.02)	−0.123** (0.06)	−0.121*** (0.03)
Constant	5.577*** (0.67)	5.577*** (0.77)	8.006*** (1.29)	6.962*** (0.95)
N. obs	677	677	677	677
R2	0.03	0.03	0.03	0.03
Adj. R2	0.03			
R. MSE	2.75	2.75		
F	5.90	4.83	8.76	

$^{*}p < 0.1$, $^{**}p < 0.05$, $^{***}p < 0.01$

with similar values. Personal income taxes have no significant relation with GD (Table 9).

Considering Immovable property taxes and profit and capital gain taxes, the results confirm those of the previous tables with similar the negative coefficients. The taxes on firms have tiny negative coefficients similar to those of Table 4.

Let us now combine the Immovable property taxes with social security contributions (Table 10).

Table 10 Economic growth, immovable property, and firm taxes

	POLS	POLSR	FE	RE
Rec. tax imm. pro. rate	−0.168 (0.13)	−0.168 (0.11)	−0.897** (0.36)	−0.412*** (0.14)
Nonrec. tax imm. pro. rate	−0.234 (0.42)	−0.234 (0.19)	0.247** (0.10)	0.052 (0.13)
Tax firm rate	−0.001 (0.00)	−0.001* (0.00)	−0.001*** (0.00)	−0.001*** (0.00)
Total tax rate	−0.073*** (0.02)	−0.073*** (0.02)	−0.131*** (0.04)	−0.105*** (0.02)
Constant	5.340*** (0.60)	5.340*** (0.71)	8.022*** (1.26)	6.729*** (0.88)
N. obs	677	677	677	677
R2	0.03	0.03	0.03	0.03
Adj. R2	0.03			
R. MSE	2.75	2.75		
F	5.85	5.93	12.55	

$^{*}p < 0.1$, $^{**}p < 0.05$, $^{***}p < 0.01$

The results confirm the negative coefficients of the relation of recurrent immovable property taxes and GD. The regressions for not recurrent immovable property taxes are no more significant. Social security contributions have negative coefficients with GDP that reach a −0.442 value with FE estimator. However, with this estimator, the negative coefficient of the recurrent immovable property taxes is almost the double; and with the other estimators, the ratio between the negative coefficients of the two class of taxes is much greater (Table 11).

Finally, we couple the immovable property taxes with consumption taxes (Table 12).

One can notice the results are much similar to those of Table 6 relating to the entire OECD panel.

To sum up, the results for the EU confirm those of the OECD, plus a negative important relation of the not recurrent immovable property taxes and GPD: a result that may depend from the greater importance that these taxes have in many EU countries.

4.3 Immovable Property Taxes as Main Independent Variable in the "Old" Eurozone Countries

Let us now consider the 11 "old" Eurozone countries member of OECD beginning with Immovable property taxes as main independent variable and the aggregate fiscal burden as control variable.

Table 11 Economic growth, immovable property, and social security contribution taxes

	POLS	POLSR	FE	RE
Rec. tax imm. pro. rate	−0.241* (0.13)	−0.241** (0.12)	−0.813** (0.36)	−0.473*** (0.10)
NonRec. tax imm. pro. rate	−0.230 (0.42)	−0.230 (0.17)	0.098 (0.12)	0.015 (0.13)
Social sec. contribution	−0.065** (0.03)	−0.065*** (0.02)	−0.442*** (0.15)	−0.125** (0.06)
Total tax rate	−0.064*** (0.02)	−0.064*** (0.02)	−0.011 (0.06)	−0.078*** (0.03)
Constant	5.734*** (0.57)	5.734*** (0.69)	8.089*** (1.39)	7.100*** (0.74)
N. obs	695	695	695	695
R2	0.05	0.05	0.03	0.05
Adj. R2	0.04			
R. MSE	2.77	2.77		
F	8.48	6.86	8.09	

$^*p < 0.1$, $^{**}p < 0.05$, $^{***}p < 0.01$

Table 12 Economic growth, immovable property, and consumption taxes

	POLS	POLSR	FE	RE
Immovable property tax Rate	−0.025 (0.06)	−0.025 (0.02)	−0.030*** (0.01)	−0.028*** (0.00)
Consumption tax rate	0.177*** (0.05)	0.177*** (0.05)	0.179 (0.14)	0.185** (0.09)
Total tax rate	−0.115*** (0.02)	−0.115*** (0.02)	−0.208*** (0.04)	−0.155*** (0.03)
Constant	4.592*** (0.61)	4.592*** (0.67)	7.920*** (1.55)	5.971*** (0.72)
N. obs	695	695	695	695
R2	0.05	0.05	0.05	0.05
Adj. R2	0.05			
R. MSE	2.76	2.76		
F	12.40	11.35	12.81	

$^*p < 0.1$, $^{**}p < 0.05$, $^{***}p < 0.01$

The negative coefficient of the recurrent taxes on immovable property now reaches a level of −1.154 with the estimator FE, while that of not recurrent taxes on immovable property arrives to −3.06.

As for immovable property taxes and aggregate taxes on income, profits and capital gains, results confirm those of Table 13 as for immovable property taxation, while Income, profit and capital gain taxes show a positive non irrelevant relation with GDP, of about 0.13.

Coupling immovable property taxes and personal income taxes, we find that recurrent taxes on immovable property, under estimator FE have a negative coefficient of 1.4 while personal income taxes have a negative relation with GDP with a coefficient of −0.26.

As for immovable property taxes and firm taxes, the results confirm those of the previous table as for the immovable property recurrent taxation, with a coefficient of 0.9 under the estimator FE. Firm taxes give a positive contribution to GDP growth with coefficients ranging from 0.36 to 0.95.

We are now considering the immovable property taxes and the social security contributions.

The results confirm those of Tables 13, 14 and 15 as for the negative relation with GDP growth of taxes on immovable property. Social security contributions too, have a negative relation with GDP, but with coefficients much lower (Table 16).

Coupling immovable property taxes and consumption taxes, we find the negative relation of taxes on immovable property with GDP of the previous with similar high coefficients, while consumption taxes give a positive contribution to GDP growth with coefficients ranging from 0.2 to 0.4 (Table 17).

To sum up, as for EU, the negative relations of taxes on immovable property and GDP have coefficients higher than those of EU and OCSE, while among the taxes that have a positive relation with GDP there appear the taxes on profits and capital gains, with not irrelevant coefficients, together with the consumption taxes. Personal Income Taxes and Social Security Contributions have negative coefficients with GDP, with values much lower than those of the taxes on immovable property (Table 18).

Table 13 EZ economic growth and immovable property taxes

	POLS	POLSR	FE	RE
Rec. tax imm. pro. rate	−0.234 (0.25)	−0.234 (0.22)	−1.154*** (0.36)	−0.667** (0.31)
Nonrec. tax imm. pro. rate	−3.061** (1.53)	−3.061*** (1.19)	−0.164 (1.78)	−1.548* (0.85)
Total tax rate	−0.092*** (0.02)	−0.092*** (0.02)	−0.126*** (0.04)	−0.108*** (0.03)
Constant	6.137*** (0.70)	6.137*** (0.83)	7.800*** (1.22)	6.904*** (0.94)
N. obs	464	464	464	464
R2	0.06	0.06	0.05	0.06
R. MSE	2.64	2.64		
F	10.10	9.10	11.14	

$^{*}p < 0.1$, $^{**}p < 0.05$, $^{***}p < 0.01$

Table 14 EZ economic growth, immovable property, and personal income, profit, capital gains taxes

	POLS	POLSR	FE	RE
Rec. tax imm. pro. rate	0.088	0.088	−1.006*	−0.277
	(0.28)	(0.27)	(0.46)	(0.38)
Nonrec. tax imm. pro. rate	−3.103** (1.52)	−3.103** (1.21)	−0.085 (1.76)	−2.086*** (0.67)
Inc. prof. ca tax rate	0.132**	0.132**	0.131	0.111
Total tax rate	(0.05)	(0.06)	(0.11)	(0.11)
	−0.147*** (0.03)	−0.147*** (0.03)	−0.182** (0.06)	−0.149*** (0.06)
Constant	6.433*** (0.71)	6.433*** (0.84)	8.258*** (1.31)	6.912*** (0.89)
N. obs	464	464	464	464
R2	0.07	0.07	0.06	0.07
R. MSE	2.62	2.62		
F	9.16	8.08	9.01	

*$p < 0.1$, **$p < 0.05$, ***$p < 0.01$

Table 15 EZ economic growth, immovable property, and personal income taxes

	POLS	POLSR	FE	RE
Rec. tax imm. pro. rate	−0.210 (0.27)	−0.210 (0.27)	−1.396*** (0.41)	−0.919** (0.46)
Nonrec. tax imm. pro. rate	−3.086** (1.50)	−3.086*** (1.20)	−0.404 (1.55)	−1.335 (0.89)
Personal income tax rate	0.021 (0.06)	0.021 (0.06)	−0.262** (0.11)	−0.105 (0.10)
Total tax rate	−0.100*** (0.03)	−0.100*** (0.03)	−0.025 (0.06)	−0.065 (0.05)
Constant	6.253*** (0.79)	6.253*** (0.89)	6.673*** (1.35)	6.411*** (1.31)
N. obs	446	446	446	446
R2	0.06	0.06	0.03	0.04
R. MSE	2.59	2.59		
F	6.52	6.82	11.31	

*$p < 0.1$, **$p < 0.05$, ***$p < 0.01$

Table 16 Economic growth, immovable property, and firm taxes

	POLS	POLSR	FE	RE
Rec. tax imm. pro. rate	−0.066 (0.24)	−0.066 (0.21)	−0.912* (0.43)	−0.602 (0.37)
Nonrec. tax imm. pro. rate	−3.134** (1.47)	−3.134** (1.23)	0.110 (1.33)	−1.255** (0.62)
Firm taxes	0.359*** (0.09)	0.359*** (0.10)	0.947*** (0.14)	0.604*** (0.13)
Total tax rate	−0.106*** (0.02)	−0.106*** (0.02)	−0.213*** (0.04)	−0.149*** (0.03)
Constant	5.606*** (0.78)	5.606*** (0.84)	8.335*** (1.32)	6.725*** (1.05)
N. obs	446	446	446	446
R2	0.09	0.09	0.07	0.08
R. MSE	2.55	2.55		
F	10.18	8.43	31.44	

$*p < 0.1$, $**p < 0.05$, $***p < 0.01$

Table 17 EZ economic growth, immovable property, and social security contribution

	POLS	POLSR	FE	RE
Rec. tax imm. pro. rate	−0.133 (0.24)	−0.133 (0.21)	−1.235*** (0.38)	−0.398 (0.26)
Nonrec. tax imm. pro. rate	−2.690* (1.49)	−2.690** (1.05)	1.382 (1.145)	−2.240** (0.95)
Social security contribution	−0.215*** (0.05)	−0.215*** (0.05)	−0.592** (0.22)	−0.249*** (0.08)
Total tax rate	−0.010 (0.03)	−0.010 (0.03)	0.058 (0.07)	−0.011 (0.04)
Constant	5.589*** (0.69)	5.589*** (0.82)	7.987*** (1.62)	6.131*** (0.70)
N. obs	464	464	464	464
R2	0.11	0.11	0.10	0.10
R. MSE	2.58	2.58		
F	13.58	12.04	11.40	

$*p < 0.1$, $**p < 0.05$, $***p < 0.01$

4.4 Immovable Property Taxes as Main Independent Variable in the Anglo Saxon Countries

Let us then consider the Anglo Saxon countries (Anglos), with the same set of equations, applied to the three previous panels, starting with immovable property taxes as main independent variable and the aggregate fiscal burden as control variable.

Table 18 EZ economic growth, immovable property, and consumption taxes

	POLS	POLSR	FE	RE
Rec. tax imm. pro. rate	−0.255 (0.24)	−0.255 (0.21)	−1.291*** (0.35)	−0.744*** (0.24)
Nonrec. tax imm. pro. rate	−2.006 (1.54)	−2.006** (0.99)	−0.890 (1.30)	−1.452 (1.16)
Consumption taxes	0.193*** (0.06)	0.193*** (0.06)	0.399* (0.20)	0.260** (0.13)
Total tax rate	−0.128*** (0.02)	−0.128*** (0.03)	−0.211*** (0.05)	−0.158*** (0.03)
Constant	5.065*** (0.73)	5.065*** (0.86)	6.200*** (1.76)	5.654*** (0.82)
N. obs	464	464	464	464
R2	0.09	0.09	0.08	0.08
R. MSE	2.49	2.49		
F	9.97	8.53	13.38	

$^*p < 0.1$, $^{**}p < 0.05$, $^{***}p < 0.01$

Table 19 Anglos' economic growth and immovable property taxes

	POLS	POLSR	FE	RE
Rec. tax imm. pro. rate	−0.666*** (0.19)	−0.666*** (0.23)	−0.242 (0.15)	−0.507*** (0.05)
Nonrec. tax imm. pro. rate	−0.657 (2.08)	−0.657 (1.84)	−7.679*** (1.26)	−3.108* (1.88)
Total tax rate	0.044	0.044	0.091	0.063
	(0.05)	(0.05)	(0.06)	(0.06)
Constant	3.351**	3.351**	1.305	2.529*
	(1.49)	(1.32)	(1.80)	(1.52)
N. obs	211	211	211	211
R2	0.06	0.06	0.02	0.06
R. MSE	2.46	2.46		
F	4.62	3.10	37.64	

$^*p < 0.1$, $^{**}p < 0.05$, $^{***}p < 0.01$

Here too recurrent taxes on immovable property have a negative effect on GD The coefficient arrive to 0.666 with POLS and POLSR. Not recurrent property taxes have a negative coefficient that one may explained considering their extremely low level. The total tax rate has no more a negative relation with GD Very likely, the reason is that its level in this group of countries is very moderate.

We now consider immovable property taxes and aggregate direct income, capital gains and profit taxes.

The results as for the immovable property taxes are similar to those of Table 19, while there is a small negative effect of the income, profit and capital gain taxes of about 0.09 with estimator RE.

As for immovable property taxes combined with personal income taxes, the results confirm the previous ones as for the taxes on immovable property, while personal income taxes show a negative relation with GDP of smaller value.

We now consider immovable property taxes coupled with profit and capital gain taxes.

The results are similar to those of the previous tables as for the negative effect on GDP of the taxes on immovable property, while both the taxes on profits and capital gains and the total tax burden do not show a significant relation with GD.

We now consider immovable property taxes coupled with social security contributions.

Recurrent taxes on immovable property have a negative relation with GDP with coefficients similar to the ones of the previous tables. Not recurrent taxes on immovable property now do not have any significant relation with GDP growth. The same is now true as for the social security contributions, as well as for the total tax burden: likely because both are quite moderate.

Let us consider immovable property taxes coupled with consumption taxes.

The results confirm those of Tables 19, 20, 21 and 22 as for the taxation of immovable property. Consumption taxes have a positive impact on GDP of about 0.18, under Panel with Fixed Effect estimator. The total tax burden has no significant relation with GDP, as in most of the previous cases, relating to the Anglo Panel (Table 23).

Table 20 Anglos' economic growth, immovable property and personal income, profit, capital gains taxes

	POLS	POLSR	FE	RE
Rec. tax imm. pro. rate	−0.713*** (0.20)	−0.713*** (0.25)	−0.095 (0.38)	−0.713*** (0.09)
Nonrec. tax imm. pro. rate	0.272 (2.29)	0.272 (2.00)	−8.298** (2.44)	0.272 (1.59)
Per.l inc., profit and ca gains taxes	−0.092 (0.10)	−0.092 (0.10)	0.175 (0.27)	−0.092* (0.05)
Total tax rate	0.056 (0.05)	0.056 (0.05)	−0.002 (0.08)	0.056 (0.05)
Constant	4.271** (1.78)	4.271** (1.74)	1.420 (2.24)	4.271*** (1.45)
N. obs	211	211	211	211
R2	0.07	0.07	0.01	0.07
R. MSE	2.46	2.46		
F	3.69	2.33	48.30	

*$p < 0.1$, **$p < 0.05$, ***$p < 0.01$

Table 21 Anglos' economic growth, immovable property personal income taxes

	POLS	POLSR	FE	RE
Rec. tax imm. pro. rate	−0.771*** (0.20)	−0.771*** (0.25)	−0.524 (0.25)	−0.771*** (0.09)
Nonrec. tax imm. pro. rate	1.500 (2.32)	1.500 (2.01)	−4.858*** (0.98)	1.500 (1.66)
Personal income taxes	−0.269** (0.13)	−0.269** (0.13)	−0.396* (0.17)	−0.269*** (1.66)
Total tax rate	−0.077 (0.05)	−0.077 (0.05)	−0.263* (0.12)	0.077 (0.05)
Constant	5.269*** (1.76)	5.269*** (1.73)	0.786 (1.94)	5.269*** (1.79)
N. obs	211	211	211	211
R2	0.08	0.08	0.04	0.08
R. MSE	2.44	2.44		
F	4.53	2.52	30.73	

$^{*}p < 0.1$, $^{**}p < 0.05$, $^{***}p < 0.01$

Table 22 Anglos' economic growth, immovable property and firm taxes

	POLS	POLSR	FE	RE
Rec. tax imm. pro. rate	−0.650*** (0.19)	−0.650*** (0.23)	−0.179 (0.28)	−0.650*** (0.17)
Nonrec. tax imm. pro. rate	−0.942 (2.11)	−0.942 (1.83)	−5.925** (1.86)	−0.942 (1.70)
Firm taxes	0.140 (0.17)	0.140 (0.14)	0.490 (0.33)	0.140 (0.23)
Total tax rate	−0.042 (0.05)	0.042 (0.05)	0.045 (0.09)	0.042 (0.06)
Constant	2.952* (1.57)	2.952** (1.41)	0.984 (3.67)	2.952* (1.55)
N. obs	211	211	211	211
R2	0.07	0.07	0.03	0.07
R. MSE	2.46	2.46		
F	3.63	2.92	14.85	

$^{*}p < 0.1$, $^{**}p < 0.05$, $^{***}p < 0.01$

In conclusion, in Anglo panel too both the recurrent and not recurrent taxes on immovable property have important negative effect on GDP, as in the Eurozone Panel, but generally those of the recurrent taxes are less high and those of not recurrent taxes are higher. The effect on GDP of total tax burden, in most cases, is not significant, nor it is significant the effect on GDP of the social security contributions. Consumption taxes have a positive effect on GDP while personal income tax have a modest negative effect with coefficient much lower than those of the taxes on the immovable properties (Table 24).

Table 23 Anglos' economic growth, immovable property taxes and social security contribution

	POLS	POLSR	FE	RE
Rec. tax imm. pro. rate	−0.669*** (0.23)	−0.669** (0.31)	−0.750 (0.47)	−0.669*** (0.10)
Nonrec. tax imm. pro. rate	−0.647 (2.14)	−0.647 (1.89)	−1.322 (3.48)	0.647 (1.67)
Social security contribution	0.002 (0.09)	0.002 (0.10)	−1.453 (0.94)	0.002 (0.12)
Total tax rate	0.044 (0.05)	0.044 (0.05)	0.275 (0.19)	0.043 (0.06)
Constant	3.357** (1.53)	3.357** (1.41)	2.551 (2.56)	3.357** (1.50)
N. obs	211	211	211	211
R2	0.06	0.06	0.03	0.06
R. MSE	2.47	2.47		
F	3.45	3.19	8.76	

$^{*}p < 0.1$, $^{**}p < 0.05$, $^{***}p < 0.01$

Table 24 Anglos' economic growth and immovable property and consumption taxes

	POLS	POLSR	FE	RE
Rec. tax imm. pro. rate	−0.490* (0.27)	−0.490* (0.30)	−0.282 (0.21)	−0.490*** (0.12)
Nonrec. tax imm. pro. rate	−0.205 (2.13)	−0.205 (2.87)	−6.022*** (1.17)	−0.205 (1.52)
Consumption taxes	0.104 (0.11)	0.104 (0.10)	0.177** (0.06)	0.104 (0.07)
Total tax rate	−0.027 (0.09)	−0.027 (0.08)	0.031 (0.06)	−0.027 (0.07)
Constant	4.062** (1.68)	4.062*** (1.48)	1.421 (1.12)	4.062** (1.76)
N. obs	211	211	211	211
R2	0.07	0.07	0.04	0.07
R. MSE	2.46	2.46		
F	3.67	2.77	8.76	

$^{*}p < 0.1$, $^{**}p < 0.05$, $^{***}p < 0.01$

5 Concluding Remarks

The exam of the basic principles of the "RN" encyclical and of the thought on which has its foundations shows that its definition of Magna Charta of the Catholic Social Principles is fully justified. Its "third way" between a completely free market economy without any rule to assert competition and any care of the social questions about the workers, and an economy with a public sector prevailing on the market economy. A basic tenet of RN is that property rights are "natural rights" of the human beings, as persons free and responsible and their spontaneous societies and associations, which the governments must respect and aid to propagate, to protect the fruits of labour too. In this context, a controversy- obviously- emerged, on the immovable property taxation, between the "RN" stand and that of Henry George and his followers that argued that a general property tax on immovable property owners would be an optimal tax because generally falls on "unearned rent".

The regressions between the direct and indirect taxes on immovable property and GDP, and of the income and profit taxes, of the social security contributions and of the consumption taxes and GDP have been tested, using different estimator, as for the OECD countries, for the Eurozone countries and the "Anglo Saxon" OECD countries. The theory that the taxes on the immovable property are favorable to growth did not pass the tests of the empirical research. The likely explanation is that these general immovable property taxes cannot distinguish the "unearned" values from the others. In conclusion, RN principles on property rights and labour rights appear actual 125 years after its promulgation.

References

Almodovar A, Texeira P (2008) The ascent and decline of Catholic economic thought, 1830–1950s. Hist Polit Econ 40(5):62–87

Angelopulos K, Economides G, Kammas P (2006) Tax-spending policies and economic growth: theoretical predictions and evidence from the OECD. Eur J Polit Econ 23

Antiseri D (2005) Cattolici a difesa del mercato. In: Felice F (ed) Rubbettino, Soveria Mannelli

Antiseri D (2010) Il liberalismo cattolico italiano dal Risorgimento ai nostri giorni. Rubbettino, Soveria Mannelli

Antiseri D, Armellini P, Krienke M, Felice F, Muratore U (2011) Perché tornare a Rosmini—collection of papers, Libertas, Cattolici per la Libertà 1, June

Arnold J (2008) Do tax structures affect aggregate economic growth? OECD economic department working paper 643

Arnold J, Brys B, Heady C, Johasson Å, Schvellnus C, Vartia L (2011) Tax policy for economic recovery and growth. Econ J 121

Bher T (2003) Luigi Taparelli D'Azeglio, S.J. (1793–1862) and the development of scholastic natural-law thought as a science of society and politics. J Markets Morality 6(1):99–115

Bher CTh (2013) Luigi Taparelli on the dignity of man, Pontificia Accademia San Tommaso—Società Internazionale Tommaso d'Aquino, Congresso Tomista Internazionale. Rome, September 21–25 2003

Burke ThP (2010) The origine of social justice. Spring 52(2)

Chafuen A (2003) Austrian economics and the Social Doctrine of the Church: a reflection based on the economic writings of Mateo Liberatore and Oswald von Nell-Breuning. Journal des Economistes et des Etudes Humaines 13(2):247–268

Charrier R (2012) Jean Baptiste Loevenbruck (1795–1876). Missionaire de France et d'ailleurs compagnon de Rosmini et de Lieberman. Karthala Edition, Paris

Costa G (2010) La Rerum Novarum e Locke: un incontro non riuscito. Filosofia e Politica 2:235–262

De Rosa G (1991) L'enciclica nella corrispondenza dei vescovi con il Papa. In: Antonazzi G, De Rosa G (eds) L'Enciclica Rerum Novarum e il suo tempo. Edizioni di Storia e letteratura, Roma

Dougherty J (1985) Von Ketteler, Leo XIII and John Paul II on the social question, Crisis magazine. A voice for the faithful Catholic Laity Northeast Catholic College, 1 Apr

E.U. Commission (2012) Report on Public Finance in EMU

Gray C (1920) A. Rosmini e L. Taparelli d'Azeglio. Rivista Rosminiana 14(2):1–16

Heritier P (2010) Il personalismo liberale italiano cattolico nell'Italia del XIX secolo. In: Nomo, Petitot J (eds) Storia del liberalismo in Europa, Rubbettino, Soveria Mannelli

Heritier P (2015) Taparelli D'Azeglio Luigi. Dizionario del Liberalismo Italiano, II. Rubbettino, Soveria Mannelli, pp 1076–1078

Hoevel C (2007) The fiscal and tributary philosophy of Antonio Rosmini. J Markets Morality 10 (1):67–84

Janz DR (1998) World Christianity and Marxism. Oxford University Press, Oxford-New York

Johansson Å, Heady C, Arnold J, Brys B, Vartia L (2008) Tax and economic growth, OECD economic paper, n. 620

Kneller R, Bleaney MF, Gemmel N (2009) Fiscal policy and growth: evidence from OECD countries. J Pub Econ

Liberatore M (1889) Principi di economia politica. Tipografia A. Befani, Roma

Liggio L (2003) Henry George, private property and the American origins of Rerum Novarum. Journal des Economistes et des Etudes Humaines XIII(2):1–21

Lisska AJ (2012) Natural law and the Roman Catholic tradition: the importance of philosophical realism. Am J Econ Sociol 71(4):745–786

Mc Kinely Brennan T (2013) Subsidiarity in the tradition of the Catholic social justice. In: Evan ME, Zimmermann A (eds) Global perspectives on subsidiarity. Ius Gentium: Comp Perspect Law Justice 37

Mingardi A (2004) A sphere around the person: Antonio Rosmini on property. J Markets Morality 7(1):63–97

Misner P (1991) The predecessors of Rerum Novarum within Catholicism. Rev Soc Econ 49 (4):444–464

Muratore U (2007) Introduzione alla figura di Antonio Rosmini, with full bibliography, Stresa, Centro Internazionale di Studi Rosminiani

Novak M (1984) Freedom with justice: Catholic social thought and liberal institutions. Harper & Row, San Francisco

Rosmini Serbati A (1996) Philosophy of law, II, vol (trans: Cleary D, Watson T). Rosmini House, Durham

Sandonà L (2013) Once upon a time: the neo-Thomist natural law approach to social economics. Int J Soc Econ 40(9):797–808

Schwarzman J (1994) Henry George, Rerum Novarum and the controversy concerning private property in land. Robert Schalken Foundation, New York

Solari S (2010) The corporative third way in social Catholicism (1830–1918). Eur J Hist Econ Thought 17(1):87–113

Sturzo L (1979) Note di economia sociale aggiunte al corso del Liberatore [1900]. In: De Rosa G (ed) Id., La battaglia meridionalista. Laterza, Bari

Summers L (1981) Capital taxation and accumulation in a life cycle growth model. Am Econ Rev 71(4)

Von Kettler WE (1864) Die Arbeiterfrage und das Christenthum. Franz Kirchheim, Mainz

Ward J (1968) Leo XIII and socialism. Rev Polit 30(3)

Xing J (2011) Does tax structure affect economic growth? Empirical evidence from OECD countries, Oxford University for Business Taxation, working paper, 11/20

Xing J (2012) Tax structure and growth: how robust is the empirical evidence? Econ Lett 117

Practical Wisdom for Social Innovation. How Christian Entrepreneurs Triggered the Emergence of the Catholic Social Tradition in Europe

André Habisch

1 Introduction

"Catholic Social Thought—our best kept secret": this salient book title of Deberri (2003) and colleagues is even more appropriate on the Eastern (European) part of the Atlantic than it used to be true in the (American) West, where it originated. Catholic Social Thought is *our* (European) secret—in the sense that its influence on social and economic decision making in many European countries century has decisively framed living and working conditions during large parts of the 20th century. For example, the German labour law and professional education, which guarantees peaceful labour relations and low youth unemployment, owe themselves in large parts to politicians and administrators directly or indirectly inspired by Catholic Social Thought. Moreover, as Harvard Legal Historian Richard Berman (1983) has intriguingly shown, even large parts of the European Business Law ultimately originate in Christian concepts of man.

However, the second aspect also holds true: Catholic Social Thought is a *secret* tradition in the sense that neither their contents nor their protagonists are much remembered in contemporary Europe. Unfortunately, the National Socialist dictatorship was ultimately successful in darkening the collective memory of important Weimar republic protagonists. Moreover, the widespread characterization of the 1950ies as "lost" years of conservative backwardness and notorious persistence of Nazi elites has contributed to this development. They have deeply blurred the fact, that most important institutional and economic frameworks in Germany after the Second World War have been created and enacted during these year.

A. Habisch (✉)
Department of Ethics, Catholic University of Eichstätt-Ingolstadt, Eichstätt, Germany
e-mail: andre.habisch@ku.de

J. Backhaus et al. (eds.), *On the Economic Significance of the Catholic Social Doctrine*, The European Heritage in Economics and the Social Sciences 19, DOI 10.1007/978-3-319-52545-7_12

This article cannot elaborate the crucial role, which Catholic Social Thought did play during these years. However, as an indispensable precondition for that still pending challenge, it elaborates the emergence of the Catholic Social tradition in times of Industrialization as well as the role of spiritually enlightened entrepreneurs in the process. Pursuing that endeavour, it reconstructs nothing less than a basic reshaping of the Christian ethical tradition in times of Industrialization and modernisation, which was brought forward not by Bishops and Popes, but by "practically wise" lay people like entrepreneurs, politicians, functionaries, journalists, administrators, university professors and others.

Following recent historical research (Clark 2007), industrialization has to be understood as what it is: the most radical transition of socio-economic living conditions in Human history. The conceptual and practical critique on religion, which arose in the context of these revolutionary developments, represented a basic challenge for Christian thought leadership. It is against this challenge that the personal testimony and innovative practice of business persons like Léon Harmel (1829–1914) in France as well as Franz Brandts (1834–1914) in Germany has to be read and understood. These personalities paved the way for new concept of Christian "social" ethics—addressing not only individual behaviour but rather the creation of institutional frameworks in society.

In order to elaborate this argument, the essay is structured as follows: A first historical approach provides an overview on the pre-modern roots of the Jewish-Christian social justice tradition. The second chapter then characterizes modernisation as a basic cut in the social role which religion plays in the intellectual history of Europe. The third chapter elaborates the innovative leadership approaches of our key persons Léon Harmel and Franz Brandts. The last chapter then briefly sketches the Catholic Social thought tradition as it developed until today—and demonstrates how their basic principles influenced the practice of our entrepreneurs.

2 Origins of the Jewish-Christian Social Ethics Tradition

2.1 Jewish Tradition

The concept of social justice is deeply rooted in the origins of the Jewish-Christian religious and spiritual tradition. The figure of Abraham, whom the three monotheist religions call their "father in faith", is required to leave the traditional social order of his home town in order to head towards an alternative one, which could only be discovered and more clearly elaborated in an attitude of faith and openness towards God's promise. Israel's covenant with God is characterized by an inseparable connection between religious bonds as well as basic requirements of social justice. For God's chosen people, staying faithful towards His covenant necessarily implies to care for the poor, for widows, orphans and strangers (Ex 22, Dtn 24). On the contrary, if the poor have to live in misery, if entrusted power is abused and unjust laws are crafted, this regularly indicates that Israel has left God's path (Jes 1, Jer 5). The inseparable link between God's covenant and the practice of social justice (and social reform) is symbolized by the charismatic figures of the prophets, who keep themselves regularly apart from the political and economic elite. The prophet manifestly represents the critical attitude of the Jewish religious tradition towards the usual social injustices of the traditional political and economic order (Kletz et al. 2012).

2.2 Early Christian Tradition

In the context of the early Christians, the linkage between religious practice and social realities and is even strengthened and re-emphasized: Nobody can state that he loves God if he does hate his brother (1 Joh 4, 21); on the contrary, loving the neighbour and giving to those in need represents the Human answer to God's anteceding love. Therefore, the disciples of Jesus give and help because they sees Jesus in every needy person (Mt 25). This becomes tangible in the social practice of the first Christian communities in Jerusalem. New testament scriptures reports, that they practiced a community of property, in which the faithful continuously cared for each other (Acts 2, 45). In the context of traditional society, such a practice of continuous and extended solidarity, which also included strangers and reached out beyond the natural bonds of family and kin, clearly represents a rather revolutionary social innovation.

2.3 Abstinence of Political and Economic Activism

Interestingly enough the first symbol Jesus employed in his early public appearance is a genuine *social* one: the *kingdom* of God ("Basileia tou theou") (Jeremias 1971). This message clearly contained general principals social ethics. Having said this, however, it also has to be stated that within the early Christian doctrinal documents we do not encounter any genuine economic or political teachings. Thus, we do not find any statement concerning social rules or institutions, which would pretend to directly embody "God's will"; nor do we find any genuine "Christian" political or economic agenda developed. Certainly early Christian communities did not call for the crafting of certain "divine" political or economic institutions—comparable to the Sharia rules in the Islam tradition. Rather a differentiation between secular and religious order prevailed, which subsequently prevented both a politicization of faith and a clericalization of politics (Stegmann and Langhorst 2005, 688).

Finally, this political and economic abstinence of the early Christian moral tradition has to do with its eschatological character: Where God is felt so near that this earth seems to come to an end soon, there is no need to waste time and effort for reflecting about a worldly socio-economic order (Jeremias 1971). Moreover, until the closure of the biblical canon, early Christian communities represented social minorities, which in general did not hold any political or economic power. Therefore, they were neither inclined nor positioned to speculate about political or economic concepts.

2.4 Constantinian Shift and Monastic Influence

This only changed during the 4th century, when Christianity became first "religio licita" and later even grew into the official religion of the late Roman Empire. Connected to these developments, Christian church hierarchies and organizational structures step by step became part of the Governance system of late ancient Roman Empire. Therefore, it does not represent an occasional coincidence that early Monasteries emerged precisely during this period—keeping the spirit of social innovation alive among the Christian communities (e.g. Benedict from Nursia founding his community at Subiaco in the year 529 AD). From now on and during the subsequent medieval times, in the context of monastic communities Christian individuals used to live together in communities explicitly dedicated to God and renouncing to personal wealth and comfort. In the totally different context of a Christian Commonwealth, monastic life represents in itself a return to the separation between politics and economy from religious live. Moreover, many of these newly emerging communities were caring for the poor and the marginalised. Representing a social innovation itself, monastic life at the same time also provided multiple impulses for innovative social practices. For example, the Wisdom of Benedictine Governance rules has recently been elaborated (Inauen et al. 2010a, b; Rost et al. 2010; Galbraith and Galbraith 2004) and even the work ethics deserves attention (Tredget 2006; Chan et al. 2011). Moreover, as Harvard Law professor Berman (1983) has intriguingly shown, in early medieval times clerical lawyers constantly influenced the emerging Western legal tradition against personal dependence of poor labourers in the context of feudalist serfdom. Consequently, within their case law court practice, they continuously fostered contractual agreements and commercial law against the feudal hand and clamping services. Well educated but nevertheless without any personal possessions, these monkish judges represented something like the 'critical intellectuals' of medieval times. Finally, it has been Franciscan monks who with their conceptual work paved the way to overcome the ban on usury in medieval history—thus paving the way to the emergence of modern financial markets (Bazzichi 2008).

2.5 Medieval Monastery Influence

Other social innovations of the medieval society included the "*Montes Pietatis*", early forms of charity—and associational banking. They might be described as predecessors of today's microfinance associations. *Montes pietatis* were lending out to the poor and disadvantaged against a (modest) payment of interest. These social innovations were brought about by Franciscan monks, who took part in the "ordo Fratrum minorum", a foundation of St. Francis of Assisi (1181–1226), who—themselves coming from Noble descent—became the symbol of a "Church for the poor" during medieval times. Subsequently, Montes Pietatis developed into Saving banks and associative banks, which played a crucial role for the economic development of small cities and villages in many parts of (especially Western) Europe (Bruni and Smerilli 2008).

Moreover, even other monastic and lay Christian communities brought forward multiple social innovations by engaging for orphans and children from very poor families, caring for poor and homeless people, creating an education and living infrastructure for young journeymen (A. Kolping) and other disintegrated groups in the pre-modern society. Many genuine social developments of the Western civilization are closely linked to the Christian concept of man as being endowed with an indelible Human dignity. For example, this concept prevented a socially legitimate practice of infanticide, as it prevailed in China, the most advanced civilisation of pre-modern times (Clark 2007).

2.6 *Civilizing the First Globalisation*

Finally, Christian religious movements and teachings in many parts of the World also inspired social practices and policies. In this sense, Latin America was not discovered by Christopher Columbus but by Bartholome de Las Casas, the Dominican friar who fought for the Human Rights of indigenous people in the Spanish colonies during the 16th century. The colonial ethics of the School of Salamanca generalized these experiences and was very influential for universalizing social ethical standards during early Modern times (Melé 1999).

It goes without saying, however, that Christianity and Churches did not only generate or support movements of social innovation. Rather, the hierarchical Church represented a powerful governance structure of the pre-modern World. In European as well as colonialized countries, church hierarchies formed an important part of the ruling elite often suppressing social as well as economic innovations. Reactionary orientations in early modern times find themselves clearly expressed e.g. in the *Syllabus Errorum* of Pope Pius IX., which condemned the modern concept of human rights, democracy, political freedom etc. as lately as 1864. Thus, in many European countries, Christian churches were perceived as conservative and oppressive forces resisting social change and opposing economic development.

3 Industrialisation and the Rise of Modern Catholic Social Thought

3.1 Industrialization as a Radical Transition

As Stanford economic historian Clark (2007) has shown, the rise of the industrial age during the late 18th century in the United Kingdom and during the 19th century in many parts of Europe and North America represents the sharpest socio-economic transformation in the history of Human civilization. In the wake of that process, economic productivity and mean income per capita rose sharply in many countries but declined in others, which did not take part in the transition processes.

It by far exceeds the possibilities of this short intervention to discuss the multiple economic, political, cultural and intellectual consequences of this "modernization" process (for a more detailed presentation see the contributions in Habisch et al. 2013). For our purpose, we can limit ourselves to the enormous social and conceptual challenges, which modernization brought about for simple people and which in different forms called for social innovations. The industrialization and modernization represented—and still represents in many countries of the world—a radical transition of the living conditions not only for a tiny elite minority, but also for the majority of poorly trained simple labourers. It is true that during the decades of the modernization process, societies are able to increase their per capita income in an unprecedented way. At the same time, however, with the emergence of the industrial world, living and working conditions regularly undergo a complete change. Intellectual, social and cultural transformations accompany the economic ones. They revolutionize the way in which the daily program is structured (now governed by the necessities of industrial production), it transforms the family life (separation of labour from the private space, segregation of sexes, lack of child care), how one perceives oneself as an individual in society (social mobility and the importance of education), and the interaction mode within the family (individualization) as well as with other people (weak ties in a modern city instead of strong ties in village life). Moreover, especially at the very beginning of that process, labourers and their families regularly found themselves in a very challenging economic, social and also spiritual situation. Lacking access to basic social security institutions, economic and social insecurity and the inability to feel at home in this new urban environment characterizes their situation (Goldschmidt et al. 2014).

3.2 Social Romanticism

These challenging transition processes in Christian circles regularly used to raise a lot of critical objections and general skepticism. Many European observers during the 19th and early 20th century—lay people as well as clerics—critizised the development path towards industrialization, which in itself had threatened basic values in society. Contemporary philosophers, preachers and public intellectuals stood in principal opposition to the emerging system of market-based enterprises and industrialized production. For them, Christian values are converted authentically only if practiced in the traditional highly integrated social context. Consequently, in the perspective of these critics, those who wanted to stay faithful within the Christian tradition should themselves abstain from taking part in the social and economic life of the industrialized cities; rather they should remain in their traditional agriculture based rural Habitats. Therefore, we call the underlying concept of thought "Social Romanticism". Criticism even kept on when (with time passing-by) the socio-economic and cultural living standards in the industrial areas and cities clearly surpassed those of rural populations. Thus, the impression could incur that economic development and Christian spirituality were rather opposites. This tendency towards social romanticism has been precisely expressed by the public-law-teacher and conservative catholic Carl Schmitt: "A union of the Catholic Church with the contemporary form of capitalist industrialism is not possible. The connection between Throne and Altar will not be followed by a union between Office and Altar, between Factory and Altar." (Schmidt 1923, S. 50). In his view, theology and jurisprudence were focused on questions of truth while economics and engineering dealt with merely conventional topics. This statement resonated with the mindset of Christian intellectuals, who perceived contemporary problems as being rooted more in a crisis of faith and values rather than in structural or economic crises. Correspondingly they expected improvements to emerge rather from a reform of inner convictions ("Gesinnungsreform") than from the reform of external—i.e. political and economic—circumstances ("Zuständereform").

3.3 Secular Critics of Religion

An opposite reaction to the transition described above was secular critics of religion, which—albeit from very different positions—propagated new values for a new World. Leading intellectuals like Karl Marx, Friedrich Nietzsche, Sigmund Freud and others called for a Humanist and scientific critique of the religious tradition as well as a new era of secular and emancipatory values.

The rather influential concept of Eugenics may serve as an example of that kind of intellectual alternative to the traditional Western-Christian social ethical tradition. Eugenic authors like Sir Francis Galton (1822–1911) called for "scientifically justified" Social Ethical perspectives—referring to the theories of Galton's half-cousin Charles Darwin. Arguing in that direction, however, they followed a crude interpretation of Darwin's theory of evolution—perceiving competition and struggle for survival as a basic selection principle of the Human race. We can hold that Eugenic philosophers and scientists effectively left the Western Christian humanistic tradition behind. They did not start with a concept of the human person but rather perceived humans as substrate of a biological optimization processes. In a comparable way even the philosopher Friedrich Nietzsche and others decried

Christian Humanism and compassion as signs of weakness and distortion: "What is good? Anything that increases the feeling of power, the will to power, power itself in man. What is bad? Everything which comes from the weakness. The weak and wayward should perish: first principle of our philanthropy. And one should even help them to do so. What is more harmful than any vice? Pity indeed with all wayward and weak—Christianity…" (Nietzsche 1999, Kapitel 2). Considering the socio-economic background and the specific motivations of thought leaders like Galton, Nietzsche, Freud and others, it is no coincidence that all these authors perceived Christianity—and religion as a whole—merely as an obstacle to human development. In accordance with that most radical criticism, 19th century's Christian communities for the first time also witnessed the massive exit of non-elites from their rows—for example workers in the socialist and communist movements.

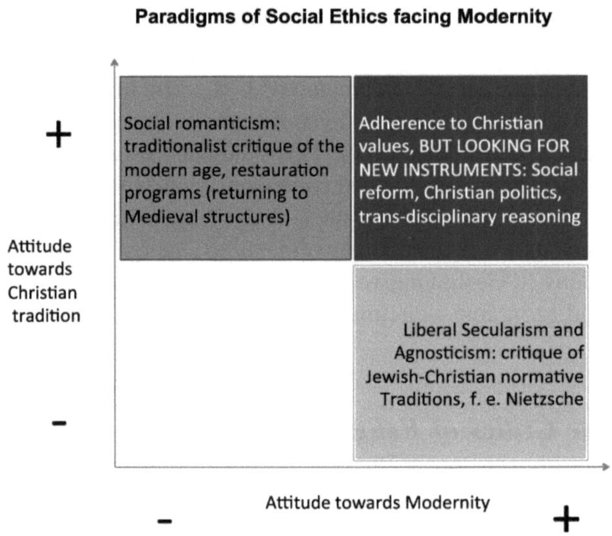

3.4 *Christian Entrepreneurs as Social and Cultural Innovators*

Our graph intends to map the resulting intellectual situation during the European industrialization. Inside of Christian communities, we find large groups of social romantics, who perceived newly emerging living conditions in sharp contrast with their own value traditions. On the other hand, we find secular thought leaders and influential scientists, who assume Western Christian traditions merely as an impediment to socio-economic progress, freedom and good life. In confrontation with both of these opposing intellectual currents, proponents of Catholic Social Thought still adhered to Christian values but at the same time also tried to actively frame the new living conditions of the emerging industrialized society out of that spirit. For that purpose, they strived to update the tradition—introducing new instruments of morality, new manifestations of faith life, etc. As "conservative innovators" (Habisch and Loza Adaui 2013), they Christian businesspersons played an import role as cultural mediators bridging the abyss, which had more and more opened up during the late 19th century (see Cornwall and Naughton 2003).

4 The Complex Role of Christian Entrepreneurs

4.1 Léon Harmel

Subsequently, two outstanding examples should be briefly sketched. The French textile entrepreneur Léon Harmel, born in 1829 at La Neuville-lès-Wasigny as a son of a wool entrepreneur, continuing his father's business at Val-des-Bois. In order to honour the social innovative endeavour of these men, a contemporary observer should keep in mind, that at that time no model or mental frame existed of how a "Christian entrepreneur" should look like. On the contrary, personalities like Harmel and Brandts—both very pious and intensely practicing Christians—had to find their own way towards Christian entrepreneurshi For example, following his moral intuition as a dedicated Christian, Harmel paid his workers a "family wage" (above the market level), installed a factory council to strengthen the worker's autonomy, created social capital around his company by empowering Catholic worker circles and Christian trade unions, appointed a factory chaplain and finally even started an ever increasing practice of workers' pilgrimages to Rome (Coffey and Harmel 2003). Particularly with the later type of activity Harmel started to develop a strong relationship to the Holy Sea—so that he was eventually even appointed "private chamberlain" of Pope Leo XIII (1878–1903). With the resulting continuous encounters, Harmel was able to create a strong emotional and cognitive bond between Catholic workers and the Roman pontiff; therefore, he rather indirectly but nevertheless substantially influenced the first Papal Social Encyclical *Rerum novarum* in 1891 and may with good reason be called a driving force behind the modern Catholic Social Thought tradition.

4.2 Franz Brandts: Life and Engagement[1]

On the other side of the French-German border, the textile entrepreneur Franz Brandts also grew up in a family of textile entrepreneurs at Gladbach. After years of education and helping out in his father's company, Brandts travelled to England in 1863 to learn more about the mechanic production techniques there. After his return

[1]This paragraph heavily relies on the publication Habisch and Loza Adaui (2011, 2012, 2013). The author thanks Cristian R. Loza Adaui who substantially contributed to this research.

to Gladbach in 1865 he convinced his father to give up the hand-weaving mill and to set up mechanical looms in the factory (Löhr 1979). As early as 1867 Franz Brandts was already one of the six entrepreneurial members of Gladbach's Chamber of Commerce who wanted to reduce the working day from more than 14 to just 12 h. Moreover, as an expression of his political responsibility he also decided to engage in the local city council of Gladbach, where he became a long-term member from 1871 until 1904. However, "neither his pioneer work as manufacturer or its local political activity would have make him famous beyond his native city if he would not have started already at a young age to care about the situation of the workers" (Löhr 1979, 92). Rather in 1872 Brandts finally left the father's company and started his own business. Right from the beginning he introduced a series of social innovations on the governance as well as operational level of his firm. Here, he was clearly inspired by Léon Harmel, whose photo was positioned on Brandts working desk.

Right from the beginning, the new Entrepreneur reduced the number of working hours in his factory to just 10, 25 compared with 11–14 at the competitors (Löhr 1974, 7). At the same time, however F. Brandts was also recognized for paying the highest wages in the city (Löhr 1979, 93). Moreover, he founded health funds with obligatory membership for every worker, installed family insurance funds and pension plans. For empowering and strengthening the personal responsibility and the general skills of his employees, he created a chapel onsite, a canteen and a sewing school, he founded an on-site music cclub, a library and saving clubs. All this was decided and implemented in the situation of fierce competition among enterprises with similar products, in which higher costs of course also result in higher prices. However, the corporate culture of solidarity and community (together with his family Brandts was even physically living amidst the workers), which resulted from these activities, also corresponded with a higher productivity and reputation of the company as an employer—effectively strengthening its economic position as well. Even if economic reasoning therefore might also have supported his decisions, it is important to see that Brandts himself never framed it that way. Rather he perceived his ample engagement as a goal in itself, which resulted from his responsibility as a dedicated Christian businessperson (Habisch and Loza Adaui 2012).

4.3 *The Corporate Level: Empowering Workers for Self-administration*

As already mentioned above, the social benefits for the workers inside of F. Brandt's factory were diverse. Documented in the "Fabrikordnung"—a kind of "constitutional" document of the new business enterprise—, the factory of Franz Brandts disposes even of a savings bank, a savings club, a kindergarten, a sewing school, a library and a music club with choir and orchestra (Löhr 1974). The employees could enjoy their lunch in a workers' restaurant, where even 86 extern workers were regularly served for just 25 pfennigs. Moreover, they could use a hospice with relaxation rooms as well as the garden and the park that where practically part of F. Brandts house (Löhr 1979, 93–94). In order to better understand the emancipative character of Brandts entrepreneurial practice, we have to analyze it in more detail. As seen above, Brandts created a health insurance fund for his workers to help them in case of sickness or necessity. Membership was obligatory for all workers of the company, who had to contribute 1–4 percent of their salary. Brandts added another 50% of the whole worker's contributions. As soon as a surplus resulted, the principal of the firm paid an interest on 5%. In case of sickness the workers received medical treatment, the cost of medicine and the half of their last four weeks' averaged income for a six-months-period (Löhr 1974, 1979; Puppke 1966, 274–275).

This practice was more or less in accordance with existing legal obligations at Gladbach. However, the obligatory character of the health and insurance funds (and of other activities) for Brandts also triggered the need to involve the employees themselves in the funds management. Here lies the heard of his social innovative practice: It lies in involving of the worker's community in the decision practice on funds expenses. The factory order ("Fabrikordnung") fixated the creation of a "Council of Elders", who was supposed to mediate between owner-entrepreneur and the workers, and to care about the worker's problems. The emancipative dynamic is manifest in the changing decision rules. Starting in 1880, the health insurance fund was managed by a board of 6 persons: 4 employees elected from the work force, the foreman and the owner-entrepreneur, who in case of election had two votes (Löhr 1979, 93). Thus, employees still held a majority vote in the fund management even in relationship to the owner-entrepreneur. Five years later, the Board now consisted of four representatives appointed from the company and eight representatives as assessors selected without the participation of the company but only from the voting members for 2 years. Moreover, the worker's committee ("Elders") of the company is involved in governing the welfare institutions of the factory (health insurance, saving club, library, kindergarten, canteen, sewing school, etc.) and in the supervision of the work order. Starting from that practice gradually a "worker's council" with co-determination rights emerged. The factory order adopted in 1885 guaranteed the workers personal responsibility and internal co-management. This emancipative institutional dynamics was indeed exceptional in an era, in which worker's benefits—if granted at all—were perceived as mere alms that fell from the patriarchal generosity of the entrepreneur.[2]

[2]Another study states that the "Fabrikordnung" of Franz Brandts is also a precursor experience of codetermination ("Mitbestimmung")—the integration of workers into the internal decision process of the firm (Puppke 1966, 271–276), which is integrated in German constitutional law.

4.4 Behavioral Rules

The social innovations of Brandts' factory aimed at increasing the social welfare of the workers. On the other hand, however, they were also accompanied by a set of rather strict behavioural regulations. For that purpose, the factory order of 1885 started with clear ethical orientations: "All supervisors have to be a model for their subordinates as far as morality and a religion is concerned" (Fabrikordnung 1885, § 1, 5, our own translation from German). Mockery of religion and morality as well as repeated scraps would induce immediate dismissal: "dissolute lifestyle, reckless debts and repeated drunkenness" had the same consequences (Fabrikordnung 1885, § 4, 6). Moreover, F. Brandts was also famous for his demanding sexual morality. Male and female labourers should be working separately if possible; moreover, illegitimate sexual relations were forbidden—even during leisure time and outside the factory (Fabrikordnung 1885, § 5, 6). From today's perspective, this regulation did indeed put major infringements on the private lives of workers. However, the precarious social situation of the workers should also be remembered, here. In a social context, in which any social security arrangement was completely lacking, an unwanted pregnancy could lead to serious economic problems especially for the unwed mother. Moreover, despite of these strict rules—or even because of them (?) —F. Brandts was revered as a father of his workers. He choose his private home directly among the residential complex of the workers. Moreover, a small Chapel was located at the centre of the small settlement, which had been constructed by F. Brandts out of his own personal expenses.

4.5 Beyond the Prototype Settlement: Mobilizing Social Networks in Germany

Obviously, Franz Brandts was not the first entrepreneurial person who was striving to make labour conditions more bearable for workers and their families. Rather tycoons like Alfred Krupp (1812–1887) served as role models for many others in that respect. However, Brandt's social engagement was not limited to his firm or to his activity as a local politician. Rather he was strongly involved in the creation of two of the most important emancipative Catholic workers organizations in Germany: "Arbeiterwohl" (1880) and the "Peoples League for Catholic Germany—Volksverein für das katholische Deutschland" (1890). When in 1880 the "Association of Catholic industrialists and worker friends Arbeiterwohl" was founded, the founding members choose Franz Brandts as a chairman. The main focus of this association should be the improvement of the situation of the working class. In 1888 nearly half (40) of the 99 representatives of the Catholic ("Center") Party in the German National Parliament were also members of that association. These included leading Catholic politicians like Ludwig Windthorst, the Centre Party Group chairman, August Reichensperger, co-founder of the party, Felix

Porsch, who later became Group President in the Prussian House of Representatives, Ernst Lieber, after the death of Windthorst the second group chairman of his party and the Social politician Christoph Moufang and Ferdinand Galen, who had formulated the first social policy request in the German Parlament in 1877. As the first secretary of the association, the young chaplain Franz Hitze was appointed. His academic studies at Rome dealt with the social question and he had moved from Rome to Moenchengladbach in 1880 in order to work with "Arbeiterwohl". Hitze later became the first professor of Christian Social Ethics at the University of Muenster/Westphalia in 1892.

At the Annual General Meetings of the Association "Arbeiterwohl" president Franz Brandt regularly held an opening address. From a historical point of view, the changing tenor of these annual speeches provides some vivid insights into the changing social ideas of the speaker. During the early years, Brandts still adhered to rather traditional social concepts. For example he believed that the social problems of workers could be solved by founding charitable organizations and by returning to a pre-industrial personal "morality". Later, however, Brandt increasingly emphasized the participation of workers themselves in the reform process and refused to subordinate them to a mere patriarchal tutelage. He called instead for respecting worker's "freedom and independence". Moreover, he also increasingly emphasized that the "moral uplift" of the workers, which was called for by conservative and clerical voices, should be complemented by a "material uplift" as well. In that sense, he stated that the social issue is closely related with socio-economic changes and even certain Entrepreneurial faults. Summing-up, according to the mature Franz Brandts, the social problem of the workers could not be solved with more education or moral preaching alone.[3]

4.6 *The People's League for the Catholic Germany*

While "Arbeiterwohl" beyond politicians and intellectual elites never succeeded to attract many working class members, the later was archived with the second association co-founded by Brandt: the "People's League for the Catholic Germany" ("Volksverein für das Katholische Deutschland"). The Franz Brandts company again financed large parts of its activities and consequently it's headquarter was established nearby at Gladbach. The objectives of the new organization were defined as follows:

> Confronting the revolutionary aspirations of the social democrats, promoting the social contract between workers and employers, offering social information and economic education through newspapers, pamphlets and to organize courses for Catholic associational functionaries, planning and leading mass meetings (Stegmann and Langhorst 2005).

[3]http://www.kas.de/wf/de/37.8053/, (22.11.16).

Serving as chairman of that larger association as well, Brandts enthusiastically supported its objectives. For that purpose the Entrepreneur even had to tolerate the opposition of fundamentalist circles and even some bishops, who generally distrusted any lay organization and publicly attacked him. Overall, however, until the year of Brandt's death (1914) the People's League grew up to more than 800,000 members mainly in Western Germany—a clear indicator of how prolific the underlying concept of a partnership between employers and employees effectively was. When in 1891 Pope Leo XIII announced the first social encyclical *Rerum novarum* dealing with the labour question, Brandt felt himself as being confirmed by his Church. He strongly agreed with the denial of the social democratic party and the moral admissibility of a governmental social policy. Consequently, he even wanted to see the principles "of the Holy Father in the labour question being set as a guiding star of the thinking and acting on the main issues of private and public life". With some time distance, his amazing civic engagement was finally honoured by the ruling elites as well. Even if the Protestant Prussian Government explicitly denied to confer the Catholic Brandts the honorary title "Kommerzienrat", in 1896 he received the rarely conferred Wilhelm medal for his social merits.

The importance of the Volksverein not only for Social Catholicism but also for democratic traditions in the western parts of Germany in the first half of the 20th century can hardly be overestimated. Activities included a grass-roots level Christian cultural engagement, which enriched the life of millions of simple workers and their families. The associational life of Social Catholicism (supported by educational and political materials produced by the Volksverein) enabled many Catholic workers to overcome widespread alienation and to resist the calls of Totalitarian voices from the Communist as well as the Nazi movement. Moreover as indicated above, "Arbeiterwohl" and "People's League" served as the civil society backbone of the Social Catholic "Centre party" and recruited many functionary elites of the Weimar republic—including the long term Labour Minister Heinrich Brauns, who laid the foundations of the German labour law (1920–1928).

4.7 *Franz Hitze*

Ethical visions play an important role for the success of any entrepreneurial innovation: social as well as economic. In the opposite direction, however, the social initiatives of Franz Brandts also (indirectly) supported the emergent tradition of academic catholic social thought in Germany. Two outstanding personalities from the People's league context especially represent this very important legacy of Brandt's activity: Franz Hitze for the academic and Heinrich Brauns for the social and labour policy development.

As mentioned above Franz Hitze started in 1880 to become the first secretary of Arbeiterwohl; ten years later in 1890, he also served as secretary and board member of the People's League for the Catholic Germany (both until his death 1921). Later in life, Hitze was elected member of the Parliaments of the Kingdom of Prussia

(1882–1893 and 1898–1912) as well as the German Empire (1884–1918 and 1920–21) for nearly 40 years. Moreover, after 1893 until his retirement in 1920 he also served as the first Professor of Christian Social Teaching at the University of Muenster. This unique combination of practical experience (resulting from his civic engagement) on the one hand and his involvement in parliamentary decision-making as well as academic teaching on the other, distinguished Hitze to become a crucial mediator of social political ideas in Germany. In 1883 he supported the centre party as an expert in the discussions on the draft for the Bismarckian statutory health insurance. Moreover, he was involved in the Parliamentary work on all social security laws. His particular point of interest, however, laid in the protection of workers. The Industrial Code of 1891 and its amendments owe a lot to the active participation of Hitze in the Parliamentary deliberations. The whole body of social legislation within the German Empire could not be conceived without the flexible and responsible negotiations of the speaker of the Centre Party. Moreover, after the First World War Hitze along with Heinrich Brauns represented the Centre Party in the negotiations of the social articles in the Constitutional Committee of the Weimar Republic National Assembly. Both were instrumental in the design of the Article 165 (workers' and economic councils) and prevented—together with other parliamentarians—that radical communist council ideas would be included in the council law of the 1920s (Gabriel and Große Kracht 2005).

4.8 Heinrich Brauns

Heinrich Brauns shares the fate of many Christian politicians of the 19th and 20th centuries: Their names are largely forgotten—even in the country of the social market economy, for which he became one of the most important predecessors. Yet Brauns was definitely one of the most prominent politicians of the German centre party and the leading figure of German labour and social politics during the Weimar Republic. Moreover, for decades Heinrich Brauns was closely connected with the history of the "People's Association for Catholic Germany".

Already during his pastoral service as a chaplain in Krefeld and as vicar in Essen-Borbeck, Brauns became familiar with the day-to-day problems of the workers and their families. Moreover, he provided active assistance in building Catholic worker associations. For example, together with August Brust he co-founded the Trade Union of Christian Miners (1894), which made him suspicious to be a "red Chaplain": a reason why Prussian authorities watched him very closely and recorded most of his speeches (Lingen 2000).

Since September 1900, Heinrich Brauns was on leave from his vicar office for health reasons serving as a "private clergyman" outside of the archbishop's authority. In that crucial moment of his life, Franz Hitze prompted Brauns' appointment as a research assistant at the central office of the People's League in Mönchengladbach.

Brauns dedicated himself with great devotion to the social education service of the "People's league". As a director, he organized and headed the economics courses, which aimed to train leaders for the Christian workers' movement. It was mainly due to his relentless effort that the People's Union experienced a rapid growth during these times. For 19 years he served as a crucial member of the management team—largely without being restricted by other commitments. However, through his work within the People's League, he came in close contact with the centre party and its leaders. Moreover, while still working in this position, from 1903 to 1905 Brauns came to study Economics and constitutional law at the Universities of Bonn and Freiburg and concluded his studies with a doctorate in economics.

With his integrative and intellectual positions, Brauns embodied the modern, social policy wing of the contemporary Catholic social movement. The concept of Solidarism, mainly developed by the Jesuit professor Heinrich Pesch, represented the driving force of Brauns' social work. Based on the Christian revelation, Christian Social ethics stresses to receive its power from religious practice and worship. Therefore, compared with all other ethical and humanitarian systems, Christian ethics seemed particularly suitable to grow the willingness for selfless altruism and sacrifice, by which alone class antagonisms could be bridged. Therefore and in accordance with the concept of solidarism, Brauns admonished unions and entrepreneurs repeatedly not to jeopardize state and economy (as basis of society) by exaggerating their financial claims. After the defeat in the First World War in 1919, Brauns entered the Weimar Republic National Assembly and subsequently became a member of the German Parliament (Reichstag) for the Catholic Centre party. Together with the workers' representatives of the Centre, he realized that in the changed political context of the Republic, the party in its old form would have no future and therefore should open itself up Consequently, in early November 1918, he proposed a democratic inter-denominational "Christian People's Party" (Christliche Volkspartei)—without success, however. Moreover, a decade later at the end the 1920s, even his second attempt to promote a new Christian People's Party, the so called "Brauns/Stegerwald project", failed.

In the National Assembly Brauns quickly came to enjoy a good reputation as a reflected and experienced social politician. Thus, it was not surprising that he was appointed as the first Imperial Minister of Labour in 1920. Heinrich Brauns uninterruptedly held this office for eight years—serving in twelve different cabinets during that time. So decisively did he coin the social policy of the Weimar Republic, that he was finally called "Henry the Eternal" and "most value stable minister". In a 1926 review of what had been achieved in the field of social policy during recent years, he named seven areas, in which substantial progress had been made: labour law, labour market policy, worker's protection, social security, welfare rights, utilities and housing and human settlements.

The record of Brauns' 8 years tenure is impressive. The Reichstag adopted more than 120 laws with social political content. Moreover, there were also about 300 regulations and official acts adopted directly by the Minister of Labour. Among the most notable were the regulation on the labour conciliation (1923), the Labour

Court Act (1926), the Law on Employment and Unemployment Insurance (1927), and the Imperial duty to care (1924). During his term as a Minister of Labour, Brauns' organizational talent came to full fruition. Right from the beginning he consciously assumed that only the core administrative work should be achieved in the central office (i.e. the Ministry of Labour), while everything else should be delegated to the subordinate authorities. This required an appropriate transfer of the decision-making and regulatory power as well as an appropriate redesign of the administrative units in a proper and efficient form. Affected were the Imperial insurance institution, the Imperial institution for employment, unemployment and some supply institutions.

The organisational model which was enforced by Heinrich Brauns represented a perfect example of applied subsidiarity—even if the concept as such was only introduced by the encyclical *Quadragesimo anno* in 1931. When Brauns in May 1928 fell prey to a political intrigue of his own party fellows and had to step down as a Minister of Labour, the German Labour and Social Law system was basically set. It is remarkable, that even his social democratic successor stated: "For Eight years, Dr. Braun held the leadership of the official German social policy in his strong hands. Eight years of life—and if we calculate with "performance years", it would probably be a multiple thereoff. When he took leave of us a few months ago, we had the impression that it is not just an office, but that he had left behind a life's work in our hands".

After his retirement as Minister of Labour, Brauns took over as head of the German delegation to the International Labour Conference in Geneva from 1929 to 1931. Subsequently he became the first German president of that institution in 1929. In 1931 the Heinrich Brüning government installed him as chairman of a commission to look for solutions to address unemployment, the "Brauns commission". Subsequently, he had many unauthorized suspicions and slanders to go through and was a defendant in the Nazi lawsuit again the People's league. The Nazi administration took away his passport and harassed him in multiple ways. In March 1933 Brauns was no longer appointed a candidate of his Centre party in the National Parliamentary elections. However, as a by-product of that outing, he also did not need to vote in favour of the fatal "Enabling Act" ("Ermächtigungsgesetz"), which paved the way for the Nazi dictatorship in summer 1933. On October 19, 1939 Heinrich Brauns died as a result of appendicitis in the hospital of Lindenberg.

4.9 The Role of the People's League in Crafting German Social Policy

With Franz Hitze and Heinrich Brauns, two leading German Social policy makers emerged from the work of People's league and their underlying social activity. However, the institutions and arrangements behind these men and the crucial role for their successful professional development is often neglected by modern historiography. Here, the Catholic entrepreneur Franz Brandts comes into play—including the multiple economic and social associations he founded. In his early theoretical elaborations about the Christian reorganization of the Company, the young Franz Hitze had still maintained rather medieval hearty ideas. Only when he turned to practical social work in the context of the association "Arbeiterwohl", Hitze's ideas approached pragmatic solutions of the burning social questions. Even for Heinrich Brauns, in the deep crisis he faced when health reasons forced him to retire from pastoral care in 1900, it was the People's League to provide him with a new framework to further develop his organizational knowledge as well as to pursue his academic studies in Economics and Constitutional law.

Recently, social historiography generally attributes social security reforms during in the German Empire exclusively to politicians. We came to interpret the emergence of social security during the 1890ies as a result of Chancellor Bismarck's aim to weaken social democrats and appease the growing labour movement. *This representation, however, ignores the crucial importance of shifting basic concepts, practical models and engaged politicians for political decision-making*. The social and economic entrepreneur Franz Brandts contributed substantially to the provision of all three important elements:

Shifting basic concepts: with his Catholic social thought concept of solidarity among classes, he laid the grounds to overcome the exploitation theory of Marx, Engels and others.

Practical models: with the innovative practices of his own Gladbach based textile company he implemented "best practice", which subsequently inspired social policy legislature. Thereby, his Christian values not only drove his own emancipative labour practices—framed by gratuitousness and a spirit of responsibility. Rather it also inspired his "Social Enterprise" People's League, which bettered the living conditions for catholic workers in early industrialized Germany.

Engaged politicians: The Economic and Social innovator Franz Brandts inspired reform minded politicians like Franz Hitze, Heinrich Brauns and others in an outstanding way. As seen above, these men later became drivers of crafting social political institutions in Germany during the first decades of the 20th century.

Summing-up, without the organizational skills and the visionary perspective of Franz Brandts the People's League would have never reached its decisive importance; nor could it have developed its emancipating dynamics for the workers and their families. Shortly after his death in 1914 the association lost much of its adaptability to a quickly changing social environment. Membership decreased and a new clerical leadership of the Volksverein slipped into a romantic anti-capitalism, which the successful Entrepreneur Brandts had always been keen to avoid (Baumgartner 1977). After the First World War, the People's League never regained its earlier strength.

5 The Emerging Tradition of Catholic Social Thought—As Realized in the Practice of Christian Entrepreneurs

Catholic entrepreneurs like Franz Brandts and Léon Harmel—together with politicians, union representatives, journalists, academic teachers etc.—became front-runners of the Catholic social thought tradition. They helped to spell out the Christian message even in the context of the completely new context of the modern industrialized society. Moreover, inspired by the Christian tradition they developed innovative social practices of "empowering" workers—for example by founding workers association of solidary but also by transferring important budgetary rights to them.

Experiences, testimonies and speeches of the Christian social movement stood in the background, when in 1891 Pope Leo XIII presented his first social encyclical *Rerum Novarum.* This was a rather innovative type of Church document, which discussed topics like the rights and duties of employers and workers, pledged against socialism, emphasized the dignity of the person with a special focus on workplace relationships, called for a joint striving for the common good, participation and solidarity, and weighed the right of private property against the universal destination of goods. As we know, with *Rerum novarum* Pope Leo XIII had only started a whole series of social encyclicals, in which the church continuously addressed contemporary social and economic issues. In 1931, Pope Pius XI. (*Quadragesimo anno*) entailed a justification of private property (against Marxism) and coined the term subsidiarity. During the 1960s, Pope John XXIII. in his *Pacem in terris* (1963) laid the emphasis on peace and relations between nations. Only 4 years later Paul VI. (*Populorum progressio*) focussed on global justice and development (1967). Pope John-Paul II. deeply impacted the social encyclical tradition with no less than three important documents: In *Laborem exercens* (1981) he depicted a (philosophically grounded) theology of labour and labour relations, in *Sollicitudo rei socialis* (1987) he dealt with issues of Global Justice thereby also mentioning the natural environment. In *Centesimus annus* (1991) he provided a reflection on the decline of socialism but also emphasized the flaws of the capitalist system. Again after a long silence, Benedict XVI. in his *Caritas in veritate* (2006) reflected the financialization and dehumanisation of companies, which became so obvious in the diverse crises of the young new century. Faced with a decay in global business culture, *Caritas in veritate* launched the topic of "gratuitousness" in business. However, Benedict did also not refrain from arguing also with new terms like corporate responsibility, socially responsible finance and investment and discussed topics of personal responsibility (like responsible consumption and live-style). Thus, the Pope emphasized the important role of civil society—calling for a new global social order and a transition towards a socially responsible globalisation (Habisch and Loza 2010; Grassl and Habisch 2011). More recently, Pope Francis within its Encyclical *Laudato si'* (2015) developed a Christian spiritually based approach towards a more comprehensive concept of sustainability—

another important step in the continuing history of the Catholic social tradition, which received widespread appraisal also from secular experts.

At the basis of this ongoing history, however, remains the basic principle, which had already been identified and transferred into business practice by our entrepreneurs mentioned above.

5.1 Human Dignity/Personality

Workers are perceived not as mere instruments as the scientific concept of "human capital" sometimes suggests. Rather as workers they are human beings endowed with a responsibility for other persons. Right at the very beginning of that evolution, this implied for Brandts and Harmel

- to provide their workers with a fair compensation, which does also take into account their family obligations;
- to grant as much *workplace security* as possible in a market economy;
- saving clubs and pension funds became predecessors of a modern social security system in order to enable a decent living even after retirement;
- to realize "work/life balance" in the sense, that also the personal (as well as spiritual) necessities of workers are taken into account; this included for example a library or a sewing-club, facilities to serve lunch for low prices etc. Also decent housing near to the production facilities has to be mentioned here in the case of both entrepreneurs;
- to provide continuous training in order to allow for job enrichment as well as professional development of workers.

5.2 Solidarity

Despite of perceiving the company merely as a network of (formal) contracts among individuals, both Harmel and Brandts developed a strong sense of community and expressed this spirit by instruments of solidarity of the stronger partner (here: the Entrepreneur) with the weaker ones (here: the workers with their families). These included:

… that the entrepreneur is not living in a remote nobel quarter of his city, but rather assumes his family home in the middle of the workers flates, which are build on factory grounds;

… instruments of elder care (like saving clubs and pension funds), even if a relatively low life expectancy at that time made it not very probable that a lot of recipients would result.

Solidary care for sick and injured workers as well as rudimentary family insurance—for example in the case of the premature death of the breadwinner.

Initiatives to improve the living conditions in the region: housing for workers and their families plaid a huge role here; moreover, education for young workers.

Regional development/citizenship: both entrepreneurs engaged in local as well as regional/national politics creating civic networks with other entrepreneurs, but also with politicians, academic teachers, civic leaders etc.

In the case of Harmel, the "semaines sociales" program for the young clergy as well as his publicly noted worker' pilgrimages to Rome have to be mentioned, with which he also raised the awareness of the church hierarchy for the social question.

5.3 Subsidiarity

The practice of subsidiary governance structure is probably one of the most remarkable aspects of the entrepreneurial decisions of Brandts and Harmel. Again it was the later to very clearly express the central thought in a programmatic way: "the welfare of the worker through the worker and, as far as it can be done, with him—never, *a fortiori, without him*" (*L. Harmel*).

Patriarchal thought dominated the activities of many worker-friendly Entrepreneurs at this time. In line with the pre-modern concept of charity and benevolence, this implied to perceive the workers as mere passive receivers of beneficiaries. Even if analogue thoughts could be identified even in early documents and speeches of our protagonists, an evolving culture of cooperation induced a clear shift of their attitudes. In that sense, Léon Harmel later expressed: "Patronage should give way for association". In his view, it is not the gracious gift of the Entrepreneur, but rather the communitarian self-help of the workers themselves, which may in the long run ease their lot. This basic drift from patronage to association becomes tangible in the tendency underlying the governance structure of Brandts' factory. As seen above, the different versions of the "Fabrikordnung" (1880 and 1885) determine more and more participatory majority rules. The influence of the company in pension money decision-making decreases meanwhile the self-administrative character is increasing. In Harmel's company, a similar dynamic is reflected in the growing role of worker's councils for collective decision-making, which step by step paved the way towards more self-administration of workers over their own concerns. This again strengthens the practical wisdom of worker's representatives who had to remember the shortage of means in their decision making.

Finally, another expression of subsidiarity is the community involvement of our entrepreneurs, who partially opened their facilities and sites to the public they supported local identity and—directly or indirectly—the creation of public goods in their regions.

6 Conclusion: Conservative Innovators and the "Inculturation" of Their Faith

Catholic social thought is more than just another line of instructional teaching of the church hierarchy. Rather, it is predominantly the result of the—today rather forgotten—testimony of Christian political and business leaders like Léon Harmel, Franz Brandts and others. Even in a context of radical socio-economic change as well as mutual contestation of believers and non-believers, they sticked to their value tradition. To verify that option, however, they had to come up with rather innovative forms of organisation and characteristic forms of "practical wisdom".

In a historical moment, in which nobody knew what "Catholic Entrepreneurship" might actually mean, Brandts and Harmel had to bring about that mental frame in a life-long and sometimes even painful trial and error process. As "conservative innovators" they practiced the "inculturation" of the faith into the modern society—a program, which was much later expressed by the documents of the Second Vatican Council as well as the International Theological commission. In their document "Faith and Inculturation" published in 1988, the Vatican based International Theological commission formulated: "The industrial revolution was also a cultural revolution. Values until then assured were brought into question, such as the sense of personal and community work, the direct relationship of man to nature, membership in a support family, (…) implantation in local and religious communities of human dimension, [and] participation in traditions, rites, ceremonies and celebrations which give a sense to the great moment of existence. Industrialization, in provoking a disordered concentrating of populations, seriously affected these age-old values without giving rise to communities capable of integrating new cultures" (1988, no. 21).

Moreover, the commission explicitly reflects on the specific role of Christian lay people to realize that challenge: "At a time when the most deprived peoples are in search of a suitable development model, the advantages as also the risks and human costs of industrialization are better perceived. We must develop a capacity to analyse cultures and to gauge their moral and spiritual indicators. A mobilization of the whole Church is called for so that the extremely complex task of the Inculturation of the Gospel in today's world may be faced with success" (IKT 1988, no. 20).

At the eve of the 21st century, this program of "inculturation" of religious traditions and value systems into the modern society is more challenging than ever. For example, facing the hardships of socio-economic modernization in their countries, the Eastern European orthodox traditions are challenged to develop similar social ethical orientations of their faith as in the West; not only theologians or politicians are potential actors, here, but rather practically wise business practitioners as well.

Moreover, this is not limited to the Christian hemisphere. In a similar way, the struggling countries of the Arab world may bring forward something like an

"Islamic Social Thought". Based on the practice of practically wise business leaders as "conservative innovators", they may spell out consequences of their religious traditions of solidarity ("Zakad") for social ethical reforms in society and economy. Can the East Asian religious traditions or even many indigenous traditions in developing economies catch back a comparable orientation function? Can they help "wise" business leaders to play their role in the modernization process of their societies—thus contributing to the "civilization of markets" in their hemisphere?

Finally: Do Christian wise business leaders in the era of another radical reform, which is the IT revolution and the emergence of "disruptive innovation", once again have the cultural strength to "inculturate" their concept of man and society? What can practical wisdom from the religious traditions mean in the global struggles of the 21st century? Overcoming oblivion and honouring the memory of courageous business leaders like Harmel and Brandts—as well as their practically wise predecessors in many parts of the World since then—might help us in facing that challenge.

References

Baumgartner A (1977) Sehnsucht nach Gemeinschaft. Ideen und Strömungen in der Sozialkatholizismus der Weimarer Republik. Schoningh, Munich

Bazzichi O (2008) Dall'usura al giusto profitto. L'etica economica della scuola francescana. Effatà, Cantalupa

Berman HJ (1983) Law and revolution. The Formation of the western legal tradition. Harvard University Press, Cambridge MA, London

Bruni L, Smerilli A (2008) Benedetta Economia. Benedetto di Norcia e Francesco d'Assisi nella Storia Economica Europea. Città Nuova, Rome

Buchholz RA, Rosenthal SB (2005) The spirit of entrepreneurship and the qualities of moral decision making: toward a unifying framework. J Bus Ethics 60(3):307–315

Chan CCA, McBey K, Scott-Ladd B (2011) Ethical leadership in modern employment relationships: lessons from St Benedict. J Bus Ethics 100(2):221–228

Clark G (2007) A farewell to alms. A brief economic history of the world. Princeton

Coffey JL, Harmel L (2003) Entrepreneur as catholic social reformer. University of Notre Dame Press, Notre Dame

Cornwall JS, Naughton MJ (2003) Who is the good entrepreneur? An exploration within the Catholic social tradition. J Bus Ethics 44(1):61–75

Deberri EP, Hug JE, Henriot J, Schultheis MJ (2003) Catholic social teaching: our best kept secret. Centre of Concern, Washington

Gabriel K, Große Kracht H-J (eds) (2005) Franz Hitze (1851–1921) Sozialpolitik und Sozialreform, Paderborn

Galbraith CS, Galbraith OI (2004) The benedictine rule of leadership: classic management secrets you can use today. Adams Media Corporation, New York

Goldschmidt N, Habisch A, Western Religion, Social Ethics and Public Economics (2014) In: Forte F, Mudambi R, Navarra P (eds) A handbook of alternative theories of public economics. Elgar, Cheltenham, pp 198–226

Grassl W, Habisch A (2011) Economics and ethics: towards a new humanistic synthesis. J Bus Ethics 99(1):37–49

Habisch A, Loza Adaui CR (2010) Seasoning business knowledge: challenging recent Catholic social thought. J Manag Dev 29(7/8):660–668

Habisch A, Loza Adaui CR (2011) Practical wisdom in management: a catholic perspective. In: Ehret J, Möde E (eds) The challenge of the catholic intellectual tradition: making a difference in contemporary academic settings. Lit Verlag, Zürich, Berlin, pp 15–38

Habisch A, Loza Adaui CR (2012) Entrepreneurial spirit and the role of gratuitousness for innovation. In: Carné DM, Dierksmeier C (eds) Human development in business: values and humanistic management in the encyclical "Caritas in Veritate"—Basingstoke et al.: Palgrave Macmillan, pp 217–236 (Humanism in Business Series 5)

Habisch A, Loza Adaui CR (2013) Konservative Innovation. Die Bedeutung christlichen Unternehmertums für die christliche-soziale Bewegung in Deutschland. In: Peter S, Arnd K (eds) Interdiziplinarität der Christlichen Sozialethik. Ferdinand Schöningh: Paderborn, pp 107–126

Habisch A, Küsters, H-J, Uertz R (eds) (2013) Tradition und Erneuerung der christlichen Sozialethik in Zeiten der Moderne. Herder, Freiburg, Basel, Vienna

Inauen E, Rost K, Frey BS, Homberg F, Osterloh M (2010a) Monastic governance: forgotten prospects for public institutions. Am Rev Public Adm 40(6):631–653

Inauen E, Rost K, Osterloh M, Frey BS (2010b) Back to the future: a monastic perspective on corporate governance. Manag Revue 21(1):38–59

International Theological Commission (1988) Document "Faith and Inculturation". Vatican

Jeremias J (1971) New testament theology: the proclamation of Jesus. Scribner's, New York

Kletz P, Almog-Bareket G, Habisch A, Lenssen G, Loza Adaui CR (2012) Practical wisdom for management from the Jewish tradition. J Manag Dev 31(9):879–885

Lingen M (2000) Heinrich Brauns und der Volksverein für das katholische Deutschland (1900–1933). In: Haas R, Rivinius KJ, Scheidgen H-J (eds) "Im Gedächtnis der Kirche neu erwachen". Studien zur Geschichte des Christentums in Mittel- und Osteuropa zum Jubeljahr 2000 als Festgabe für Gabriel Adriányi zum 65. Geburtstag (Bonner Beiträge zur Kirchengeschichte, Band 22), Cologne, Weimar, Vienna, pp 235–264

Löhr W (ed) (1974) Die Fabrikordnung der Firma F. Brandts zu Mönchengladbach. Unveränderte Nachdruck der Ausgabe von 1885, Stadtarchiv Mönchengladbach

Löhr W (1979) Franz Brandts (1834–1914). In: Aretz J, Morsey R, Rauscher A (eds) Zeitgeschichte in Lebensbildern. Aus dem deutschen Katholizismus des 19. und 20. Jahrhunderts, Mainz: Matthias-Grünewald, pp 91–105

Melé D (1999) Early business ethics in Spain: The Salamanca School (1526–1614). J Bus Ethics 22(3):175–189

Nell-Breuning O (1969) The image of the entrepreneur in catholic social teaching. Manag Int Rev 9(2/3):35–47

Nietzsche F (1999) The anti-christ, Trans. H. L. Mencken, See Sharp

Percy A (2010) Entrepreneurship and catholic social teaching. In: Gasparski W, Ryan LV, Kwiatkowski S (eds) Entrepreneurship: values and responsibility (praxiology), transaction, New Jersey, pp 195–210

Puppke L (1966) Sozialpolitik und Soziale Anschauungen Frühindustrieller Unternehmer in Rheinland-Westfalen, Rheinisch-Westfälischen Wirtschaftsarchiv zu Köln, Cologne

Rost K, Inauen E, Osterloh M, Frey BS (2010) The corporate governance of Benedictine abbeys: what can stock corporations learn from monasteries? J Manag Hist 16(1):90–115

Schmidt C (1923) Römischer Katholizismus und Politische Form, 1 edn. Paderborn

Stegmann F, Langhorst P (2005) Geschichte der Sozialen Ideen im deutschen Katholizismus. In: Euchner W, Grebing H, Stegmann F, Langhorst P, Jähnichen T, Norbert F (eds) Geschichte der sozialen Ideen in Deutschland: Sozialismus - katholische Soziallehre - protestantische Sozialethik: ein Handbuch,: VS Verlag für Sozialwissenschaften, Wiesbaden, pp 559–866

Tredget DA (2006) Benedictines in business and business as a vocation: the evolution of an ethical framework for the new economy. In: Tredget DAI benedittini negli affati e gli affari come vocazione: l'evoluzione di un quadro etico per la nuova economia, Università Cattolica del Sacro Cuore & Associazione per lo Sviluppo di Banca e Borsa, Milano, pp 27–45

MIX
Papier aus verantwortungsvollen Quellen
Paper from responsible sources
FSC® C105338
FSC
www.fsc.org

If you have any concerns about our products,
you can contact us on
ProductSafety@springernature.com

In case Publisher is established outside the EU,
the EU authorized representative is:
Springer Nature Customer Service Center GmbH
Europaplatz 3, 69115 Heidelberg, Germany

Printed by Libri Plureos GmbH
in Hamburg, Germany